Unaccompanied asylum seeking children
The response of social work services

Jim Wade, Fiona Mitchell and Graeme Baylis

BAAF
ADOPTION
& FOSTERING

Published by British Association
for Adoption and Fostering
(BAAF)
Skyline House
200 Union Street
London SE1 0LX
www.baaf.org.uk

Charity registration 275689

© Jim Wade, Fiona Mitchell and
Graeme Baylis, 2005

British Library Cataloguing in Publication Data
A catalogue record for this book is available
from the British Library

ISBN 1 903699 86 X

Editorial project management by Miranda Davies
Cover photo of boy posed by model,
John Birdsall Photography; photo of girl
courtesy of Exile Images
Designed by Andrew Haig & Associates
Typeset by Avon DataSet, Bidford on Avon
Printed in Great Britain by Creative Print
and Design Group

BAAF is the leading UK-wide membership
organisation for all those concerned with
adoption, fostering and child care issues.

Contents

Acknowledgements

A great many people have helped to make this study possible. First, we would like to thank the Nuffield Foundation, which funded the research, and in particular Sharon Witherspoon for her support throughout the course of the study.

The study could not have taken place without the commitment and support of managers, social work practitioners and administrators working within the three participating local authorities. Their co-operation was grounded in a strong desire to improve services for unaccompanied young asylum seekers and they responded to our persistent requests for information and provided time to talk to us with remarkable grace and good humour.

Special thanks go to the members of our advisory group who provided consistent support, advice and encouragement throughout the study and provided detailed and insightful comments on earlier drafts of these chapters. Many thanks then to Judith Dennis (Refugee Council), Selam Kidane (BAAF), Ravi Kohli (Royal Holloway College, University of London), Kate Stanley (Institute for Public Policy Research) and to Tessa Ing and Ilan Katz (Department of Health) who were involved in earlier stages of the study.

Gwyther Rees (The Children's Society) designed and developed the Access databases that were used for collecting the case file and interview data and we are very appreciative of his expertise and helpfulness. Our thanks also go to Helen Jacobs and Dawn Rowley in the Social Work Research and Development Unit (SWRDU) at the University of York who provided us with excellent administrative support throughout the project. Thanks especially to Dawn for her skill in proofreading and formatting the final report.

Most of all we are indebted to the young people who participated in our study. Without their willingness to share time with us and speak openly about their experiences, this book could not have been written. We hope that we have been able to do justice to their views and to their quest to rebuild their lives in calmer water.

Jim Wade, Fiona Mitchell and Graeme Baylis
September 2005

Notes about the authors

Jim Wade is a Senior Research Fellow in the Social Work Research and Development Unit (SWRDU), University of York. For the past 15 years he has researched and published widely in the area of social work and related services for vulnerable groups of children and young people, including looked after children, care leavers, young runaways and unaccompanied asylum seeking children. He has been involved in the preparation of best practice guides and official guidance on services for care leavers and young runaways and has acted as consultant to other national and international research initiatives in these areas.

Fiona Mitchell, formerly a Research Fellow at the SWRDU, has spent six years working as a social researcher. She has worked on studies of homelessness, social exclusion, missing persons and young runaways. Her most recent work has focused on service provision to unaccompanied children. Fiona is currently working as a freelance researcher and training to become a social work practitioner.

Graeme Baylis, formerly a Research Fellow at the SWRDU, also has several years' research experience. In addition to her work on unaccompanied children, she has a keen interest in qualitative research and has previously researched and published in the area of parenting and community at Birkbeck College, University of London. Having worked closely alongside social work practitioners for the current study, Graeme decided to retrain and is now also studying for a social work qualification.

List of tables

1 Introduction

It really happened fast, when our aunt sent us with the agent to come here. It was more like a movie. I was just thinking, is this real or am I dreaming? We were just thinking about home . . . and my sister was basically a bit frightened. That night we slept . . . well I don't know if she slept, I didn't sleep as I was wondering about the future for us . . . I was confused, you know, 'cos when we came here we had to go to all sorts of people. People taking me to all these places, and it's like: tomorrow, where am I going to go? (Abdi reflecting on his arrival with his younger sister)

The Immigration and Nationality Directorate (IND) defines an unaccompanied asylum seeking child as a person below the age of 18 (or who appears to be if proof is lacking) who is making a claim for asylum in their own right and who has no adult relative or guardian to turn to in this country (Home Office, 2002).[1] As was the case with Abdi and his sister, not all young people physically arrive alone. They frequently arrive in the company of a sibling, a relative, a benefactor, a family friend or an agent who has arranged their travel. In most cases, however, these people are unwilling, unable or unsuitable to provide continuing care for young people in the country of destination (Ayotte and Williamson, 2001). In most cases, children and young people are left to negotiate a route map for themselves.

Unaccompanied young people have formed part of the population of forced migrants throughout the last century. Their displacement to countries near or far from their own may occur for a number of often interrelated reasons (Russell, 1999; Ayotte, 2000). The need to seek safety

---

[1] The terms children and young people are sometimes used interchangeably in this text. Although legally an unaccompanied minor below the age of 18 is considered a "child", given that the vast majority are in the 14–17 age range, we predominantly refer to them as "young people". Equally, though not all unaccompanied minors claim asylum, all the young people in this study did make a claim.

from armed conflicts, political upheavals, persecution or natural disasters are frequently cited as major factors leading to departure. However, there are also others, including escape from serious poverty and deprivation, limited opportunities for the future connected to breakdowns in civil society and trafficking for the purposes of exploitation. Although young people may arrive for a variety of different reasons, what unites them is the experience of separation from their families, of being uprooted from their homes and cultures and most of that which is familiar, and the search for safety and asylum in countries that are often far removed from their countries of origin.

Separation from parents and caregivers may also occur in a variety of circumstances and often some time before young people finally leave (Ayotte, 2000; Ayotte and Williamson, 2001). Their parents may be dead, missing, imprisoned or ill and unable to provide care. They may be sent away by their parents or by other close relatives who perceive them to be in danger, whether directly or indirectly, or who select them to leave for economic reasons. In a few instances, as was the case in this study, young people may also flee dangerous or abusive family environments. In these divergent scenarios, young people are often reliant on help from family members, strangers or agencies or on their own resources for survival for some time before they finally leave their country of origin.

Once young people arrive, it is not surprising to find that, like Abdi, they are infused with feelings of confusion, even bewilderment, and of uncertainty for the future. The literature has understandably stressed their vulnerability as children who are alone and as children seeking asylum (Ruxton, 2000; Stone, 2000). It has also emphasised the emotional consequences of separation and flight. The journeys themselves are often long and arduous, made in the company of strangers, and may expose young people to risk. They also carry with them a physical and emotional legacy from their past experiences. They may have experienced several periods of disruption, their loved ones may be dead or missing, they may have experienced torture or physical injury, or been forced to engage in violence themselves. They are very likely to carry feelings of worry, loss or perhaps guilt at their own survival or escape. Where an economic subtext exists, they may also be burdened with the expectations of family members to make a return on their investment.

Once they do arrive as strangers in an unfamiliar landscape, as Abdi clearly describes, they are then confronted with navigating the maze of immigration rules and of our systems of care and protection in a society that has unfamiliar customs and practices. Troubles arising from the past coalesce with uncertainty about the future, about whether their asylum claims will be believed and accepted, and about whether the support they need in the present to reconfigure their lives will be met and by whom. It is in this context that unaccompanied young people first come to the attention of social services – at ports of entry and duty desks – and it is in this context that social workers first attempt to assess these needs and develop strategies to aid young people's settlement.

Resettlement

The term resettlement will be employed in subsequent chapters to capture the complex transitions necessary for young people to adjust to life in a new land. In its original coinage, it was used to describe international arrangements through which some governments permitted the development of resettlement programmes to provide durable solutions to the needs of some groups of "quota refugees". Aspects of this meaning find an echo in the UK Government's development of a national strategy for refugee integration (Home Office, 2000a, 2004b).

Over time, however, the meaning of resettlement has become more elastic, less confined to officially designated refugees, and used to describe the processes by which refugees and asylum seekers attempt to re-root their lives within host countries over time.[2] Although as a concept it connotes permanence, the transitions made by unaccompanied asylum seeking young people are not dissimilar, even though outcomes for them may be uncertain. Used in this way it may embrace the different forms of support and services young people may need to manage a successful transition. Resettlement is a multi-faceted process that, in the case of unaccompanied young people, implies a range of practical, psychosocial and cultural needs:

---

[2] Extracts from Ravi Kohli's work on resettlement were helpful in situating this discussion (to be published as: *Social Work Practice with Unaccompanied Refugee Children*, Palgrave Macmillan).

- for a safe and supportive place to live;
- for access to purposeful education or training;
- for continuities with past relationships, customs and cultures and opportunities to create new ones; and
- for opportunities to move forward from troubling experiences, re-centre their lives and find new purpose in everyday routines and activities.

These complex processes are what can be encapsulated in the simple word "resettlement". This is how it is used in this text. It also helps to define the caring and enabling role of social workers and allied professionals. Helping young people to settle, to find peace and purpose, is at the centre of the social work task with unaccompanied young people.

However, this work needs to be undertaken in partnership with young people. Although studies have understandably foregrounded the vulnerability of young people, greater attention has only more recently been given to their resilience and capacities to meet the challenges of resettlement (see Kohli and Mather, 2003). Rather than conceptualise young people as passive in relation to social work services, we need to understand more about the ways in which refugees – and young people in particular – use their own creativity and resources to reconstruct and resettle their lives eventually (Carey-Wood *et al*, 1995; Bloch and Shuster, 2002).

Resettlement occurs gradually over time. There is evidence that, even for "quota refugees" settling in more favourable circumstances of permanent residency and full access to employment, it can take up to a decade for them to relocate themselves within host communities (Silove and Ekblad, 2002). This study therefore only casts a light on the very early stages of settlement, ranging across a period of four to 30 months after young people had first arrived in the UK, and on the work of social workers and other professionals to help guide young people's first steps on this journey.

Ascertaining numbers

A major difficulty for service planners (and researchers) has stemmed from the lack of consistent national data on the numbers and characteristics of unaccompanied young people being supported by local authorities. Up to the present, there have been several official sources of data, none of which have provided a complete picture.

The Home Office produces annual statistical reports on the number of asylum applications made by unaccompanied young people. Over the period covered by this research study (2001–2003), they point to a rapid and, from the perspective of local authorities, unexpected rise in the numbers of young people arriving in search of asylum. They also indicate that, in the latter stages of the research, numbers of new arrivals had once again started to decline. The flow of applications increased from an estimate of 3,469 in 2001 to 6,200 in 2002 and declined once more during 2003 to 3,180 (Heath and Hill, 2002; Heath et al, 2003, 2004). Considerable caution is needed when interpreting this pattern. The figures produced for 2001 were the product of a manual count and excluded some applications, and are therefore not comparable to those generated in later years and provide only an approximate indication of numbers. However, the flow they describe fits the experience of our participating local authorities. As we shall see further in subsequent chapters, these local authorities were faced with a rapid increase in new referrals at a time when they were relatively ill-equipped to meet the challenges this presented. Towards the close of the study, meanwhile, the decline in new arrivals created a window of opportunity to consolidate, review and realign their services for unaccompanied children.

The Department for Education and Skills (DfES) provides two sources of information on asylum seeking children supported by local authorities. The first relates to unaccompanied "looked after" children and provides a snapshot at 31 March based on annual local authority returns. These show a slight, if steady, increase in the number looked after in recent years, from 2,200 in 2002, to 2,400 in 2003 and 2,800 in 2004. Furthermore, they consistently show that the majority of young people (around 70 per cent) were located in London, that a further minority (16–17 per cent) were located elsewhere in the South East and that the majority were male.[3] However, these statistics obviously take no account of unaccompanied young people "in need" who are being supported by local authorities in the community.

The second Departmental source of information relates to this population of children "in need" through a census of children in receipt of social services during a one-week period. Unfortunately the census does not identify *unaccompanied* asylum seeking children separately from those living with families. Data for February 2003 suggested that there were 12,500 asylum seeking children in receipt of services and that 83 per cent of these were being supported in families or independently, most likely under s17 arrangements.[4]

A further source of data has been provided by the London Asylum Seekers Consortium (LASC) and relates to unaccompanied children supported by London boroughs. Figures for March 2004 suggested that 4,252 young people were being supported by London boroughs at that time and that three-quarters of these young people (75 per cent) were aged 16 or 17.[5]

Taken together, what these sources of information suggest is that there are significant numbers of unaccompanied children being supported by local authorities, predominantly in London and the South East, but that there has also been a significant and growing spread of smaller numbers to other parts of the country. Most unaccompanied young people are male and aged 16 or over and it *may* be that the number of these young people being looked after is slowly increasing. However, it is evident that more accurate national information is needed to aid resource allocation and service planning by local authorities. At the time of writing, a new *National Register for Unaccompanied Children* (NRUC) is about to be launched, combining IND and social services information on unaccompanied children with the aim of improving the co-ordination and exchange of information. It is to be hoped that this register will meet some of the shortfalls of the data sources that have been available up until now.[6]

---

[3] See: DfES, *Statistics of Education: Children Looked After by Local Authorities* London: DfES – for these year endings. Available: http://www.dfes.gov.uk/rsgateway/DB/VOL/

[4] The DfES census findings for February 2003 are available at: http://www.dfes.gov.uk/rsgateway/DB/VOL/v000451/CINIE2004_final.pdf

[5] LASC data are available from: http://www.westminster.gov.uk/lasc/

[6] Information on NRUC is available at: http://www.nruc.gov.uk/default.htm

The legislative context for social services

Once a young person has been accepted as an unaccompanied asylum seeking child, they have the same rights and entitlements to welfare services as other young citizens. Local authorities have a statutory duty under the Children Act 1989 to safeguard and promote the welfare of all children "in need". Children "in need" are those whose health and development would suffer without the provision of services. Unaccompanied children and young people, lacking the presence of parents or customary caregivers, are by definition children "in need" (Department of Health, 1995; Kidane, 2001b). As such, social services have a responsibility to assess these needs and provide services appropriate to them. The *Framework for the Assessment of Children in Need and their Families* should provide the framework for these assessments and makes specific mention of unaccompanied children as one of the groups that is at risk of falling through the assessment net and therefore requiring "particular care and attention during assessment" (Department of Health *et al*, 2000, p. 47). The Department of Health has also endorsed an updated guide to conducting assessments for unaccompanied children that builds on its earlier official guidance (Department of Health, 1995; Kidane, 2001b).

Gaining acceptance from IND as an unaccompanied asylum seeking child is an important factor in accessing social services, since the responsibilities of local authorities are clearly defined for this group of asylum seekers and they are then able to claim payment for accommodation and support services through the Special Grant that is administered by the Home Office. Where a young person claims to be a minor but is considered by IND to be older than 18, they are treated as an adult asylum seeker until such time as sufficient evidence is provided to substantiate their claimed age. The burden of proof lies with the young person, although it is Home Office policy to accept the outcome of age assessments undertaken by social services (Home Office, 2000b). Such disputes are not uncommon and young people may be refused access to a service until this is clarified (Munoz, 1999; Dennis, 2002). Levels of payment under the Special Grant are also age related. A higher level is paid for young people who first applied for asylum below the age of 16 and a lower level is paid for those aged 16 or 17. Studies have identified this distinction as an important driver of differentiated services for unaccompanied young people, with local authorities making extensive use of community support provisions within the Children Act (s17) to provide accommodation to older teenagers in the community (Audit Commission, 2000; Stone, 2000; Stanley, 2001). The regulatory framework for support provided under these arrangements is considerably weaker than is the case for young people looked after (s20).

Local authorities have specific duties with respect to looked after children that do not apply to those supported in the community. These include, amongst other things, requirements for child care planning and review, allocated social work support and contact, and for promoting the health, education and training of young people. Local authorities have to account for progress in these areas through the Government's *Performance Assessment Framework*.

Those looked after also have eligibility for leaving care services up to the age of 21, and beyond if they continue in education. The Children (Leaving Care) Act 2000, building on the Department of Health's *Quality Protects* initiative, introduced new duties that were designed to respond to consistent evidence highlighting the poor outcomes achieved by young people leaving care (Biehal *et al*, 1995; Broad, 1998; Pinkerton and McCrea, 1999). These duties apply to "eligible", "relevant" and "former relevant" young people and include requirements to prepare young people for adult life, to assess and meet their needs and to provide pathway plans and personal advisers (Department of Health, 2001). Where unaccompanied young people have been looked after, they are eligible to receive these services at least to the point where they receive a final negative adjudication on their asylum claims and fail to comply with removal directions (Children's Legal Centre, 2004). No such obligations have been attached to young people supported in the community (s17) who have formed the majority of the population of unaccompanied young people and for whom, as our findings will reinforce, case closure at the age of 18 has been commonplace.

However, recent guidance may be effecting some change in the numbers of young people looked after and therefore eligible for leaving care services. In June 2003, the Department of Health issued guidance on the appropriate use of s17 accommodation (LAC(2003)13, Department of

Health, 2003). The guidance was issued in response to s116 of the Adoption and Children Act 2002 which had the effect of amending the Children Act 1989 to expressly permit the use of accommodation for children and families under s17. The guidance clarified that, in the case of lone children (defined as those under 18), there should be a *presumption* for the use of s20 accommodation and support unless clear contraindications were uncovered during assessment and, as such, clearly questioned the routine placement of older teenagers under s17 arrangements. What this guidance will mean in practice for unaccompanied young people lies outside the scope of the present study, although early evidence suggests that some gradual progress is being made in the numbers looked after (Refugee Council, 2005).

At the time of writing, large-scale changes to the child welfare system are also being envisaged through the *Every Child Matters* agenda and the Children Act 2004 (Department for Education and Skills, 2003b). It remains to be seen how these will affect services for unaccompanied young people. At present, the proposed changes would appear to reflect the continuing ambivalence towards the care and protection of unaccompanied children that has marked policy-making in the immigration and social work arenas. Although improvements to safeguarding arrangements, to assessment and multidisciplinary working are likely to be helpful developments, the exclusion of immigration and asylum agencies from duties to safeguard and promote the welfare of children and from involvement in local safeguarding boards points to a more limited safeguarding framework for unaccompanied children and young people that may adversely affect their welfare.

The research context

This study was designed and conducted at a time when, from a research perspective, little was known about how social services were attempting to meet their obligations to unaccompanied young people. Although the need to develop positive policy and practice in this area had been frequently highlighted (Parker, 2001; Christie, 2002; Okitikpi and Aymer, 2003), the evidence base to inform these developments was relatively weak (Mitchell, 2003).

Reports on refugee and asylum seeking children, in the main emanating from non-governmental organisations, have often been policy focused and prescriptive, concerned with identifying what legislation and guidance suggest should happen and outlining principles of good practice based on these.[7] While this material has been helpful in establishing the parameters of positive practice and in reinforcing rights and entitlements, it has not enabled us to understand very much about how services are provided in practice, why they vary in the way that they do, and the range of factors that may constrain work with unaccompanied children.

During the course of the study, research in the UK on refugee children and, in particular, on the lives and concerns of unaccompanied asylum seeking children has started to emerge in a more systematic way, and reference to this growing body of literature is integrated into the chapters that follow.[8] However, at the outset of the study, the knowledge base was considerably more limited. A small number of studies or reviews about refugee children more generally had provided a focus on their educational needs and experiences (Rutter and Jones, 1998; Candappa, 2000), on issues associated with their physical, mental and emotional well-being (Blackwell, 1997; Ahearn (ed), 2000; Gosling, 2000; Hodes, 2000) and on their social adjustment to life in the UK (Candappa and Egharevba, 2000). Work had also been completed on the support needs of unaccompanied asylum seeking children in the asylum process (Ayotte, 1998; Russell, 1999). This body of work was helpful in alerting us to the diversity that exists amongst unaccompanied young people, to the complexity of the transitions made by them and to the range of issues that service providers might need to take account of when planning support.

However, research exploring the nature of social services responses to unaccompanied children was thin on the ground and largely confined to a small number of inspection reports (Audit Commission, 2000), brief surveys of local authorities (Stone, 2000) and an in-depth qualitative study exploring young people's experiences of service provision (Stanley, 2001).

---

[7] Examples of this policy-based work include: Rutter, 2003a; Save the Children, 2003; Separated Children in Europe Programme, 2004.

[8] See, for example, the special issue of *Child & Family Social Work* (8:3, August 2003) for reviews of these developments.

Taken as a whole, this work highlighted positive pockets of social work practice with unaccompanied children, especially within newly emerging specialist children's teams, but also highlighted weaknesses in the policy framework, organisation and delivery of these services. In brief summary, the studies pointed to variations in:

- the quality of assessments undertaken with young people, especially for those in the older age range, and to inconsistencies in the conduct of age assessments;
- the pathways that young people subsequently took and, in particular, the tendency for older teenagers to be placed in unsupported housing of variable quality (under s17);
- the arrangements for social work contact, planning and review;
- the degree to which young people could be culturally matched to place-ment providers, in the overall range of placements available, in the use of out-of-authority placements and in the conduct of pre-placement risk assessments;
- the access to education and health care; and
- the arrangements to plan and support young people's transitions to adulthood.

Although these studies were able to identify areas of strength and weak-ness in existing local authority provision – and highlight areas of positive practice – they were limited by their design and purpose. There was a need to understand in greater depth how social services were discharging their responsibilities to unaccompanied children and young people. We needed to know more about how young people's needs were defined and assessed, how different cases were prioritised and managed by social services, how the services that were provided related to young people's progress and welfare, and about the context and constraints associated with this service provision. This is the contribution to know-ledge that the current study has sought to make. In doing so, it also has much to say about the ways in which young people themselves attempt to negotiate the transitions that are associated with resettlement, using their own resources and those of others they make contact with, and about the complexities involved for social workers in helping young people to reconstruct their lives in new and unfamiliar surroundings.

Subsequent chapters will explore the connections between the assessments that were made, the support and services that flowed from them, and the experiences and progress of young people in key areas of their lives – in their placement careers, in education and training, in health and well-being, in their social lives and in their transition to adulthood. Before doing so, however, the next chapter describes the design of the study and the methods that were employed to collect information about young people. It also helps to set the scene for these later chapters by describing the characteristics of the young people and important aspects of the service context in each of our three participating local authorities.

2 The study design and context

In view of the limited data available on social work services for unaccompanied asylum seeking children and young people, there was a clear need for an exploratory study to map out how local authorities were attempting to meet their responsibilities to them under the Children Act 1989. This study attempts to meet this aim and, in so doing, to understand more about the ways in which these young people try to negotiate the complex and difficult transitions associated with their resettlement and how they are (and may be better) supported by social services in this process.

This chapter seeks to provide context to the more substantive chapters that follow. It provides an outline of the overall study design and includes a description of how the sample of young people was obtained, the methodology that was employed to collect information about them and how this information was analysed. In order to set the scene for later chapters, it also provides a brief description of the characteristics of the sample and of the service contexts in the participating local authorities.

All research studies are bound by the timeframe within which information is collected. This has a particular resonance when investigating services that are relatively new or emerging. As we have seen, the relatively sudden and rapid rise in the numbers of unaccompanied young people arriving in the UK created significant challenges for some local authorities. New responses, including the development of specialist asylum teams for unaccompanied children, were needed to meet these challenges. The emergence and consolidation of these teams, often from uncertain beginnings, was occurring in tandem with the research. Changes in service organisation, approach and procedure were common, as existing practices were considered inadequate or new challenges emerged. In the asylum field, continuing change is also a feature of immigration and asylum policy-making that requires service providers to react to events that emanate from this broader political arena.

These factors inevitably place limits on research studies. This study commenced in June 2002 and all data collection was completed by March

2004, although the bulk of the fieldwork was undertaken in 2002–2003. At this time, in particular, the participating authorities were in the process of digesting the implications of the new Department of Health guidance (LAC(2003)13), issued in June 2003, and the findings from the Hillingdon judicial review (August 2003).[1] Although, towards the end of data collection, there was evidence of these local authorities initiating policy reviews in light of these developments, the longer-term implications for the care of unaccompanied young people lie beyond the scope of the present study. These are important questions that require further assessment.

The study provides a benchmark of the state of social work services for unaccompanied young people at that point, and considerable insight into how these services vary for different segments of the overall population, and the effects that these variations have on young people's lives. By focusing on the more enduring aspects of social work relationships with unaccompanied young people and the complexities inherent in helping, it is to be hoped that the study will provide a range of messages to support good practice that will have a lasting relevance, irrespective of the twists and turns that social work and asylum policies may take in the near future.

The study design

The study sought answers to a number of closely interrelated questions:
- How were young people first referred to social services and how were these referrals managed? How were young people's needs assessed and how did variations in assessment and procedure relate to the services young people subsequently received?
- What services did young people receive over the period of time they were supported by social services and in relation to what areas of their lives? How did these vary for different groups within the population and how did they affect young people's progress and well-being?
- Why were services provided in the way that they were? What factors constrained or facilitated the support that was provided?

---

[1] *R (Behre and others) v Hillingdon London Borough Council (2003)* EWHC 2075 (Admin)

The research was conducted in three local authorities – a southern county, a London borough and a northern city. These were selected to provide both a reasonable geographical spread across England and also of different types of authority. The design comprised a multi-method approach. An analysis of social work case files for the whole sample yielded quantitative and qualitative data that enabled us to map how young people's needs were defined and the services that were provided, and to identify variations in these services to sub-groups within the population. This analysis was undertaken retrospectively and therefore covered social work involvement from the point of referral through to case closure or the point of data collection (for cases that remained open) – a period of time ranging from four to 30 months after initial referral.

The case file study was complemented by in-depth interviews with a sub-sample of young people, drawn from this larger population, and with their current or most recent support workers. Drawing on the perspectives of young people and workers, the interviews provided a deeper understanding of young people's experiences since arrival, of how and why events had taken the course they had and how the support they had received (from all sources) related to the progress they had made (for good or ill). The design was completed by a policy study undertaken in each authority, drawing on analysis of policy documents and focus groups held with social work practitioners in each authority. This methodological triangulation enabled us to explore the research questions from different angles and take account of differing service contexts. Quantitative methods were used to map patterns of settlement and service provision and qualitative methods to explore the social processes involved in the relationship between young people and social services over time (Denzin, 1971; Hammersley and Atkinson, 1983; Mason, 1994).

Sampling

The sampling frame for the study comprised all new referrals of "unaccompanied children" to the three participating local authorities over a retrospective period of 18 months, from 1 March 2001 to 31 August 2002. The sampling frame was restricted to cases where a) the local authority

15

defined the young person as an "unaccompanied child" and b) it provided some form of service following referral.

This creates some limitations. First, the study is unable to take account of cases where social services reject a referral or fail to provide a service. Previous studies have suggested that some local authorities have been reluctant to take responsibility for the care of unaccompanied young people (Williamson, 2000; Stanley, 2001). However, despite the sampling strategy, there was evidence of some young people being initially denied support or experiencing a protracted referral process, especially where their age was disputed or they lacked appropriate documentation. These issues will be returned to in Chapter 3. Second, the local authorities were not provided with a specific definition of an "unaccompanied child" by the research team, nor was there a stipulation that these young people should be "asylum seekers", since we were keen to explore the range of cases accepted for a service. In effect, the local authorities tended to operate with a broad definition of "unaccompanied child". The one characteristic shared by all was that they had become separated from their parents or customary caregivers. However, the sample included young people who were identified as being alone at a port of entry or subsequently, who had been abandoned by adults who had accompanied them to the UK, who were living with a "responsible adult" who may or may not have been previously known to them and young people who were living with relatives but in circumstances where they had made an asylum claim in their own right. All the young people had made an asylum application at some point, 95 per cent at or before the point of referral.

The local authorities provided an anonymous data transfer on all new referrals during the sampling period. The information included date of birth, date of referral, sex and country of origin. The sampling frame was used to construct a stratified random sample of cases for inclusion in the study. Four stratification criteria were employed – local authority, age at referral (whether under 16 or 16 plus), sex (80 per cent male and 20 per cent female) and length of time since referral (greater or less than nine months). These criteria were selected to ensure the inclusion of a good cross-section of the cases managed by social services and to take account of factors that were thought likely to be associated with different service responses. Age had been considered a key determinant of the type and level of service young people received (Audit Commission, 2000; Stone, 2000). Sex was necessary to ensure the presence of females in the sample. Males constituted an overwhelming majority in the sampling frame, ranging from 80–95 per cent of referrals across the three authorities, and a simple random sample might therefore have generated an all-male sample.

Length of time since referral was selected to ensure we included young people positioned at various points along different service pathways – some referred relatively recently, others accommodated under s20 of the Children Act 1989 for varying lengths of time and some who had been assisted under community provisions (s17). The sampling strategy was designed to ensure a spread of cases that were reasonably representative of those dealt with by social services departments and of the range of services provided at that time. It also helped to ensure that all aspects of children's services would come under scrutiny – from assessment through family support and the looked after system to leaving care.

Our intention was to select a sample of 240 young people for the case file study (80 per local authority). This did not prove feasible and Table 2.1 shows the final sample obtained (n = 212). This includes a slightly uneven distribution across the three authorities (Area 1 – 72 cases; Area 2 – 72 cases; Area 3 – 68 cases).

Table 2.1
The case file sample

	Case file sample (number)				
	Case duration				
Age at referral	*Less than 9 months*		*More than 9 months*		*Total*
	Male	**Female**	**Male**	**Female**	
Under 16	34	16	39	4	93
16–17	49	13	47	10	119
Total	**83**	**29**	**86**	**14**	**212**

The final size of the sample was affected by time and resource constraints associated with conducting the fieldwork. Arranging access to social work case files was time consuming and the time necessary to carefully analyse each file and record thematic quantitative and qualitative information from the files on to a database created a heavy workload for a small research team. However, the profile of the final sample and the numbers represented in particular cells were affected by other factors. In some categories there was a simple lack of numbers available, for example, in the numbers of females referred in the first half of the sampling period and, in Areas 2 and 3, in the number of males referred below the age of 16. There were also inaccuracies in the information forwarded from local authorities – in sex, dates of birth and so on – that could only be discovered once case files were being scrutinised. Finally, the profile of the overall sample was also affected by the interview sample achieved (see below).

A purposive interview sample (selected by sex and age at referral) was recruited from *within* the overall case file sample prior to the start of data collection. Our intention was to attain a sample of 36 young people (12 per authority). We were aware that some young people would prove difficult to trace and that others might decline to participate. In these circumstances, we hoped to select a suitable substitute. However, given the small numbers in some categories, this was not always possible. A total of 57 young people were approached for interview. Some had to be excluded after repeated attempts to contact them proved unsuccessful, a smaller number refused to participate and three were excluded at the point of selection as practitioners felt that their circumstances made it unsuitable to include them. Table 2.2 shows that interviews were successfully completed with 31 young people. Although matched interviews were carried out with their current or most recent support workers, it was not always possible to find a practitioner who had knowledge of the case. Interviews were therefore completed with 27 practitioners.

Table 2.2
The interview sample

| | Interview sample (number) | | |
	Male	Female	Total
Under 16	9	9	18
16–17	7	6	13
Total	**16**	**15**	**31**

The case file study

A retrospective analysis of the social work case files held on all 212 young people was conducted. This was a complex task that involved a careful appraisal of the information recorded in each file. A detailed schedule was developed to guide the collection of quantitative and qualitative data and to provide for consistency of interpretation by the two researchers who were working at different sites. The information drawn from files was entered on to a customised Access database specifically designed for the purpose. The schedule and database were piloted and refined at the start of fieldwork and as issues of interpretation arose these were discussed within the research team and a consensus was reached.

The design of the database was based on a review of existing empirical research and practice guidance on the services provided to unaccompanied children. Information was collated under a series of descriptive categories that linked important aspects of the social work process (such as referral, assessment and care planning) to key life areas for young people (such as placement, education, health, risks, social support and immigration). Information under these categories was also collated across time, from the point of referral through to transition for those who reached 18 during the fieldwork cycle. Detailed chronologies were, as far as possible, constructed of young people's placement, education and health histories, linking where and when events occurred to the issues that appeared to have arisen and the responses that were made by social services. In this way, a more or less complete narrative was constructed for each young person covering the period of time they had been supported by social services. The database contained memo fields for each theme to record qualitative information, and statistical variables were completed to record more objective information about the young person (age, sex, date of referral, placement history and so on) and judgements that were reached by researchers based on a careful reading of the file (for example, whether an initial assessment of needs had taken place, whether there was evidence of a young person having contact with friends or family and so on).

Once this detailed phase of data collection was completed, a second phase of analysis was undertaken. This involved a re-appraisal of the data in order to construct summaries for each case within each of the themes and to derive further variables based on a careful reading of the case. The database was used to display the "chunks" of data collected during the first phase of data collection with the aim of reducing this to an organised and compressed assembly of information that would permit conclusion drawing and action (Miles and Huberman, 1994). The resulting "action" was an account that focused upon a description of what had occurred in the case, so far as this could be surmised, what may have influenced the responses made by social services and the level of support provided to each young person on the basis of the evidence recorded on file. Pen pictures were also constructed to provide an overview of the main issues for each case and to retain a sense of the whole "story" for each individual.

Where statistical variables called for researcher judgements, the basis for these judgements and the criteria that would be used to make them were discussed within the team to enhance consistency of interpretation. For instance, we were keen to get some statistical purchase on the overall support package provided to each young person. In order to achieve this, separate judgements were made about the adequacy of support provided over time to each young person in each of ten areas (initial assessment, placements, education, family, friends, community, health, emotional and personal issues, life skills and immigration). Overall, support in each area was rated as "less than adequate" where there was either no evidence that an assessment of need had taken place in this area (at any point) or where there was evidence of an inadequate response to needs that were identified. Support was rated "adequate or better" in each area if there was evidence that some assessment had taken place and that the subsequent response was adequate to need. Where no information was recorded in a particular area, support was rated as "less than adequate". The ten areas were then summed to provide an overall score that approximated the support package provided to each young person that could be used in further analysis.

As a check on inter-rater reliability, 11 cases were piloted with each of the three researchers simultaneously (but separately) rating the support provided in each area for each case and providing an overall support package score. The findings from the pilot suggested that, while there was considerable variation in the judgements made about specific variables, there was a good degree of consistency in the overall rank ordering of cases using the Spearman's Rho test.[2] In other words, while there were differences in the judgements about the adequacy, for example, of placement support in a particular case, the assessment of overall support packages was reasonably consistent across the research team – suggesting broad agreement about those that were more and those that were less comprehensive.

Once this phase of analysis was completed, the dataset was ready for final analysis. The qualitative data in the Access database were subject to content analysis across the cases, using the statistical variables to select clusters of cases for further analysis. For statistical analysis, the variables were transferred into SPSS (Statistical Package for the Social Sciences). Given the nature of the data generated from case files, we mainly utilised non-parametric statistical tests.[3] Some multivariate analysis was also undertaken using partial correlation, log-linear analysis and logistic regression. The sample size and the level of missing data often presented problems in using these techniques and we therefore regard the findings based on multivariate analysis as indicative rather than conclusive.

In general, for all these tests we regarded a test result as statistically significant where the p value was less than 0.05. Put another way, this is regarded as a 95 per cent level of confidence. However, in a few instances we have included data with a p value of less than 0.1. All test results are included in the text to enable readers to draw their own conclusions about the strength of the associations identified. Not all tables presented total exactly 100 per cent due to rounding.

Inevitably, the analysis of case files has limitations. Although it is an accepted strategy within social work research for generating mapping data on populations in need, it is limited to what is recorded on file and to a social work perspective on the course of events. It is a textual analysis that deals with narratives about events rather than the events themselves and it is important to bear in mind that recordings may not provide an

---

[2] Associations for the Spearman's Rho test were: Researcher 1 x Researcher 2 (correlation coefficient 0.863; p = 0.001); Researcher 1 x Researcher 3 (0.601; p = 0.05); Researcher 2 x Researcher 3 (0.803; p = 0.003).

[3] These included Pearson's chi-square (or Fisher's Exact where analysis involved smaller sub samples), Mann-Whitney, Kruskal-Wallis and Kendall's tau-b.

accurate portrayal of events that have occurred (Kagle, 1984; Ames, 1999). A recent inspection of the quality of case file recording categorised recordings into "poor", "weak", "good" or "superior" (Goldsmith and Beaver, 1999). The case file records scrutinised in this study spanned the spectrum identified in the inspection report although, in the main, they tended to range from "weak" to "good". There were a few instances of "poor" recording, with no information recorded beyond the young person's biographical details, and of "superior" recording, where there was evidence of detailed recording and of its continuous use for analysis, review and decision-making. In general terms, as might be expected, the standard of recording tended to be better for "looked after" children when compared to those supported in the community (s17), reflecting the additional statutory responsibilities attached to these cases. However, there was also considerable variability in the case records of both groups of young people.

An appraisal of the information that was recorded on file, including omissions, formed an important part of the analytic process. We were mindful of the level of detail recorded, the timing of recordings and of any disparities or incongruities in the information that was recorded. We were also mindful that what is not recorded may have something telling to say about the relative priorities social workers give to particular kinds of cases. Where no information existed, this was also noted. The interviews also provided an opportunity to cross-check the stories told by young people and workers with the case recordings for those cases. These suggested that, in the main, the information held on file was likely to be broadly indicative of the services provided to young people. Where case file recordings were scant, this tended to correspond to interviews where the allocated support worker had limited knowledge of the young person and where contact with them had been infrequent over the period of time they were supported. In the remaining cases, the interviews with young people and practitioners provided a richer experiential account of events that had transpired, offering different angles and perspectives, but rarely contradicted the essential account drawn from the case files. More detailed recordings therefore tended to reflect greater social work activity in practice with a young person.

The interviews

Semi-structured interviews were conducted with a sub-sample of 31 young people, selected by age at referral and sex, and with their current or most recent support workers. The purpose of the interviews was to trace each young person's history from the point of arrival in the UK, to gain an understanding of their subsequent experiences and the meaning and significance these had for them, to obtain insight into the progress they felt they were making in key areas of their lives and how this progress may have related to the support (or lack of support) they had received from social services and other sources. The practitioner interviews provided a different angle or perspective on the same course of events. These interviews also charted young people's experiences in the UK, sought to elucidate the support that had been provided and to identify factors that had enhanced or constrained this support role. At a broader level, the practitioner interviews also explored aspects of the organisation and delivery of services to unaccompanied children that influenced their work and the support they could provide.

While the process of reconstructing this history with young people was relatively straightforward, with practitioners it was considerably more complex. Many young people had experienced several changes of worker. In these circumstances, the current support worker was often relatively new to the scene and their knowledge of young people's pasts was sometimes uncertain. This was exacerbated where detailed case file recordings were lacking. In other scenarios, where cases had been closed sometime previously, workers were sometimes unaware of how young people's lives had progressed subsequently. In four cases, it was simply not possible to identify a worker who had knowledge of the case and a worker interview was therefore impractical.

The interview sample was identified at the sampling stage, before the commencement of fieldwork. We wanted to interview the young person first and then seek their consent to interview their support worker and access their case files. The process of seeking consent from young people was protracted and provided different opportunities to clarify understanding and agreement. An initial approach was made through a known practitioner. Each practitioner was briefed by a member of the research team and given two leaflets – one for the young person and one for themselves clarifying what we wanted them to do. The young person's leaflet was written in plain English and translated into two further languages (appropriate for the majority of our original sample). In other cases, interpreters were used. The leaflet stated the study's purpose, what participation would mean, our confidentiality policy and the right of young people to opt out at any point or to refuse to answer questions that made them uncomfortable. Once agreement was initially secured, the name and contact details of the young person were supplied to the research team (for the first time) and a researcher contacted the young person to arrange a suitable time and place for interview. Consent was reviewed again at this point and also at the time of the interview appointment.

The process worked well, although it proved time consuming and demanded considerable commitment from practitioners in the participating authorities. However, it was significantly more difficult where young people had infrequent contact with social services or where their cases had been previously closed. With respect to the latter group, a number of those selected for interview eventually had to be excluded as there was no way of tracing them. We were unable to make a direct approach to these young people as, consistent with data protection requirements, we could not have access to their names or contact details without their prior consent.

All information collected during the interviews was confidential to the research team. Although a policy was developed to cover circumstances where a breach of confidentiality might be necessary if a young person was found to be at serious risk of harm, this did not need to be formally implemented. A guarantee of anonymity was provided to all participants. In this context, although young people in the interview sample have been ascribed names, these are purely fictitious and some of the details provided in case illustrations have been changed to protect the identities of those concerned. Letters (such as "F" or "L") ascribed to cases drawn from the case file sample are also purely random and may be repeated, given the limitations of the alphabet.

A schedule was developed to guide the interviews with young people and practitioners and to ensure coverage of the main research questions. The vast majority of interviews were tape-recorded (only three young people refused), although many were conducted through the medium of interpreters. The information provided by the interviews was transferred directly from tape on to a specifically designed Access database after careful (and often repeated) listening. A guide was developed to assist the process of analysis and provided notes and definitions for each indexing category to ensure consistency of interpretation across the team. The guide was then refined through conducting a pilot of a small number of interviews.

The analysis of qualitative data involved two stages. First, data from the tapes were summarised separately on to two distinct interfaces within the database (one for the young person and one for the worker). The data was summarised in "chunks" and quotes under coded categories. These largely mirrored those employed in the case file study, since we hoped to be able to relate back the interview material to the case file recordings for these cases. However, the coding schema also allowed for new qualitative themes and issues to emerge and provided space for researcher observations to be made. In this way, observations could be made about the mood and tenor of the interview, the interviewees' reactions to certain questions or could identify emerging themes and issues.

The second phase of analysis brought together the information drawn from young person and worker into one combined interface. The analysis involved a process of data reduction, creating summaries under each theme that juxtaposed the perspectives of young person and worker to provide a rounded appreciation of the issues arising from the case in relation to each theme. Brief pen pictures had also been created for each case so that this analysis could be placed in the context of the whole "story" for each young person. This approach permitted each theme to be analysed in the context of the whole complex set of issues for each young person. Once completed, the collated data for all cases (including lengthy textual quotations) were printed out on a theme-by-theme basis in order to undertake a cross-sectional analysis for each theme.

The policy study

A detailed policy study was undertaken in each of the three authorities to provide context to the case study material. This incorporated an analysis of all the relevant policy documents that were available in each authority.

These documents provided an understanding of the development of services over time, developments in policy and procedure and insight into issues affecting resources, and the organisation and delivery of services to unaccompanied children. Further insights were obtained from the practitioner interviews and from focus groups held in each authority at an early stage of the study. The material from the focus groups was also used to inform the development of the research instruments necessary for the case file study and the interviews. These strategies were also supplemented by non-participant observation of team practices during the course of fieldwork. Researchers were based in social work offices for considerable periods of time during the fieldwork cycle and the insights gained from their engagement with teams therefore provided an important source of data.

Material generated from the policy study was entered on to an Access database and organised under a range of descriptive categories. Once data entry was complete, the information was printed out for each local authority and analysed alongside the case study material drawn from the case files and interviews. The triangulation of methods meant that it was possible to situate patterns identified across the sample and distinctive features of the careers of individual young people in the context of the wider service environments in these local authorities.

The local authorities

The three local authorities were selected to reflect a range of socio-geographical contexts and included a southern county, a London borough and a northern city. The location of these authorities also meant that they had different historical traditions in the services they provided to unaccompanied children and that they received varying numbers of referrals. As we shall see in later chapters, there were also significant differences in the way young people were referred or found their way to social services in these authorities and, in consequence, in how these referrals were initially managed.

Area 1 is a county-based local authority that has supported fairly high numbers of unaccompanied children and young people in recent years. A majority of referrals to this authority had been identified at a port of entry.

Area 2 is an inner London borough that has supported varying numbers of unaccompanied children over the last decade and all the young people referred to this authority did so after making their way to London.

Area 3 is a city authority in northern England. Historically, this authority has supported lower numbers of unaccompanied children, although its responsibilities have increased in recent years. Most, although not all, referrals of young people to this authority were made "in country" after young people had travelled there.

The local authorities participating in the research were provided with a guarantee that we would seek to protect their identities. In consequence, it is not possible to provide a detailed account of the organisation and delivery of services within them, since it is likely that this would make them clearly identifiable. However, in order to provide some context to the chapters that follow, this section provides a brief overview of some of the service characteristics and developments that were common to the authorities.

The development of specialist services

The sampling for the study (March 2001 to August 2002) coincided with a period of significant change in the services provided to unaccompanied children and young people. Social services departments have had a long-standing responsibility for the support of unaccompanied children arriving in the UK and, since the introduction of the Children Act 1989, they have had a clear duty to safeguard and promote their welfare. Until the late 1990s, local authorities based in London were largely responsible for discharging these duties to the majority of unaccompanied children. However, at this time, two things changed. First, there was a rapid increase in the numbers of unaccompanied children seeking asylum between 2001 and 2002 (Heath *et al*, 2003). As a result, the authorities most affected faced a sharp increase in new referrals. Second, there was a significant spread throughout England in the range of local authorities supporting unaccompanied children, many for the first time.

These changes meant slightly different things for the three participating local authorities. For the first time, Area 1 was faced with a dramatic increase in the numbers of unaccompanied young people seeking services. Area 2, although it had greater experience of providing services to refugee children, became responsible for a larger number of unaccompanied children than had previously been the case. Area 3, for the first time, began to pick up smaller numbers of children and young people over time.

None of the local authorities were particularly well positioned to meet these challenges. New policies, procedures and guidance to manage these referrals were needed at a time when few signposts existed and, in response, embryonic specialist services were initiated. The interviews with practitioners pointed to the sense of crisis and confusion that surrounded these early developments. Staff numbers were very low and caseloads were high. Overstretched workers often lacked basic facilities, such as office space, paperwork or telephones. Policies and procedures had to be developed "on the run" and amended in the light of experience. Coping with the new referrals was difficult:

> *It's not an exaggeration to say there was probably . . . there could have been five or six new young people coming in every day, [and] this was on top of your normal duties as a social worker.* (Support worker, Area 2)

In circumstances such as these, case planning and sound record-keeping were difficult to achieve and the legacy of these early days was evident in the comments of some practitioners:

> *Every team is running to stand still, to keep up with the stuff that's coming in . . . If we'd known how many [young people] we were going to have four years ago, it could have been planned, you could have put things in place. But the first year I was here, we were struggling just not having enough files and forms. There were not enough printed because the numbers we were dealing with, it wasn't planned. So if you go back over the files, you might think they're in a right state, but we physically didn't have the files or filing cabinets. That was a time when we had three social workers with one room and one mobile phone.* (Social worker, Area 1)

Over the course of the study, these services evolved. New services, policies and procedures were developed and refined in the light of subsequent experiences or in response to new challenges. Although the organisation and delivery of these services varied in each authority, they shared some common characteristics that will be considered further below.

Specialist children and families teams

All of the local authorities had developed at least one specialist "children's asylum team". In two areas, these teams worked solely with unaccompanied asylum seeking children and young people while, in the other, the team also provided services for asylum seeking children who had arrived together with their families. These teams were located and managed within the children and families sections of social services. However, they also operated within the context of broader asylum services in each authority.

The specialist teams were staffed by qualified social workers and by unqualified support workers. In general terms, social workers tended to hold case responsibility for young people who were "looked after" (s20), while support workers often had responsibility for young people who were supported under s17. However, cases were sometimes co-worked, with support workers providing the day-to-day support for young people irrespective of their care status.

Language support was a critical issue for these teams. In most instances, interpreters were employed to facilitate meetings with young people. However, where young people had established some links with their own communities of origin or had been placed by agencies within these communities, community or agency representatives sometimes provided these services. In one team, the first language of three members of staff was appropriate for the majority of young people who were referred. They worked as language support assistants or as support workers to children and young people. This had a number of advantages. Staff members were able to call on them to provide interpreting services at short notice. Their role was also valuable to young people, since they were able to provide a welcome link with young people's homelands in the early stages of resettlement and help to guide their first steps when confusion and disorientation were common experiences. However, it did not generally appear to be the case that recruitment of practitioners from within the refugee communities was pursued as a matter of policy.

Alongside one-to-one casework, some teams had also experimented with group work. These groups were aimed at reducing the social isolation many young people experienced soon after arrival and provided some essential life skills training (cooking, managing money, health promotion). As we shall see in later chapters, group-based services and organised social activities were often appreciated by young people and provided welcome opportunities for social engagement, especially where young people lacked networks of their own.

Other asylum teams

Despite the existence of child-focused asylum teams, unaccompanied young people were not always supported within these teams. In particular, some young people aged 16 or 17 at referral were supported by teams that worked with asylum seeking adults and families under the interim arrangements of the Immigration and Asylum Act 1999. These teams provided a community care role. Direct support to young people came largely from support workers. Professionally qualified social workers were rare amongst the frontline staff in these teams, although team managers tended to be qualified senior social workers.

The client base of these teams was large and practitioners were working directly with unaccompanied young people, single adults and families. The support provided by these teams was variable and did not appear to be tailored to the particular needs of young people. There was also evidence that practitioners did not always understand the rights and entitlements of unaccompanied children and confused them with the complex policy and legal systems in operation for adults and families. For example, the initial assessment paperwork in one team often recorded information that was not relevant to the provision of services to young people below the age of 18, by designating them as "destitute" following an assessment of their financial circumstances. In these teams it was also quite common for assessment responses to appear more procedural, to be led by the accommodation and other resources available to the team rather than by the needs of young people as individuals, and these issues will be considered further in later chapters.

Contracted-out services

All of the participating local authorities used formal contractual agreements to commission and govern services provided by independent fostering providers and by private or voluntary housing providers that gave key worker support to individual young people placed with them. Issues arising from the use of these housing providers, in particular, will be considered in later chapters.

However, in two local authorities there was also an historic reliance on agencies that provided a range of services which, in many respects, meant that they were occupying the place of social services. In one local authority, this took the form of a reliance on refugee or community-based agencies that had often placed young people prior to their referral to social services. In the other, it took the form of a dedicated agency that provided accommodation and broader support services mainly to older teenagers across the local authority. The origins of these services lay in the crisis response to increased numbers of referrals and, in the former case, to the presence of active communities of origin within the locality. Whether by design or as a result of *de facto* arrangements, these agencies had assumed some responsibility for the reception and assessment of certain referrals and, whether formally or informally, seemed to have largely taken the place of social services over the period of time young people were supported. In some instances, it was clear that young people had no contact in person with social services, although their placements and allowances continued to be funded by them. In other instances, young people were transferred to these external agencies once an initial assessment had been completed.

The quality of care provided by these agencies varied considerably. As we shall see in subsequent chapters, some young people settled well in their placements and received positive support and contact that addressed important areas of their lives (including education, health, immigration and social support). Others, however, were less fortunate and found the support provided by these agencies to be less than adequate. As the specialist services provided by social services evolved over the course of the fieldwork, the relationship with and reliance on these agencies changed. Concerns about the variable support provided by refugee and community agencies led to increased regulation. Although the services of these agencies continued to be used, there was clear evidence in later case files of social services assuming greater control and adopting *de facto* rather than just *de jure* case responsibility. In the other authority, the contract with the dedicated agency was ended and social services assumed direct case responsibility for all new referrals.

At least in part, this realignment of services was facilitated by a decline in the numbers of new referrals that occurred in late 2003 and early 2004. This created greater space for services to be reviewed and revised. This opportunity to rationalise service structures also coincided with the advent of national policy developments that were significant to the support of unaccompanied children and young people and that prompted the local authorities to rethink and reorganise the provision of services.[4] Although each of the local authorities has responded to these challenges in different ways, it does appear to be resulting in service structures that will increase the likelihood of unaccompanied young people below the age of 18 being supported by specialist children's and families social work teams. How these services develop in practice and the implications they may have for the experience and progress of young people, however, will need to be appraised through future research and inspection.

Characteristics of the sample

The final sample of 212 young people was inevitably influenced by the stratification criteria that were employed. Just over one-half of the sample (52 per cent) was referred in the first half of the sampling period of 18 months and just under half (48 per cent) in the second nine months. As we intended, one-fifth of the sample (20 per cent) was female and 80 per cent was male. Just over half of the young people (56 per cent) were aged 16 or 17 at referral and the remainder were below this age. However, the ages of young people included in the study ranged from infancy, the youngest being one year old, through to young people in their late teens (Table 2.3). The majority of referrals (89 per cent), however, concerned those aged between 14 and 17 years old. Only a small minority (5 per

---

[4] These include changes to interim arrangements, LAC(2003)13 and the outcome of the Hillingdon judicial review (see p. 188).

cent) were aged ten or under and all of these children, with just one exception, were referred to Area 3.

Table 2.3
Age at referral (n = 212)

	Number
Under 5 years	2
5–9 years	4
10–12 years	9
13 years	8
14 years	27
15 years	43
16 years	64
17 years	55

The children and young people came to the UK from a total of 23 different countries. The main countries of origin included the former Federal Republic of Yugoslavia (20 per cent), Afghanistan (12 per cent) and Iraq (12 per cent).[5] The sample was quite evenly split according to region of origin. Similar proportions of unaccompanied young people came from Africa (27 per cent) and the Middle East (26 per cent), a slightly higher proportion (32 per cent) originated from Europe, a smaller proportion (15 per cent) from Asia and very few young people (1 per cent) arrived from the Americas. Region of origin was also associated with differences in gender. The overwhelming majority of young people who originated from Europe were male (96 per cent), as were those arriving from Asia (90 per cent) and the Middle East (84 per cent). However, almost half the young people who originated from Africa were female (48 per cent).

Young people from the same country of origin were often concentrated in particular local authorities and formed a significant proportion of the cases supported in that area. For example, in one local authority two-fifths (41 per cent) of the cases included in the sample were from the

---

[5] Referrals from a fourth country of origin formed a significant proportion of the sample (13 per cent). However, this country is not specified to protect the anonymity of one of our participating authorities.

same country of origin. In another area, young people drawn from two countries of origin formed a majority of cases included in the study from that authority (64 per cent). However, despite these concentrations, it was also the case that these young people and others included within the sample were from a diverse range of ethnic communities and had diverse linguistic, economic, cultural and religious backgrounds.

Summary

The study was conducted between late 2001 and early 2004 and coincided with a period of significant change in the development of services for unaccompanied children and young people. Its purpose was to explore how social services were attempting to meet their responsibilities to unaccompanied children, to assess why services were provided in the way that they were, how services varied for different sub-groups within the overall population and how these services inter-played with the progress of young people's lives.

The study design comprised a multi-method approach. A retrospective analysis of the social work case files of 212 young people referred to three local authorities was undertaken. The sample was stratified to provide a good cross-section of the cases managed by social services. This analysis yielded quantitative and qualitative data that enabled us to map out the services provided to young people in key areas of their lives from the point of referral to the point of data collection or case closure, which ranged from four to 30 months later.

The case file study was complemented by in-depth interviews with 31 young people and their current or most recent support workers and by a policy study undertaken in each local authority. This triangulation of methods enabled us to explore the main research questions from different angles and perspectives and take account of differing service contexts. Quantitative methods were used to map patterns of settlement and service provision and qualitative methods to explore the social processes involved in the relationship between young people and social services over time, taking account of factors that enhanced or constrained the support provided.

The final sample of young people obtained was influenced by the stratification criteria that were employed in sampling – sex, age at referral and length of time since referral. One-fifth of the sample was female and just over one-half of the sample was aged 16 or 17 at referral. The majority of referrals (89 per cent) related to young people aged 14 to 17. The children and young people came to the UK from a total of 23 different countries and were quite evenly distributed across the main regions of origin (Europe, Africa and the Middle East), with smaller proportions originating from Asia and the Americas.

3 Referral and assessment

Assessment is a continuous process that starts with an initial contact or referral. At the point of initial contact, several questions need to be decided. Is it appropriate to provide any service? Is an immediate intervention needed? What further information needs to be collected to guide the assessment of need? For many observers, the quality of the needs assessment and, in light of this, the section of the Children Act 1989 under which services are provided represent the crux of the controversy that surrounds the provision of services and support to unaccompanied children.

Studies have pointed to variability in the occurrence of needs assessments, in the procedures that are employed and in the overall quality of assessments within and between local authorities in England (Munoz, 1999; Stanley, 2001; Children's Legal Centre, 2003). For example, the Audit Commission (2000) suggested that, 'many authorities, for example, do not offer 16- and 17-year-old unaccompanied children a full needs assessment' (p. 66). Stone (2000) reported that almost three-quarters of the 54 local authorities surveyed were not assessing the needs of unaccompanied children with reference to the recently introduced Assessment Framework. Studies have also inferred from evidence about young people's later lives that needs assessments either may not have taken place, were ineffective or were not adequately implemented to meet the needs of these children and young people (Refugee Council, 2000; Kidane, 2001a; Stanley, 2001; Dennis, 2002). However, there is limited empirical evidence to help us understand the ways in which the needs of this group of children and young people have been assessed and, consequently, how responses to their needs have been planned. With regard to the gaps identified in the research, the study aimed to identify *if* needs assessments occurred at the point of referral and to explore the nature of the assessments that were undertaken.

Background information recorded on file

An initial referral to social services provides an opportunity for practitioners to gather basic information to inform their decision making. The following account provides a brief overview of the information recorded on file about the basic characteristics of young people. This information was not necessarily gathered or recorded at the point of referral, although in many cases it is likely that it was.[1]

A **date of birth** was always recorded. It was clear that these dates were sometimes estimated and that the date of birth recorded did not always reflect the age that practitioners believed young people to be. Sometimes practitioners believed young people were actually younger or older than their official papers suggested.

Sex and **country of origin** were always recorded. Recording on **ethnic origin** was not as widespread and occurred in a variety of ways. Some use was made of the Department of Health classification system but this was not systematic and appeared to have limited relevance to direct work, since children were often simply recorded as "other". However, practitioners also recorded information in a more meaningful way in 42 per cent of the cases. For example, practitioners working with children and young people from the former Federal Republic of Yugoslavia often recorded whether or not they were ethnic Albanian, Serb or Roma. Similarly, case recordings on young people from Afghanistan distinguished between different groups (e.g. Pashtun, Tajik, Hazara and Uzbek).

The **language(s)** spoken by young people were almost always recorded (96 per cent of cases). However, it was notable that where young people spoke a number of languages the language of preference was not always clearly noted. The degree of fluency in English was seldom recorded.

References to **religion** were common (72 per cent) and ranged from simple classifications, such as 'Christian' or 'Buddhist', to more detailed descriptions of a young person's relationship to a religion. For example, a recording may have noted that a young person identified as Muslim and

---

[1] These data were collected from referral and initial assessment records as well as from other forms and case notes on file. The point at which information was first recorded by a practitioner was not always clear.

wished to maintain a halal diet but did not wish to pray or attend mosque.

Immigration status at the point of referral was recorded. At the point of referral, 94 per cent of children and young people had lodged a claim for asylum. The remaining young people had either not yet made an application for asylum (5 per cent) or had already been granted "exceptional leave to remain" (1 per cent).

The **date of arrival** was not always clearly recorded and was omitted in 5 per cent of cases. There was also considerable variation in the level of detail recorded regarding the circumstances of the child and the source of referral. In 15 per cent of cases, there was no detail recorded on the referral although it was possible, in some cases, to construct an account of the source or timing of the referral. In 9 per cent of cases no **date of referral** was recorded.[2]

When and how referrals were made

More than one-quarter (28 per cent) of the referrals concerned young people who had been identified at the point they arrived in the country (see Table 3.1). The overwhelming majority (89 per cent) of these referrals originated from immigration services. The remaining 11 per cent resulted from a combination of community representatives, the police and housing agencies. The majority (91 per cent) of referrals made on arrival were received in Area 1, where a "port of entry" is located, although a small number were also received in Area 3.

The majority (72 per cent) of children and young people, however, were referred to social services sometime after they had arrived in the country. They often came into contact with social services as a result of links with other services, such as immigration services, legal services, the Refugee Council Panel of Advisers or community organisations. In other cases, however, referral was due to relatives, friends or strangers taking them to social services to request assistance.

---

[2] Referral dates were calculated with reference to dates of arrival, initial assessment or first placement for the purposes of the research. Data in the next section relate to cases where it was possible to discern approximate date of arrival and source of referral (n = 203).

Table 3.1
Referrals to the local authorities (n = 203)

Type of referral	*Number of referrals to local authority*			*Totals Number (%)*
	Area 1	*Area 2*	*Area 3*	
On arrival	52	–	5	57 (28)
In country	18	70	58	146 (72)
Total referrals	**70**	**70**	**63**	**203**

The source of referral was partly linked to the geographical location of the local authorities and the resources available within them, as illustrated by Table 3.2. For example, the only local authority to receive referrals from the Refugee Council's Panel of Advisers was based in London where the Panel operates a rota system. Similarly, legal advisers figured as a main source of referral in this authority where young people may have been required to provide proof of a local connection or had sought help with their asylum claim before referral to social services. The propensity for referrals to be made by relatives, friends or community organisations in Area 3 was a function of the way in which the children and young people came to be in this area and of the role of refugee community associations in brokering relationships between young people and social services at this time.

Young people who were referred "in country" came to the attention of social services after varying lengths of time in the UK, ranging from a few days to more than a year after entry. Most, however, had been referred within a relatively short time of arriving. Just over one-half (52 per cent) had been referred within one week, almost three-quarters (72 per cent) within two weeks and a total of 85 per cent within one month of arrival. A small proportion of young people (11 per cent) came into contact with social services after a number of months and just 4 per cent were referred after a year or more.

Table 3.2
Source of "in-country" referrals to local authority (n = 136)**

Source of referral	Number of referrals to local authority			Total (%)
	Area 1	Area 2	Area 3	
Immigration services	9	1	1	8
Legal adviser	1	16	4	15
Panel of Advisers	–	13	–	10
Community representative	–	3	23	19
Self	–	22	10	24
Relative or friend	–	2	11	10
Stranger	–	3	3	4
Other service*	8	2	4	10
Total	**18**	**62**	**56**	

*Includes the National Asylum Support Service (NASS), other social services department or housing agency.
**10 cases had no record of referral source.

The circumstances of young people at referral

The circumstances of young people tended to vary according to the length of time they had been living in the UK. Where young people were identified at a port of entry, referral to a duty social worker at the immigration holding area was normally immediate. However, some young people identified at port of entry and referred to Area 3 by immigration services had to travel north to that authority. In addition, some young people made their own way there and were referred immediately, once contact had been made with relatives, with other adults or with refugee community organisations located in the authority.

Where the gap between arrival and referral to social services was more significant, young people's circumstances varied more considerably. Where it was shorter, ranging from a few days to three weeks or so, most young people in Areas 1 and 3 had accessed support from housing or refugee agencies prior to referral. In Area 1, this largely stemmed from a formal arrangement with a specialist housing/support agency that acted on behalf of the local authority in "processing" some referrals received from the port of entry. In Area 3, young people tended to come into contact with refugee agencies through contact with siblings, friends or adult contacts who were already supported by these agencies in partnership with the local authority. In Area 2, fewer formal arrangements existed and young people were more likely to have slept rough or stayed with strangers they had met on the streets before being referred to social services.

Where young people had been in the UK for around a month or more before referral, some differences in circumstances were apparent. These young people were more likely to have been staying with relatives or family friends and only approached social services when it when it was no longer possible to do so. This was sometimes prompted by a change in household composition, where another person joined the household, or by a change in circumstances, such as the effect of overcrowding or of increased financial difficulties. A smaller number of referrals in this group concerned age disputed young people who had been referred to the National Asylum Support Service (NASS). In some instances, social services only assumed responsibility when these decisions had been challenged and a decision was made to accept the young person as a minor.

Referrals made after a year or more included a few cases where young people were referred back from adult to children's teams for further assessment, where referrals were made by external agencies for young people living in informal settings with insufficient support, and one case where a parent with two children had gone missing and left them alone.

The immediate response to referrals

While the response of some practitioners to these referrals captured the elements of "speed, sensitivity and security" that are advocated in current guidance and training materials, others were less sensitive to young people's immediate needs (Department of Health, 1995; Kidane, 2001b). The challenge facing local authorities is not straightforward. Two immediate and difficult questions need to be answered at the point of referral. Is the child eligible for services as an "unaccompanied asylum seeking child" who is "in need" under the terms of the Children Act 1989? And if so, what particular needs should be addressed immediately, prior to any further assessment?

Eligibility for services

Guidance has consistently stated that unaccompanied asylum seeking children are, by definition, children "in need" (Department of Health, 1995; Kidane, 2001b; Department of Health, 2003). However, a key issue for social services is to determine whether an individual qualifies as an unaccompanied asylum seeking child. To do this, an assessment is needed of the age of a child and their status as both an asylum seeker and as unaccompanied. Approaches to these problems varied between teams. Some teams adopted a more flexible approach. In these teams, where a young person appeared to be alone and without parental support, this tended to be sufficient to trigger an initial assessment of them as a potential child "in need". Other teams operated a narrower definition, requiring proof of a young person's eligibility for services before any response was made.

Case files contained notes on practitioners' perceptions of the ages of young people, including estimations of the age or age range that they considered young people to be. The process of determining age appeared unsatisfactory for a number of reasons. Judgements about a young person's age were sometimes made on the basis of a single meeting. Recordings on age varied from those providing a clear rationale for the decisions made, although the rationale may itself have been ill founded, to those with simple and sometimes categorical statements that offered little insight into the decision-making process. Examples included: 'it was immediately clear that he is not his stated age of 15, he is 17 or 18 and could be older'; 'we do not believe this young person is 13 years old, nearer to 15/16 but we erred on the side of caution and placed him at [a residential unit]'. There was also evidence of practitioners giving some young people the "benefit of doubt", continuing to treat them as minors even though there was some concern that they were older than their stated age.

Some young people were required to demonstrate their status as an "asylum seeker". This differed across the authorities and appeared to relate to the geographical location of the authority and to a preoccupation with establishing a "duty" to a particular young person. This was not an issue in Area 1, as young people were usually identified at port of entry and referred by the Immigration Authority. It also did not appear to have been a major issue for practitioners working in Area 3, who tended to prioritise consideration of whether or not a referral concerned someone who was "in need". However, in Area 2, while practice varied across the teams, it was more likely that young people needed to establish their status as an asylum seeker as well as demonstrate a "local connection" to the area. This was taken to extremes in some cases, where young people were refused assistance until they presented at the office with their original immigration paperwork or some "proof" of their local connection (in the form of letters of referral from their solicitors or from acquaintances they had been staying with). This often resulted in a protracted process of referral and caused considerable distress to some young people.

"S" first made contact with a children's team. They advised that, since he was 16, he would be supported by a generic asylum team and was given directions to their offices. He returned later that day and explained to the social worker that he had got lost. He was trying to find the Refugee Council offices, as the other team had refused him help as he lacked formal immigration paperwork (only an IND compliments slip stating that they had been unable to process his application on the day he had attended and advising him to return on a specific date). The social worker provided him with the fare and directions to get to the Refugee Council offices, while noting that he was 'very anxious'.

There appears to have been considerable flexibility, however, in the interpretation of who constituted an "unaccompanied" child. Practitioners tended to consider children to be "unaccompanied" where they were without their parents or the person who had been previously taking care of them in their country of origin. The sample included cases of young people who were referred after being abandoned by adults who had accompanied them here, who were living with a "responsible adult" who had some connection to the young person but was previously not known to them, who were living with relatives but had apparently made asylum claims in their own right and cases where young people had become separated from their parents subsequent to their arrival in the UK. This suggests that, in general, the three authorities operated with a broad definition of an unaccompanied child; one that tended to increase the proportion of young people eligible to access services.

Immediate responses to need

At the point of referral, judgements also had to be made about the need for immediate service responses, especially in relation to placement and financial assistance. Where young people were referred on the day they arrived in the UK, the vast majority (90 per cent) were provided with an immediate placement. However, the way in which these referrals were managed differed according to the authority and the young person's circumstances at the time.

Young people referred to Area 1 were initially contacted by a duty social worker at the immigration holding area. What occurred at this stage varied according to the time of day or night, the physical or emotional state of the child and the availability of an interpreter. In some cases, a brief interview took place to gather basic details. In others, the social worker depended upon information provided by immigration services and their own visual assessment of the young person's age and physical condition. In all cases, a very basic assessment was made as to whether the referral concerned a "child" and, in most cases, an immediate placement was provided. Young people were initially placed in a foster or residential placement or in a supported hostel or hotel accommodation. Further assessment interviews were usually scheduled to happen within a few days of the young person's placement.

In Area 3, as we have seen, young people referred on the day they arrived within the authority may have been initially referred by immigration services or may have made their own way to relatives, family contacts or refugee agencies. Most were initially housed in accommodation managed by refugee community organisations and, although these placements appear to have been planned and funded by social services, it was often unclear whether social services' practitioners had physically met these young people prior to placement. A few referrals concerned young people who were coming to meet adult relatives living in the area and, in these cases, placements were not provided although initial assessments were conducted.

A good proportion (42 per cent) of "in country" referrals were also provided with an immediate placement on the day they were referred. A majority of these young people had been referred (or referred themselves) within one week of arriving in the UK. Where young people had been in the UK for a longer period pre-referral, they were more likely to have found a settled placement or at least a temporary living situation that made the provision of immediate placements less likely, even though some of these settings were not entirely risk free.

Young people's experiences of first contact

Eight young people within the interview sample had been referred to social services when they first arrived in England.[3] They themselves provided only a brief description of this first point of contact. All had been referred to the same social services department and had been identified at port of entry. Most described being confused and having little understanding of what was happening. They remembered meeting a man or a woman, who asked some questions, and then they recalled being taken to stay somewhere – to a foster or residential placement or to a hotel.

One boy remembers being scared when he first arrived at a residential unit because he arrived in the middle of the night and the home was in an isolated place. Another describes the same home but tells of being taken to a "refugee centre". The two boys who were taken to hotels remember going there with other boys; neither spoke much about this time but focused on later meetings when they felt that they began to understand more about was going to happen. Most did not understand until later who was involved or how they were going to help:

I didn't understand what happened, just that the interpreter took me there [to the foster home]. (Da-xia, who understood this family to be friends of a woman who had helped her previously)

The guy on the phone was meant to be an interpreter but he wasn't. [Well] he was an interpreter, but he couldn't speak my language ... I just understood that he said, 'you will go to an English family', just

---

[3] None of the practitioners interviewed were involved with these young people at the point when they were initially referred to social services.

that. I didn't even know what he was on about . . . A couple of hours later, a man, he was a bit older. . . took me, he put me in his car and he drove two hours, I guess, two hours and a half, and he brought me here [to the foster home]. (Kamuran)

Despite feeling confused about what was happening, many young people felt reassured that someone was going to help them:
No idea what's taking place in my life at that time. But I am happy that that man tried to explain what is going to take place . . . How they talk to you, you get confident. (Miremba on her first experience of social services)

The experiences of those who were referred after spending time in the community were similar. They also often spoke of being confused about the role of social services and of feeling reassured or comforted by the approaches taken by the practitioners. They felt that they listened and asked questions in a sensitive way: 'the way she spoke to us was like a mother'; '. . . they just talked calmly and listened to us calmly'. Others remember being given explanations of social services' role, such as: 'they said we are here to care for you'; 'the interpreter told me they are looking after children and that they would find me a placement, somewhere to stay'.

Not all young people were provided with assistance or accommodation on the day they were first referred. In some cases, the first referral interview involved establishing whether it was appropriate for a young person to remain where they were while a further assessment was undertaken. Some were keen to stay with the people whom they knew or had recently met while this assessment was completed. However, others were in situations to which they were reluctant or unable to return, but were nonetheless initially refused help or accommodation:
And then it was hard for me because I don't know where to go and the people I had been with refused me also – 'you can't sleep with us anymore'. They had a lot of children, you know . . . (Ghedi was initially refused any assistance from social services because he did not have the photographic ID card issued by the IND)

Initial refusal of assistance tended to occur for two reasons. First, as we have seen, some young people were told to return with correct paperwork (e.g. an IND identity card). In the meantime, some had to remain in insecure and potentially unsafe situations (for example, with strangers they had met). Second, some were advised that they could not be assisted on that day as there was no accommodation available. Some young people challenged this decision, often with the help of an adult (an interpreter, a community representative or a solicitor) who had accompanied them to the office – and two young people described "waiting it out" at the office for hours until they were eventually provided with somewhere to stay.

First impressions are vital and help to set the tone for the work that may follow. Young people were often understandably confused and wary during their first encounters with social services, but were also seeking reassurance, comfort and care. Where these initial interviews were conducted with sensitivity, calmness and an appreciation of the need to explain the role of social services, young people often felt reassured that the help they needed would be at hand. Where young people were forced to clear unnecessary eligibility hurdles or were turned away, as was the case with Ghedi, the opposite conclusion often had to be drawn.

The assessment of need

The *Framework for the Assessment of Children in Need and their Families* defines an initial assessment of need as:

> A brief assessment of each child referred to social services with a request for services to be provided . . . [which should determine] whether the child is in need, the nature of any services required, from where and within what timescales, and whether a further, more detailed core assessment should be undertaken. (Department of Health *et al*, 2000, p. 31)

Although this study was not linked to the implementation of the Assessment Framework, we were keen to assess how young people's needs were assessed. Analysis of case files was undertaken to identify the proportion of cases in which initial and core assessments had been carried out, the timing of these assessments and who was involved in conducting them.

47

These issues will form the substance of this section. Later sections will explore the different approaches to assessment that were evident across the authorities and will identify some of the practical difficulties of conducting assessments with unaccompanied young people.

Detailed information was also collected on how these assessments addressed (or failed to address) important needs arising from discrete areas of young people's lives. This included young people's needs for placement, health and emotional well-being, education and training, family and social relationships, personal development (including emotional and behavioural development, social presentation and self-care skills), immigration and risk. This chapter, however, focuses on the overall *process* of assessment, and data concerning these discrete areas are included in subsequent chapters where they provide an important context to young people's later experiences in these key life areas and to the services provided to them.

Initial and core assessments

The vast majority of young people (88 per cent) had received some initial assessment of their needs. Although their age, sex or region of origin were not associated with the likelihood of receiving an initial assessment, there was some variation by local authority (p = 0.01; n = 212), with young people referred to Area 2 being the most likely to have received an initial assessment.

For around one in eight young people there was no recorded evidence of an initial assessment having taken place. In these cases (n = 26) a variety of factors appeared to have been at play. First, and mainly in Area 1, young people were often assessed by a duty team before being referred on to other social work teams or for placement at some distance from the local authority under the supervision of housing agencies. In some of these cases there was no paperwork on file recording that an assessment had occurred and, if it had in reality, it would therefore have been of limited use in planning for the child. Second, and mainly in Area 3, there was evidence that some assessments had been planned but had not been carried out for several months. These cases constituted early referrals within our sampling period, before a specialist asylum team was in existence. Once the team was established, there was evidence of these cases being reviewed. Finally, in a small number of cases the original paperwork had simply been lost and no detail existed on file of events around the time of referral and assessment.

Core assessments were rarely undertaken with unaccompanied young people and case file records suggested that these had only been completed in 8 per cent of cases. Core assessments were more likely to have been carried out by specialist children's teams and for young people who were below the age of 16 at referral. They were more likely to feature for young people who subsequently went on to be looked after under s20 of the Children Act 1989 when compared to those who were supported under s17 arrangements – although they were still only evident in 18 per cent of s20 cases compared to 5 per cent of s17 cases.[4] Information from case files suggests that core assessments were conducted where there was emerging evidence of young people having more complex needs, especially in relation to physical or mental health, or where more in-depth assessments were necessary to inform planning – for example, where reunification with relatives was proposed or an assessment of pre-existing informal care arrangements was necessary.

Who conducted the assessments and when?

Initial assessments were mostly conducted by qualified social workers or by unqualified support workers within social services (see Table 3.3). However, this was not always the case. There was also evidence of a group of young people (n = 19) who did not appear to have had much (if any) direct social services contact, even for assessment. It was clear that these cases had been formally referred to social services (as they were included within our sample) even though the only case records available were held by another agency. This agency was subcontracted by social services to provide housing and key work support to unaccompanied children as a crisis response to a sudden escalation in the numbers of referrals received by the local authority, and (so far as they occurred) they appear to have largely conducted their own independent assessments.[5]

---

[4] Associations for core assessments were as follows: children's teams (p = 0.02; n = 202); age at referral (p<0.01; n = 202); care status (p = 0.01; n = 189).

[5] Towards the close of the study, the contract with this agency was ended and social services took formal responsibility for all initial assessments.

Table 3.3
Practitioner and teams responsible for assessment (n = 161)

Practitioner	Numbers of cases per agency/team			Total (%)
	SSD children's team	SSD other team	Other agency	
Social worker	77	7		53
Support worker	18	40	19	47

Although it was difficult from case files to identify when initial assessments were completed, information was collected on when the assessment process *began*. Table 3.4 shows that the majority (71 per cent) of assessments began within seven days of the referral date. In 18 per cent of cases initial assessments were not initiated until at least 15 days had passed and 11 per cent were not initiated for more than 31 days. These latter cases were mainly the responsibility of Area 3 and most related to the transitional period prior to the establishment of the specialist team. Late assessments in Area 1 and Area 2 concerned cases of young people whose ages had been disputed. It appears that social services departments did not formally intervene in these cases until the age dispute was finally resolved.

Table 3.4
Timing of initial assessments (n = 154)*

Time since referral	Number of cases per local authority			Total (%)
	Area 1	Area 2	Area 3	
Within 7 days	33	62	15	71
8–14 days	2	1	14	11
15–31 days	1	2	7	7
More than 31 days	1	–	16	11
Total cases	**37**	**65**	**52**	

*There was no information recorded on the point at which assessments began in 19 per cent (32/186) of the cases with assessments recorded on file.

Inter-agency collaboration

The level of inter-agency and inter-professional collaboration in the assessment process was difficult to establish from the data available. It was apparent that assessments often involved information gathering from other agencies. For example, some practitioners consulted with the Immigration and Nationality Directorate (IND) to establish the status of an individual's application for asylum. There was also evidence of practitioners gathering information from those initially caring for young people in foster and residential placements or from agency workers within specialist refugee community organisations. There was also some evidence of involvement from external professionals in cases where special needs or risk assessments were undertaken.

Involvement of external professionals was more likely where young people already had some connection with them at the point of referral. For example, there was evidence of immigration services identifying cases where they believed that a young person was particularly "at risk". In such cases, representatives of the IND often became further involved in joint planning. Similarly, there was multiple agency involvement in cases that concerned young people whose ages had been formally disputed by immigration services. There was also evidence of a pattern of inter-agency collaboration linked to the "accommodation" of a child or young person, as this often prompted liaison with local authority education and health practitioners who have responsibility for "looked after" children. Liaison with external agencies also occurred when practitioners identified concerns regarding the physical or mental health of young people. In some cases, this was prompted by immigration solicitors acting upon information acquired while assisting a young person with their asylum claim. Referrals for assessment were also made to specialist health agencies, such as the Medical Foundation for the Care of Victims of Torture or Child and Adolescent Mental Health Services.

Models of assessment

Analysis of the interview data suggested that approaches to assessment differed both within and between authorities. Smale and Tuson (1993) have identified three broad models of assessment: the "questioning

model", the "procedural model" and the "exchange model". In the questioning model, the social worker as expert asks questions of those to be
assessed, collates and analyses the information and produces conclusions.
In the procedural model, the social worker follows a clear format to gather
information and to assess whether standard thresholds have been reached.
The exchange model, however, places emphasis on the assessed person as
expert about their situation and the need to aid them in planning how to
reach their goals. Milner and O'Bryne (2002) suggest that the models are
closely linked to the salience given by social workers to the different
factors of risk, resources or needs. This corresponds with the patterns that
are evident in this study.

Procedures within two of the authorities varied according to age and
perceived vulnerability. The procedures for those aged under 16 involved
an assessment of need to inform a long-term plan for care. Comparatively,
these assessments were more in-depth and were more often characterised
by the "exchange model" of assessment. The procedures for those aged
16 or 17 tended to provide less scope for the needs assessment to inform
a plan for care. For example, within one generic asylum team in Area 2,
the focus of assessment was primarily to determine the local authority's
duty to a young person rather than to explore their needs *per se*. The
assessment procedures within Area 3, however, did not vary greatly
according to age and in the main appear to have followed an "exchange
model" of practice.

The procedural model

The "procedural model" of practice was more likely to be adopted in
response to referrals of older teenagers.[6] The practitioners conducting
these initial assessments were more likely to be social care practitioners
rather than qualified social workers. Initial assessments were frequently

---

[6] The practice of two teams, in particular, tended to follow this model. One was a social
services team that had a primary responsibility for placing teenagers, often out of
authority, and had little direct involvement in these cases subsequently. The other was a
generic asylum team supporting adults, families and older unaccompanied minors. By
the close of the study, neither of these teams retained a role in assessments. However,
there was greater variability in initial assessments for older teenagers more generally.

conducted on the basis of a single interview that resulted in decisions affecting the long-term placement and support of young people. Many of these young people were then placed at some distance from the local authority and/or in the care of external housing agencies acting on behalf of the authority without further assessment of their needs. Procedural assessments could therefore be described primarily as a "screening process" used to determine a young person's eligibility for services:

The initial assessment is just straightforward – your name, got any money, any health issues – it is just a standard form for everyone on whether they would be accepted for a service. (Ghedi's support worker)

The services subsequently provided were also procedural and principally resource-led. A room in a shared flat or house was allocated without formal support, a standard weekly allowance was granted, standard referral letters were issued that stated a young person's need to be registered with health and dental practices and their need to access an English for Speakers of Other Languages (ESOL) class. The provision of services under s17 of the Children Act 1989 was 'standard practice; it was actually part of the assessment form'. At the time of the study, these young people were not allocated a support worker unless they were considered to be vulnerable. One practitioner explained:

I think there was a real variation in different approaches to assessment by the workers. Like, for example, some workers may have been from a social work background or may have had a lot of experience so they would have picked up on someone's vulnerability. Whereas other workers would be much more aware of the immigration side of things so they would have been approaching it from a different angle . . . [and] focus on different issues. (Duty social worker, Area 2)

Young people who experienced this model of assessment often lacked understanding of their rights and entitlements and of the alternatives in placement and support that might have been available to them. Although some were not critical of social services, as they had been given some-where to stay and something to eat and without such help they might have been "on the streets", others, who had gradually developed greater awareness of their rights, were more reflective about their experiences. One young person said that he was not asked about his health, his educational needs or aspirations nor about how he was managing living alone and supporting himself: 'I didn't think I had all those options, you know.' Another described how she had to take care of herself in the beginning and only came to realise what she had missed when her tutor explained social services' role and helped her to access mainstream education. She felt that she might have managed her life better if she had been given the option of foster care.

The exchange model

Practitioners working within children and families teams were more likely to have adopted the "exchange model" of assessment. Using this model, practitioners tended to work with children and young people to identify their needs and to assist them to work with or restore their own problem-solving potential. The analysis of young people's accounts suggests that the foundations for this "exchange" were laid by practitioners through the calm and sensitive manner in which they first approached young people and through the ways in which they informed them of their choices. Many young people described a period of time characterised by feelings of isolation, which they associated with language difficulties and a realisation that they were "alone", lacking a family upon which they could depend. However, during this time they also became aware of how social services could help them and some felt able to articulate their own needs and plan for the future together with practitioners, as illustrated in the following case examples.

Miremba, aged 16, was identified as at risk of being trafficked for prostitution and was placed in foster care. As a result of attending a health screening, she was found to be pregnant. Miremba described this as a time of confusion and worry. She was well supported by her foster carer and social worker who explained the different choices that she could make. However, during this time she felt increasingly isolated and uncomfortable living in a family in a predominantly white area. She wanted to live independently, as she had done for a number of years in Africa, and to be living in an area where "other African people live". Her social worker assisted her to move to a semi-independent placement, where she shared with another girl who was also pregnant and had recently arrived from another African country. They both received support from a female African support worker. Miremba said that she felt better able to deal with her situation after this move.

Ana Paula was placed in foster care with her two sisters. Although her initial assessment was delayed for some time, Ana Paula was happy with the process. She remembered that her worker spent time getting to know them and what they liked. Her worker said that their plan to move into an independent placement when her eldest sister reached 18 was formulated with the three girls together: 'Their aim was . . . to stay together as a family, to establish their life and get a good education.' Although all three may have been better supported in foster care, it was not possible for the eldest sister to remain beyond 18. The proposed response represented a compromise, but it focused upon the priorities that were set by the young people themselves.

However, this was not always the case. Some young people described being unable to tell practitioners about how they felt in their placements or about what they wanted, although the assessment itself was characterised by an "exchange model". Both of the following quotes come from interviews with young people who described being told very clearly that they could make choices about what should happen. They were aged under 16 and both described having to accept that they had to go to school and that they could not live alone. However, neither elected to inform their social workers about needs that they wanted help with:

After I went there [to the children's home], nobody came back until after a week or so. So I didn't tell anybody about what I want. (Desta, who wanted to try and trace her father as soon as possible)

At that time, I was feeling really stressed actually. I wasn't really liking it. I was going to say, 'I don't want to live in this family'. (Kamuran, who wanted to live with a family who spoke his language and could understand him)

In these cases, young people generally described a process of assessment that appears to have been protracted and/or disrupted due to a change in practitioner. This affected the relationships that they had with their social workers and Desta, in particular, emphasised that she thought it was important that a social worker should help young people to talk earlier and to ask questions. She said that she had wanted to talk about her father but no one had asked and she felt that she could not raise the issue with anyone. Desta's experience corresponds with concerns expressed by practitioners that they were reluctant to gather information about, or to "delve too deeply" into, young people's families and personal histories at such an early stage in the relationship. Some practitioners suggested that this was an issue particular to assessing the needs of unaccompanied children.

Conducting assessments

Guidance available on working with unaccompanied children and young people emphasises the importance of taking account of their needs as children, first and foremost, but it also draws attention to them as children in "special circumstances" (Department of Health, 1995; Department of Health *et al*, 2000; Kidane, 2001b).

Many practitioners described a need to take things slowly. They often felt it appropriate to focus initially on immediate needs relating to young people's current circumstances. Some described the process of assessment as characterised by a sudden flurry of activity focused upon gathering basic information about the young person and ensuring that their basic needs were met: 'to make sure that housing, education, referral to solicitors and doctors, medical and all that is set up straight away'. In general, they were reluctant to broach more complex emotional issues until later. However, some young people themselves felt that there could have been more recognition of their social needs at an earlier stage and some, like Desta, had wanted an opportunity to talk about some of the difficulties they had experienced. They had felt unable to raise these issues but had hoped that their social workers would ask them. However, in other cases practitioners had made attempts to explore young people's experiences of their past and it was apparent from the information recorded on case files that many had received some account of past family relationships and/or of young people's experiences of becoming exiled.

Practitioners felt that assessments were challenging due to uncertainty surrounding their knowledge of the young people. Some practitioners were preoccupied with uncertainties surrounding age. There was agreement that assessing age was difficult and some referred to a lack of training or guidance on how to make an age assessment. It was suggested that some of the age assessments initially undertaken were problematic and that the decisions made at the time of referral or initial assessment were difficult to work with. For example, a social worker believed that a boy with whom he was working was older than his presenting age and connected this to many of the subsequent difficulties that the young person had experienced relating to peers and to living in a foster placement:

They assess age based on one interview. I don't think anyone can do it. I think it is very hard and that's why I think the system is wrong. I have also said that to management and policy officers. I think there needs to be more liaison with the health service and different agencies, and also an assessment done over a period of time. (Joseph's social worker)

Joseph's social worker felt that it was only possible to work with him in a way that reflected the age that he was "on paper", as it was a legal requirement for young people under the age of 16 to be "looked after". Some workers resented age assessments and considered it more appropriate to focus on the person and their apparent needs to determine the services that were required:

This is happening more and more, especially with this age group, that we have to be detectives rather than social workers. It is horrible and I can't stand it, I just hate it, hate it. (Meena's social worker)

Other practitioners adopted a more pragmatic approach, whereby, following a further process of assessment, they agreed with the young person the age that they believed them to be and worked with them accordingly. This was considered a necessary step towards identifying their "real" needs and planning responses accordingly. Provided the agreed age was below 18, this was generally done without informing immigration services to prevent any jeopardy to their asylum claims.

Many practitioners found it difficult to work with a lack of information about young people's pasts or were made uneasy about the formal stories young people had presented to them. They dealt with this uncertainty in different ways. Some suspended their "need to know" and focused on building a relationship with the young person. Others constructed their own stories, although it is unclear how they formulated these judgements or how these influenced their responses to young people. Some were more understanding than others of the predicament that young people faced and of the pressure that this placed on them:

Quite often they can't tell us everything anyway or they have been told to tell us a different story to the reality of their situations. But you kind of pick things up. I mean, I can tell that she comes from quite a nice family environment, she has obviously had some good parenting. (Desta's social worker)

At first I don't think he trusted anyone at all, so he didn't want to speak. He actually lied about his story when he first came to the UK. That's one of his big problems, he lied and made the same story that we hear from a lot of people, that they were getting attacked by people there and he gave a false name as well. (Social worker to Abdulaziz, who later revealed that his father had killed his mother and a neighbour as they were known to be having an affair and that his father had then been killed by the neighbour's family)

Others felt that it was sometimes impossible to adequately assess young people's needs or to respond to them appropriately. Some young people remained private, enclosed and reluctant to engage or share information with social workers. Some workers also offered examples of cases where they believed that young people were in contact with their families, but were uncertain about the extent and nature of this contact or its implications for young people's ability to cope and settle in the UK.

The issues identified here also point to a need for initial assessments to be revisited over time. As was the case with Abdulaziz, young people's stories and needs changed or emerged over time as practitioners gradually built more trusting relationships with them. Initial assessments must therefore be seen as provisional and subject to a continuing and careful process of review.

The overall quality of assessments

Information from their case files was used to construct an overall measure of the adequacy of assessment carried out for each young person. The measure was derived by judgements made by the research team and based on a reading of the case files. Checks for inter-rater reliability were carried out through a pilot of 11 cases as a means for checking for consistency of interpretation (see Chapter 2 for further details). Assessments were classified as "adequate or better" where there was evidence that a needs assessment had been conducted (addressing the key areas of a young person's life) *and* that an adequate plan to respond to any identified needs had been made. They were considered "less than adequate" where the evidence available demonstrated a poor assessment of need *and/or* a poor response to any needs identified (for example, where an identifiable outcome to the assessment was lacking). Although this can only constitute an approximate measure, it is helpful in highlighting factors associated with better assessments.

Better assessments were more likely to have been carried out by qualified social workers (p<0.001; n = 166). Almost three-fifths (59 per cent) of assessments conducted by social workers were "adequate or better" compared to just 14 per cent of those conducted by unqualified practitioners. Linked to this, assessments were consistently better when they were undertaken in children's teams (p<0.001; n = 212) and for younger children (p<0.001; n = 212). These findings are not surprising and reflect the different responsibilities and staff backgrounds of the respective teams. Younger children were more likely to fall within the remit of children's teams and, in these teams, assessments were more likely to be the province of qualified social workers adopting an "exchange model" of assessment. What is at issue here, in particular, is the need to improve the scope and quality of assessments provided to older teenagers, many of whom experienced a "procedural" assessment and went on to receive standardised and resource-led service responses that may or may not have been appropriate for their needs.

In these respects, the findings confirm those of earlier studies that highlighted the variable nature of assessments for young people referred at 16 or 17 years of age. However, our findings suggest that this should occur in the context of improving the quality of assessments available to all unaccompanied young people. After all, it was still the case that fewer than one-half of those aged under 16 received an "adequate or better" assessment (48 per cent) and that two-fifths of assessments conducted by qualified social workers were less than adequate. In this sense, there is little room for complacency.

More comprehensive assessments tended to share a range of characteristics. The information recorded reflected a timely response to a referral or at least accounted for apparent delays in the assessment process. For example, practitioners documented the dates of initial interviews and any subsequent interviews, as well as the dates of interviews that had been planned but not realised. The information gathered was clearly recorded and, consequently, it was possible to gain an understanding of the needs of each young person and of the decision-making process that had underpinned the actions that were planned or taken. There was clear evidence of practitioners considering a range of development needs, even where knowledge of young people's pasts was limited, and taking account of young people's current and future placement needs by exploring their feelings and experiences of placement. Practitioners were often able to document young people's accounts of their journeys from their countries of origin, their current and past health, their past experiences of education and their future aspirations, as well as basic information on family members and any other relatives or contacts they had. There was also evidence of practitioners "weighing-up" this information and formulating a plan to meet the needs identified through a range of clearly defined short- and long-term actions.

In contrast, less adequate assessments were poorly recorded. In many of these cases, there was evidence of worrying gaps in information on assessment or on planned responses to potential risks or needs. In some instances, young people had gone to live with adult relatives without any assessment of these relationships or the capacity of the adult to care for the young person. In others, young people were identified as having a particular need but there was no evidence of any actual or planned follow-up (for example, to chronic health issues or experiences of social isolation). Some assessments failed to take account of young people's ability to manage and/or their experience within their current living arrangements. Siblings were often only assessed as a group, although it was clear that they had different needs in relation to their roles within the family unit. Furthermore, poor assessments were sometimes dominated by a single issue to the apparent detriment of young people's other needs, such as working towards a kinship placement in the longer term. The recordings on these assessments suggested that the process itself was relatively brief, often based upon a single interview at the referral stage, and that the information gathered was generally basic. In more extreme cases, as we have seen, it was sufficient only to screen for young people's entitlements to services and to enable a standard menu of services to be delivered.

Summary

There is limited evidence about how assessments of unaccompanied young people have been carried out, how and why they may vary, and how responses to their needs are planned.

Most young people were referred to social services relatively soon after arriving in the UK (72 per cent within two weeks). Approaches to initial assessment varied across teams. Many practitioners focused on establishing whether the young person was "unaccompanied" and "in need". Teams generally worked with a broad definition of "unaccompanied" to include children living with responsible adults, extended family members or family friends, as well as with those who were alone. Some teams, however, gave greater priority to establishing the eligibility of young people for services, requiring proof of their age, their status as asylum seekers or of their local connection, sometimes refusing services until these credentials were established.

Age assessments were difficult to conduct and were often unsatisfactory, decisions sometimes originating from a single meeting. Case files often failed to provide a clear rationale for age-related decisions and further guidance and training are likely to be necessary to improve the quality of age assessments.

Although most young people (88 per cent) received some initial assessment, core assessments were rarely undertaken in line with the Assessment Framework – amounting to only 8 per cent of the whole sample and 18 per cent of those who were subsequently looked after. Core assessments were more likely to take place for younger children, for young people with more complex health and welfare needs or for those placed informally or seeking family reunification.

Different models of assessment were evident across teams. A "procedural model", following a standardised format to determine eligibility for services and leading to a standardised menu of services was more likely for those aged 16 or 17 and often amounted to little more than a "screening process". An "exchange model" was more often adopted by children's teams and involved working with young people to inform them of their options and to help them articulate their own needs and aspirations over time. This model was generally more satisfactory for young people.

Better overall assessments were undertaken in children's teams, by qualified social workers and for younger children. This reflects the different roles and responsibilities of teams. While there is clearly a need to improve the scope and quality of assessments for older teenagers, many of whom received only basic and resource-led assessments, this should be placed in the context of improvement for all. After all, only 48 per cent of those below the age of 16 received an "adequate or better" needs assessment (as rated by the research team) and two-fifths of assessments conducted by qualified social workers were "less than adequate".

Assessments were too commonly a one-off event. Young people's stories and needs often changed over time as relationships and levels of trust grew. Initial assessments should therefore be seen as provisional and be subject to a continuing process of review.

4 Patterns of placement

Unaccompanied young people who arrive in the UK are likely to feel anxious, confused and disoriented. They also face uncertainty about their futures. A pressing need for young people is to find a place to live that can provide sanctuary, a chance to re-centre their lives and opportunities to form new attachments as part of their resettlement. Decisions affecting the placement of young people were amongst the most critical that were taken by practitioners during assessment. This chapter considers this aspect of the assessment process in more detail and identifies some factors associated with "better" assessments. We explore patterns of placement for young people over the period of time they were supported by social services and identify differences in their experiences and the support provided in different placement settings, taking account of the constraints that may limit accommodation options for unaccompanied young people.[1]

Legislation and guidance

The Children Act 1989 and its associated regulations and guidance give local authorities a duty to provide services necessary to safeguard and promote the welfare of children "in need". Lacking the presence of their parents or customary caregivers, unaccompanied minors are by definition children "in need" (Department of Health, 1995). A careful assessment of need is required to determine what services are necessary and whether these would best be met by providing them with accommodation as a "looked after" child (s20) or as a child "in need" in the community (s17). The implications of these distinctions for the nature and level of social work support young people are likely to receive, including their eligibility

---

[1] Immigration rules are a major factor constraining accommodation options for unaccompanied young people at 18. Chapter 8 explores these issues at the "leaving care" stage. This chapter focuses on the use of placement settings while young people were formally supported by social services from initial referral onwards.

for services under the Children (Leaving Care) Act 2000, were discussed in Chapter 1.

Although research into the use of placement resources for unaccompanied young people is limited (Mitchell, 2003), what there is has tended to suggest that this distinction is a key one that is defined largely by age at referral, by placement supply factors and by differences in age-related funding for unaccompanied asylum seeking young people through the Home Office Special Grant.[2] Studies have suggested that, where young people have been referred at 16 or 17 years of age, they are much more likely to have been provided with accommodation under s17, more often in unsupported accommodation of variable quality and with inconsistent or inadequate levels of social work support (Stone, 2000; Stanley, 2001; Dennis, 2002).

The legality of providing accommodation to lone children under s17 had been open to some question. The Adoption and Children Act 2002 amended s17 of the Children Act 1989 to make it permissible to use accommodation in this way (Children's Legal Centre, 2004). However, guidance issued by the Department of Health in June 2003 made clear that provision of accommodation under s17 should *almost always* concern children needing to be accommodated with their families and that, in the case of lone children under the age of 18, there should be a *presumption* for them to be accommodated and looked after under s20. Only where clear contraindications are uncovered during a thorough assessment – for example, where the child refuses to accept being looked after *and* they are considered competent to look after themselves – should accommodation and support under s17 be considered (Department of Health, 2003).[3]

Over the past decade guidance has been made available to assist local authorities when considering care arrangements for unaccompanied

---

[2] The Special Grant provides two distinct levels of remuneration to local authorities for support of unaccompanied minors according to whether they were first supported before or after the age of 16. Studies have suggested persuasively that the lower level of grant for those aged 16 or over has affected placement options for this age group.

[3] This guidance and its potential impact on services for unaccompanied children and young people largely post-dates data collection for this study. In general, information presented in this and other chapters provides a benchmark for the state of services at that point.

minors. The *Framework for the Assessment of Children in Need and their Families* draws particular attention to the importance of conducting careful assessments for unaccompanied asylum seeking children before reaching decisions about appropriate placement (Department of Health *et al*, 2000). Official practice guidance was first issued in 1995 (Department of Health, 1995) and a more recent supplementary guide, taking account of changes in policy and law, has been endorsed by the Government (Kidane, 2001b). Guidelines to support good practice have also been issued by the Separated Children in Europe Programme (2004), the United Nations High Commissioner for Refugees (1994) and by the Council of the European Union (2003). In addition, a training resource has more recently been developed for foster carers (Kidane and Amerena, 2004). Some broad consensual messages have emerged from this work that may assist practitioners when thinking about placement arrangements for unaccompanied young people:

- There is a need for speedy but well-informed, immediate responses to young people's needs for appropriate placement.
- Unless the assessment and care plan demonstrate that these needs can be met in some other way, the local authority should accommodate the child under s20. For younger children under 16 or those lacking experience of living outside the family, foster care should be the placement of first choice. Adoption will rarely be appropriate. Some older young people, or those less able to cope with the intimacy of a family setting, may prefer an alternative supported or residential environment.
- Efforts should be made to keep sibling groups together, provided this is consistent with their wishes, although account should be taken of the caring capacities and responsibilities of older siblings when placing sibling groups together in more independent settings.
- Placement decisions should take account of the wishes and feelings of the child and of their cultural, linguistic and religious needs. Efforts should be made to build links with their communities of origin.
- Where young people have been living with friends or relatives, these carers should be properly assessed for their ability to provide suitable care. These placements should be supported and monitored so as to provide continuity for young people.
- Placement decisions should be supported by a written care plan and

regular arrangements for review. Placement changes should be kept to a minimum.

• Young people aged 16–17 should not be treated as *de facto* adults and placed on their own without access to adult support.[4] Their apparent maturity may conceal other vulnerabilities.

Assessment

Information on the assessment of young people's need for placement was drawn from recordings in case files and related primarily to the period of initial assessment soon after referral.[5] Where there was evidence that some initial assessment of young people's needs had been conducted, consideration of placement almost always occurred (96 per cent of these cases; 89 per cent of cases overall). However, even where placement needs had been considered, in 10 per cent of these cases no outcome of this assessment was recorded on file (20 per cent of cases overall).

Local authority placement procedures

Almost one-half of the young people (47 per cent) were provided with accommodation on the same day as referral. Many, therefore, arrived at social services in emergency circumstances needing immediate placement. The management of referral, initial assessment and placement varied according to a number of factors: the place and nature of young people's arrival in the UK; their age; team policies and procedures; the placement resources available; and whether or not young people already had some form of pre-referral placement.

In Area 1, three-quarters of the young people (74 per cent) were identified at point of arrival in the UK and immediately referred to social services. Initial assessment on the day was usually undertaken by a duty service and young people were provided with a temporary placement pending further assessment. Where young people were placed depended

---

[4] The Council of the European Union (2003) deferred on this point, suggesting it may be acceptable to place this age group in accommodation centres for adult asylum seekers, an approach that would contravene the principles underpinning the Children Act 1989.

[5] The importance of arrangements for ongoing assessment and review is considered later in the chapter.

on age, sex, time of arrival and evolving team procedures. Females under 18 were more likely to be provided with an emergency foster placement, as were young boys under 13. Males aged 13 or over were likely to be placed in temporary residential placements before moving on to host families, supported housing or for placement out of authority.[6]

In Areas 2 and 3, referral at the point of arrival was rare (92 per cent of referrals in Area 3 and 100 per cent of referrals in Area 2 were made "in country"). The predominant pattern was for young people to make their way to these authorities, usually due to a local connection. At referral some of these young people required immediate placement, either they had nowhere to stay or had stayed temporarily with people they had met. Age and team procedures also influenced patterns of initial placement in these areas.

In Area 2, age largely determined which of two teams managed the referral. Where young people were considered to be below age 16, referrals were generally managed by a children's team. Where they were considered older, young people tended to be referred to an asylum team for older asylum seekers, unless they were thought to be particularly vulnerable. This latter team relied heavily upon private sector shared housing for unaccompanied minors, a form of housing that usually lacked direct placement support, and young people were routinely placed in these settings at referral. The children's team generally managed referrals according to age and perceived vulnerability. Younger children tended to be placed initially in foster or residential placements. Those who were older – and assessed as having adequate life skills – were sometimes placed in supported housing with key worker support.

In Area 3, all new referrals were managed by a children's team. A greater proportion of referrals to this authority (and to a lesser extent in Area 2) involved young people who were already living in informal or unregulated placements with extended kin, with adults they had met post-arrival or with host families/carers accessed through community or refugee organisations. In these circumstances, the primary challenge for

---

[6] "Host families" constituted placements that fell somewhere between informal foster care and supported lodgings, were often provided by refugee community associations and frequently recruited "carers" from within these communities.

practitioners at referral was to assess the suitability of these living arrangements and their potential for providing the forms of stability and continuity for young people envisaged in official guidance. In Area 3, where young people lacked potential carers at referral, those under 16 were more likely to be placed initially in foster or residential placements (although this was not always the case). Those aged 16 plus (and some who were younger) were likely to access shared, supported housing, often managed by community organisations, for a period of preparation prior to independence.

Shortages in the supply of appropriate placements affected all authorities. In these circumstances, *ad hoc* interim arrangements were made for initial placements, including use of hotels or other forms of temporary accommodation, especially for older males.

In all authorities, policies and procedures for managing referrals and placements evolved over the course of the study as teams adapted to new challenges or perceived weaknesses in existing strategies. For example, in Area 1 new lines of responsibility between intake and long-term teams were established to improve procedures, a major housing support agency closed and new forms of core and cluster supported housing were being envisaged. In Area 2, the adult asylum team ceased to work with unaccompanied minors and all new referrals of under-18s were being managed by the children's team. In Area 3, new supported housing with on-site key work support was being developed to reduce the reliance on community organisations, whose support to young people was perceived as inconsistent. Most of these changes were occurring at or after the end of data collection and are therefore not fully represented in our findings. However, they do reflect the fact that, in a fast-moving area of social work practice, nothing stands still for long.

Variations in assessment

Although assessments constituted the primary strategies for responding to young people's initial placement needs, there was considerable variation in quality. The likelihood of young people receiving some initial assessment of their placement needs was significantly associated with age ($p<0.01$; $n = 212$) and, to a lesser extent, with sex ($p = 0.05$; $n = 212$).

Older young people were less likely to receive an assessment before placement, perhaps especially older males.

In general terms, young people who were referred before the age of 16 were more likely to have received a thorough initial assessment; one that situated their need for placement in the context of an assessment of their broader needs and which attempted to take into account their wishes and feelings. However, many young people required an immediate emergency placement. In these circumstances, practitioners were constrained by available resources. Although mindful of the value of matching young people to potential foster carers, this was not always feasible. While placements with white British families or in placements with the closest available match by ethnic origin, country of origin or religion often worked quite successfully, in some other cases they did not and, in a few cases, led to breakdown.

In extremis, practitioners were also reliant on emergency placements in hotels or bed and breakfast accommodation (especially in Areas 1 and 2). Usually young people were placed in accommodation reserved specifically for unaccompanied minors although, in some hotels, adult asylum seekers were also present. Recent reports have been critical of the use of these kinds of accommodation for unaccompanied young people (Audit Commission, 2000; Stanley, 2001). These placements were intended as short-term solutions allowing for further assessment and a move on to more suitable alternative accommodation. However, there were several instances where these placements subsequently drifted, where there was little evidence of follow-up or further assessment and where young people remained *in situ* for quite lengthy periods.

Temporary accommodation of this kind was less commonly used for older females and there was evidence of older females moving straight to emergency foster or residential placements at referral. This was especially the case in Area 1 and reflected procedures for older females identified at point of arrival. Initial placements of this kind were also used where young women were thought to be vulnerable as a result of their past experiences or where there were suspicions that they may have been trafficked to the UK. These were often short-term arrangements, allowing for a period of recuperation and preparation before young people moved on to semi-independent placements.

Some older young people, more often male, received only a minimal assessment of their needs and their transition from referral to placement appeared largely procedural. In most instances, these young people moved straight to private shared housing that was either unsupported or provided only a low level of support. From the case file evidence, it was not clear that in many of these cases there had been an adequate (or any) assessment of their capacity to live independently before placing them. In some instances, young people were just given written directions to the placement and were told to make their own way there. This added greatly to the anxiety and confusion young people were inevitably feeling at this time. Once placed, there was also often little evidence of further follow-up or assessment.

Where young people already had informal placements at the time of referral, there was evidence of considerable variation in the quality of assessment. In some cases, relatively careful assessments were undertaken involving several home visits, checks with relevant authorities and, where necessary, liaison with other local authorities. In others, private fostering arrangements or placements with host families appeared to be ratified too readily. A major concern for practitioners centred on the credentials of the "carer" and the relationship between them and the young person. Extended kin relationships were often unclear. Where young people had been placed by community organisations, an assessment of the carer's capacity to provide suitable care was necessary. From the perspective of practitioners, this was made more difficult when these organisations brokered the relationship between them and the young person, sometimes acting as interpreters in all encounters. Although an arrangement of this kind could be positive for the young person, it made an independent assessment of the young person's wishes, the carer's abilities and the organisation's support role more difficult to achieve. In these circum-stances, the placement was sometimes approved and supported without sufficient evidence that it was the best option for the young person at that time.

Recent reports have highlighted the lack of regulation that currently exists in private fostering, the failure of carers to comply with notification and limitations in current arrangements for the assessment and monitoring of private fostering arrangements (Philpot, 2001; Clarke, 2002; Bostock,

2003). Although the Children Act 2004 has introduced a tighter framework, it still falls short of the formal registration scheme recommended in these reports. Concerns about these limitations were also reflected in comments made by some practitioners in this study:

> *In some ways it is such a dangerous set-up for the authority...*
> *because up until they are 16 the authority is still responsible if*
> *something happens ... I don't even know what background checks they*
> *do ... It just seems very loose.* (Social worker, Area 2)

These findings point to the significant challenges presented to practitioners when attempting to reconcile needs, process and placement resources in individual cases. In overall terms, better assessments tended to situate young people's placement needs as part of a broader assessment that engaged with all aspects of their lives. Where an emergency placement was required or where young people were already placed, this could take place over time, taking account of young people's wishes and capacities. Careful and thorough checks were made of carers and an assessment of how young people were faring in placement, including regular home visits and independent time with the young person, tended to follow.

Poorer assessments also tended to share certain features. Lack of recording in case files tended to be indicative that only a brief consideration of young people's needs and capacities had taken place and this was more likely where older young people had been moved on immediately to shared housing in a procedural manner. Brief assessments often failed to take account of young people's broader needs and young people appeared to have fewer choices about placement options. Where young people were already in informal living situations, assessments were also marked by a failure to adequately assess the placement or, where young people were proposing to live with family members, friends or older carers, by a limited assessment of the proposed placement and of arrangements for monitoring it.

Finally, in circumstances where a young person's exact age was disputed, procedures for their referral, assessment and placement could also be affected. Disputes of this kind are not uncommon and young people may be refused access to a service until this is clarified (Munoz, 1999;

71

Dennis, 2002). Local authorities have lacked clear guidelines for conducting age assessments and, in any event, these assessments are subject to a considerable margin of error (Levenson and Sharma, 1999). In this study, informal or formal concerns about age were evident for over one-quarter of the young people (26 per cent). While this did not always affect acceptance for a service, it sometimes affected the type of placement provided by social services. There were also instances where the ages of individuals had been formally challenged by the Home Office at the point of entry or where younger children had arrived with older siblings who were thought to be 18 or over. In these circumstances, young people spent periods of time in accommodation provided by the National Asylum Support Service (NASS) before being referred to or accepted for a service by social services, usually only after an age assessment had been completed by a paediatrician. This process often resulted in a considerable delay before their needs could be assessed and met.

Patterns of placement

There is a lack of detailed information about how placement resources are used for unaccompanied children and young people and how these placements are deployed for different sub-groups within the overall population (Mitchell, 2003). This section uses the case file data to provide an overview of the main forms of accommodation accessed by young people over the period of time they had been supported by social services – a period ranging from four to 30 months across the sample as a whole.

First and last placement

Table 4.1 shows the first and last placement for the sample as a whole. First placement relates to the first placement provided or approved by social services after initial referral, taking account of the fact that some young people were already placed informally at that stage. Last placement relates to the last known placement for young people at the point of data collection (for those cases that remained open) or at the point of case closure (if this had occurred earlier). Cases classified as "no clear evidence" refer to those where it was impossible to discern from the case file the precise type of accommodation used by young people at either time point.

Table 4.1
First and last placement (n = 212)

	First placement	Last placement
	Per cent	
Foster care	10	9
Residential care	10	2
Supported accommodation	22	26
Unsupported accommodation	29	33
Kinship placement	11	14
No clear evidence	18	17

In overview, Table 4.1 points to the changes in placement usage associated with young people "ageing out" of the care system. Over three-quarters of young people (77 per cent) at the point of data collection were aged 17 or over and, of those with a last placement in foster care, 58 per cent were aged 16 or 17 at this point and preparing for later independence. This helps to explain the small rise in the proportion of young people living in supported or unsupported accommodation at the close of the study. The small rise in the number of young people living in kinship placements reflects the later identification of extended family members and attempts by local authorities to promote reunification.

Placement usage

Access to a first placement in these different types of accommodation varied by age at referral (p<0.001; n = 173), sex (p<0.01; n = 173) and care status (p<0.001; n = 161). The range of foster placements used varied considerably and included local authority foster carers, carers provided by independent fostering providers (IFPs), both within and outside local authority boundaries, and the approval of more informal care arrangements under fostering regulations. It was not surprising to find that the vast majority of young people with a first placement in foster care (91 per cent) were looked after under s20 and were younger – over three-quarters

(77 per cent) were below the age of 16. Furthermore, as previously suggested, initial placements in foster care were more likely to be made for young women, almost one-third of whom (30 per cent) were placed in foster care compared to just 8 per cent of young men.

Two local authorities used residential units for unaccompanied minors and, in addition, some use was made of private and voluntary sector children's homes. Residential care was mainly used for an initial period of assessment and preparation before young people moved to semi-independent settings. They were mainly reserved for younger males accommodated under s20. Almost three-quarters (71 per cent) of those who accessed a residential placement were looked after (s20) and were both predominantly under 16 (81 per cent) and male (91 per cent). The mainly short-term nature of these placements is reflected in the very small proportion of the sample in residential settings at data collection (Table 4.1).

Around one in nine young people first lived in kinship settings (Table 4.1). Young people may have travelled to the UK with an intention to live with these relatives and be residing with them prior to referral or, in one or two cases, were quickly transferred to them at the point of referral. This pattern was more common in Areas 2 and 3 where there was a greater proportion of "in country" referrals. A wide range of extended relatives was involved, including grandparents, aunts, uncles, older cousins and more distant relatives where the status of the relationship was more uncertain. Young people also sometimes arrived in sibling groups and the eldest sibling was approved as carer for the family unit. As indicated in Table 4.1, some young people were provided with temporary placements and then moved on to relatives at a later point. Active pursuit of the possibilities for reunification was more common in Area 1. In this authority, kinship placements only accounted for 2 per cent of all initial placements but, at the point of data collection, they accounted for more than one in five (22 per cent).

Obviously, the possibility of a kinship placement depends upon the presence of relatives in the first place. However, a majority of those placed tended to be under the age of 16 (65 per cent) and were somewhat more likely to be female (22 per cent of females) than male (11 per cent). Arrangements for supporting these placements tended to vary, although the majority of longer-term kinship placements were supported under s17 (58 per cent). In some instances they were treated as private fostering arrangements although, towards the end of the study, there was movement towards approving some as s20 foster placements. This not only affords young people greater care and protection and strengthens arrangements for social work support, but it also provides young people with later access to leaving care services should they require them. However, not all families appreciate the direct involvement of social services and, inevitably, the negotiation of these arrangements is a matter of some delicacy.

More than one in five young people moved straight to supported accommodation (Table 4.1). The provision of supported accommodation varied considerably. It included specialist housing projects with on-site support and supported hostels (YMCA hostels or foyers, for example). However, the predominant form was the provision of shared housing for groups of unaccompanied minors with floating support given by key workers. Accommodation of this kind was provided both within and outside the responsible authority, and was offered directly by social services or, more commonly, through the medium of private or voluntary housing agencies. Young people provided with a first placement in these settings were almost always supported under s17 (97 per cent) and were rather more likely to be male – 29 per cent of males had a first placement in supported housing compared to 16 per cent of females. While more than one-half of these young people were aged 16 or over at referral (59 per cent), it was perhaps more surprising to find that 28 per cent were aged 15 and 11 per cent were younger than this. A majority of these cases resided in Area 3 and related to unregulated pre-referral placements arranged by community organisations in shared housing with nominated "carers" – placements that were subsequently approved or changed at a later date by social services.

Nearly one-third of the sample was placed at referral in unsupported shared housing, mostly managed by private landlords or housing agencies (Table 4.1). In a smaller number of cases, it also included young people placed initially in hotels. Three-quarters of these young people were aged 16 or over at referral (74 per cent) and were almost always supported under s17 arrangements (98 per cent). There was no great difference in the likelihood of males or females being placed in these settings – 38 per cent of males compared to 27 per cent of females. Young people below the age of 16 (mostly aged 15) had either been subject to an age dispute and transferred to a team for older asylum seekers (Area 2) or had been placed in hotel accommodation after being identified at point of arrival (Area 1).

Placement pathways

The placement careers of young people were complex and, for many, involved moves within and between different types of placement. Although one in five young people (20 per cent) made no moves throughout the time they were supported, more than one-half of the sample (56 per cent) made one or two moves and one-quarter (25 per cent) made three or more. Table 4.2 shows the "main type" of placement in which young people lived while supported by social services or by agencies on their behalf. This was constructed from a detailed chronology of all placements for each young person and identifies the placement type in which they had spent the majority of their time. In one in seven cases (15 per cent) it was not possible to discern this pattern from case file recordings. Although this still tends to flatten out the complexity of young people's placement careers, it does provide a basis for identifying factors in young people's characteristics and experiences associated with different placement settings.

Table 4.2
Main type of placement (n = 212)

	Per cent
Mainly care*	11
Mainly supported accommodation	29
Mainly unsupported accommodation	31
Mainly kinship	14
No clear evidence	15

*Only four young people were mainly in a residential placement and 20 in foster care.

As we have just seen, these main placement pathways were rooted in the interplay between the placement resources available in different local authorities, team policies and procedures, the age of young people at referral and, linked to this, the section of the Children Act under which young people were subsequently supported.[7] In essence, where young people were referred below the age of 16, their cases were more likely to have been managed by a children's team and to have followed a s20 pathway. In consequence, these young people were more likely to have had a main placement in foster or residential care and, once they moved on, they were more likely to have moved on to forms of supported rather than unsupported accommodation. In contrast, older young people supported under s17 were much more likely to have spent the majority of their time in unsupported or supported housing (see Table 4.3).

Table 4.3

Main type of placement by care status (n = 168)

Main type of placement	S20 pathway*	S17 pathway
	per cent	
Mainly care	45	2
Mainly supported accommodation	24	40
Mainly unsupported accommodation	3	46
Mainly kinship	29	12

*Only a minority of young people followed a s20 pathway (n = 38). Large percentage differences therefore relate to quite small numbers. For example, only 11 young people (29 per cent) mainly lived in a kinship placement compared to 15 (12 per cent) of those supported under s17.

Other factors were also associated with these different placement settings. Where young people were mainly placed was also associated with other key aspects of their lives. First, the additional support provided to young people in care and kinship placements helped their engagement with

---

[7] Associations with "main type" of placement were as follows: local authority (p<0.001; n = 180); team (p<0.001; n = 180); age at referral (p<0.001; n = 180); care status (p<0.001; n = 168). It was interesting to find that, once young people had been placed, the pattern of these placement careers was no longer associated with sex (p = 0.63).

education (p<0.01; n = 102). No young people who predominantly lived in care placements and just 6 per cent of those in kinship placements spent a majority of their time out of education, compared to 32 per cent of those who mainly lived in supported settings and 33 per cent of those in unsupported accommodation. Second, young people living in care and kin settings also appeared to have stronger networks of social support (p<0.001; n = 180). These young people appeared to be more integrated (with carers, friends and community) and less prone to isolation than were those who lived mainly in semi-independent or independent placements. In these respects at least, care and kin placements seemed to offer more protection.

For young people living mainly in care and, to a lesser extent, kinship placements, support provided by professionals was more likely to form part of a broader package of care that addressed more aspects of young people's lives than was the case for those mainly in supported or unsupported accommodation (p<0.001; n = 180).[8] To a large degree, this pattern reflected the statutory responsibilities associated with being looked after (s20). Young people in care placements were more likely than any other group to have had care plans, regular reviews and regular contact with an allocated social worker over the time they were supported.[9] While young people in kinship settings were also more likely to have arrangements of this kind, when compared to those in either supported or unsupported accommodation, patterns of ongoing assessment, review and contact were considerably more irregular than for those in care, reflecting the greater proportion of kinship placements that were supported under s17.[10]

---

[8] This measure of overall support package was derived by the research team from a reading of case files. Judgements were reached about the adequacy of professional support provided to each young person in ten separate life areas and was then summed to provide an overall score per case on a scale of 0–10 (see Chapter 2 for further details).

[9] Associations with "main type" of placement were as follows: care plan (p<0.001; n = 180); reviews (p<0.001; n = 180); allocated social worker (p<0.001; n = 173).

[10] The findings based on a comparison of care and kinship settings should be treated with caution as numbers were low (n = 54). Fisher's Exact tests were used in an effort to compensate for this. Associations for care and kinship placements were as follows: care plan (p<0.01; n = 54); reviews (p<0.001; n = 54); allocated social worker (p<0.01; n = 50).

Finally, there is some research evidence that the placement of unaccompanied young people outside of the responsible authority has been quite commonplace, that it presents significant challenges to social workers when supporting young people in these settings and that young people may find it harder to access support (Audit Commission 2000; Stone, 2000; Stanley, 2001). Where it was possible to discern from case files where young people's placements were located (n = 153), around two-fifths (41 per cent) had been placed mainly out of authority during the time they were supported by social services. The decision to place young people out of authority seemed primarily to have been resource led, linked to the large numbers needing placement and to limitations in the local availability of placements. While many young people were placed in neighbouring authorities, others were moved to quite distant parts of the country. There was no association between placement out of authority and young people's personal characteristics (sex, age at referral, health status and so on) or according to whether they were looked after under s20 or supported under s17. It affected all categories of placement in a broadly similar way. For example, while 51 per cent of young people in unsupported accommodation were mainly located out of authority, this also applied to 36 per cent of those in supported accommodation and 32 per cent of those predominantly in care placements.

However, placement out of authority did require social services to place more reliance on the role of external agencies to provide for young people's day-to-day support and there was some evidence of variation in the support that was available to young people. In these circumstances, young people were much less likely to have had access to an allocated key worker (p<0.001; n = 153) – 11 per cent did so compared to 47 per cent placed within the authority – or to have had regular contact with them (p<0.01; n = 153). Although a similar pattern was evident in relation to access to allocated social workers, this did not reach the threshold for significance (p = 0.09). It would seem, therefore, that the provision of consistent support to young people placed out of authority was often more difficult to achieve.

Experiences of placement and support

The interviews with young people and practitioners shed further light on young people's experiences of living in different placement settings. This section looks at each of the main types of placement and identifies issues arising from differences in young people's experiences and in the support that was provided to them.

Residential care

Previous studies have suggested that unaccompanied children and young people are relatively unlikely to be placed in residential settings and that, where they are, they are most likely to be used for short-term periods of assessment soon after arrival (Williamson, 1998; Stanley, 2001). This picture is consistent with findings from this study. Twenty-one young people (10 per cent of the sample) had a first placement in residential care, mostly in units housing other unaccompanied young people. Use of placements in mainstream children's homes was rare. Most stays were for a relatively short period, although one or two young people stayed for five to six months before moving on to supported accommodation, kinship or foster placements.

Placements of this type provided a bridge to assist young people's initial adjustment to life in the UK and, where young people lacked the practical skills to manage in more independent settings, it offered opportunities for an intensive period of preparation. Comfort was also often found in the companionship of other young people from similar backgrounds who were facing similar challenges:

It was kind of good, for the first few months. Having people with you . . . speaking the same language, from the same country. It was good fun for a few months but, after a few months, you get bored. Same for everyone I think. (Amir)

Although young people often valued the care and support provided by residential social workers in these early days, boredom and frustration often set in and was accentuated where units were situated in more remote areas, isolated from the social links and connections that were of increasing importance to young people.

Some young people found the nature of residential regimes too constricting. Others found these environments and their relationships with peers quite stressful and were relieved when social workers, responding to their concerns, were able to identify more suitable placements. Research on mainstream children's homes has pointed to the importance of considering the mix of young residents and the implications this may have for the culture of the home and the quality of life experienced within it (Berridge and Brodie, 1998; Sinclair and Gibbs, 1998). What constitutes an appropriate mix can be a complex question for unaccompanied young people, especially given the limited residential (and supported hostel) resources available. However, there were several instances where young people felt unsettled and fearful as a result of turbulence generated between residents from different ethnic or national groups. Placement of unaccompanied young people in residential units (or indeed in shared housing) can allow for their more specific needs to be met and provide a welcome source of support and solidarity, but this needs to be set against a recognition of the heterogeneity within this population and the potential for tensions to arise (see also Khan, 2000; Stanley, 2001). The quality of leadership in well-run children's homes has also been identified as an important factor that can reduce tension and provide a positive culture (Sinclair and Gibbs, 1998).

Foster care

As we have seen, foster placements were the preferred option for younger "looked after" children and for the initial placement of some older females. Limitations in the supply of placements meant there was a considerable reliance on the role of independent fostering providers (IFPs) and on placements out of authority. For older young people, these were often short-term placements allowing for a period of adjustment and preparation before moving on, primarily to supported accommodation or kinship placements.

Where foster placements worked well, young people tended to value the support that was available from foster carers and social workers. For young people wanting and able to manage in a family setting, they often provided a feeling of safety and security and an opportunity to build attachments to an alternative family:

81

If it is [to be a] family, then it is this one . . . My background is that I come from a family, I liked being with my dad and everything . . . Yes, I like it. (Desta)

Desta, who arrived from Eritrea aged 15, was placed out of authority with Ethiopian carers through the medium of an IFP. She had lived there for 15 months, after an unhappy time spent in a residential unit. Her feelings about her carers were strengthened through close cultural ties, the ease of communication they afforded and the day-to-day care they provided:

They help me with everything, like how I do my hair. They offer advice; they help me with everything.

Practitioners were generally aware of the potential value of placements that met young people's cultural, religious and language needs. These were often in short supply and, as other research has found, efforts were often made to identify carers from young people's communities of origin, either directly or through links with external fostering agencies (Williamson, 1998). Sometimes the priority given to cultural matching involved compromising on other aspects of a placement and there were examples of young people living in overcrowded conditions, sharing two or three to a bedroom, or lacking private space or facilities for study. As we have also seen, especially in the context of private fostering arrangements or placements with host families, a desire to provide continuity for young people sometimes overrode the need for an adequate assessment of the carer's capacity to provide suitable care. The potential risks to young people when difficulties are underplayed in order to make a culturally appropriate placement have also been highlighted in official guidance (Department of Health, 1995).

In some cases only a broad cultural match could be made and, while this sometimes worked well, in a few cases it did not. Bacia, from Uganda, was placed with a black couple of West African and Jamaican descent. As she said: 'We had nothing in common, other than the man being African.' The tensions that grew between them eventually led to a breakdown and her move to supported accommodation. In some cases, therefore, broad matching policies may create difficulties for young people unless they take proper account of their wishes and feelings and are based on a careful assessment of individual needs. Bacia did not feel she had been given a great deal of choice about this placement.

The majority of young people moved into mainstream cross-cultural placements. Some young people prioritised living with an "English" family in order to learn the language and take full advantage of the possibilities for education. Although young people often spoke fondly of the kindness and support they had received, it often involved considerable sacrifice, as young people found communication difficult, struggled to adjust to new customs, expectations and norms of behaviour and, especially in more isolated locations, to cope with the effects of cultural isolation:

I really had the feeling of being like a family but, at the same time, because I [did] not speak any English and we have different cultural backgrounds . . . I did feel a bit lonely and afraid of doing something wrong. (Da-xia)

Occasionally, the links young people did have with their own communities could create additional pressure to remain in such placements at a time when young people were struggling to adjust:

I [felt] sad. I was wishing that I could be with someone I could under-stand at that time. But when I was speaking to anyone in my language, they were saying, 'Don't move away from this family because you need them to learn English.' (Kamuran)

In many cases, time aided young people's adjustment and these foster placements lasted quite successfully. Kamuran's placement, for example, had provided a stable home base for over two years at interview and, although as an older teenager he was finding it restrictive, he appreciated the care that had been provided. In some instances, young people's sense of isolation and their desire to be closer to their own communities grew over time, creating a restlessness or desire to move on to semi-independent settings. Da-xia was ultimately unable to resolve the cultural tensions inherent in her placement and opted to move to supported accommodation in an area with a stronger Chinese community. Even Kamuran, reflecting on plans to move on in the future, felt that he would move to an area where he could establish stronger links with the Kurdish community.

The Children Act (1989) makes provision for looked after children to have access to independent visitors. In keeping with recent research (Stanley, 2001), little use appeared to be made of these provisions for unaccompanied young people in this study. Some young people, however, were allocated support workers from the same or similar countries of origin and, in some cases, the emotional support provided by adults acting as interpreters proved helpful in guiding young people through the maze of resettlement. The development of independent visitor or befriending schemes, drawing on approved adults from young people's countries of origin, may therefore prove helpful in reducing the cultural isolation experienced by young people in circumstances where cross-cultural placements need to be made.

Some young people found the boundaries and controls attached to family placements increasingly frustrating, especially where carers were inflexible or failed to negotiate with them as older teenagers. Tensions of this kind created a dilemma for social workers who, on the one hand, were keen to maintain the placement and, on the other, needed to acknowledge the frustrations felt by young people. Efforts at mediation were sometimes successful, some inflexibility being counterbalanced by the all-round support the placement provided. In others, it was not and young people felt relieved to move to supported accommodation where they had greater freedom and control over their lives. These issues appeared to be particularly acute where young people had previously experienced a considerable degree of independence and responsibility, either before arriving in the UK or subsequently, or where there were continuing doubts about a young person's age. In these circumstances, practitioners were sometimes forced to recognise that a foster (or residential) placement was not the best environment in which to meet a young person's needs.

Reliance on independent fostering providers could also make social workers' lives more complicated, especially for placements out of authority where direct monitoring and support were more difficult. In these situations, good liaison and communication were essential but were not always forthcoming. The recent proliferation of IFPs also made the search for placements more complicated. Each time a new agency was approached, negotiations had to be conducted to build new relationships, understand how the agency operated and assess the varying levels of support and finance provided to carers and young people. Negotiating individual packages of care was time consuming, more costly and more formal than the relationships that existed with in-house fostering teams: *So it is much more about mediating and finding out how different agencies work, because they all offer different amounts of support and different levels of money to the carers and to the young people . . . Each time you have a new placement, unless it is an agency you have used before, you have to get to know the organisation as well.* (Social worker, Area 2)

Kinship placements

A significant minority of young people were placed with extended relatives. Either they had been living with them prior to referral (mainly Areas 2 and 3) or these moves had been planned after a stay in a short-term placement (Area 1). Where they worked well, they provided young people with stable and familiar attachments and, in a similar manner to care placements, tended to provide greater support for education and a stronger network of social support than that which was generally available to young people in more independent environments. The majority of these placements were supported under s17 arrangements.

Previous studies have raised concerns about the potential risk of abuse or exploitation that can arise in kinship or private foster placements, especially where adequate assessment of the capacities of carers has been lacking (Ayotte and Williamson, 2001; Dawson and Holding, 2001). Studies have also pointed to the lack of a statutory duty to monitor these placements once they are established and have highlighted a tendency for social work support to withdraw (Williamson, 1998). We have pointed to considerable variability in the nature of the assessments that were undertaken in these cases. This is a difficult task. These adults may have only recently arrived in the UK themselves, documentary evidence of the relationship may not exist and they may come from cultures where family ties and obligations are strong and may be reluctant to co-operate with an investigation that they consider to be unnecessary or overly intrusive (Mitchell, 2003). Assessments also take time and this can be intensely frustrating for young people waiting to join relatives. In one or two cases, this process was truncated as growing concerns were raised about the deteriorating mental health of young people awaiting a placement.

The costs to young people of not providing adequate assessments or monitoring placements effectively once they are made was, however, evident in several cases. Hassan, for example, when aged 15 spent a disastrous year in London with an adult cousin who lived in a shared house with other friends. Although Hassan had wanted this move, the assessment of the cousin appeared rudimentary, no transfer arrangements were negotiated with the receiving authority and no follow-up support was provided. In effect, he was cut adrift, unable to speak English and dependent personally and financially on his cousin:

> *I couldn't speak any English. I wanted to go to social services to see if they could help but I wasn't able to express myself . . . Every day I felt like going back, but eventually it was a year.*

It was only when he was finally able to approach the local social services that his circumstances changed for the better. A return to his own authority was negotiated and he settled more successfully into supported accommodation. Hellen's story is equally worrying. She was identified at point of arrival and placed in foster care for two nights from where she was collected by her sister and taken to live with her family in another area. After four months, she was re-referred on child protection grounds by a teacher and she was then moved to supported housing. This had all appeared to occur without any assessment, planning or follow-up, as a team manager later made clear:

> *There is no care plan on file and there is no review to make clear how those plans were made or how any of that actually happened.*

The quality of accommodation generally available to adult asylum seekers and refugees meant that young people's living situations with family were often overcrowded and under strain. In some instances, concerned social workers helped families to move to better accommodation. In others, however, these strains sometimes led to a breakdown in relationships as young people were eventually pressured to leave.

Social services also often relied upon the strength of close familial ties and obligations when deciding levels of financial assistance for these placements. Where they were supported under s17 provisions, the level of remuneration to families was often lower than for other foster placements. Some private fostering arrangements were not financially assisted at all and social workers expressed concern about the hardship this inflicted on families that were already struggling to manage on a low income:

> *You know it is a huge sacrifice when you already have four children to take on two more and to find you are not going to receive any financial support for them and you have to do it all on your own.* (Social worker to Clara and her sister)

These decisions appeared to be primarily resource driven, borne of a concern to avoid setting precedents that might persuade families or other close adults that public funding would be available to support children brought to the UK in the future.

Supported and independent accommodation

A majority of the young people had a main placement in supported or unsupervised housing. Most of them were aged 16 or over at referral, were supported under s17 arrangements and often moved into these forms of accommodation as a matter of team procedure. However, supported accommodation was also used for young people moving on from care placements and these young people rarely accessed unsupervised housing.

The range of supported accommodation used included host families (often recruited by community organisations and bridging aspects of fostering and supported lodgings), supported hostels for young people (foyers and YMCAs) and floating support schemes (mainly utilising private sector shared housing). Most independent accommodation relied upon private shared housing, usually sourced through private or voluntary housing agencies. However, some young people moved on to independent council tenancies and emergency use was made of hotels and other forms of temporary accommodation, including hostels for the homeless.

Supported hostels were mainly used for young people approaching 18 who either lacked skills or confidence for independent living or, more commonly, for young people whose lack of a settled asylum status precluded access to council tenancies.[11] Difficulties accessing such tenancies had led Area 2 to negotiate an agreed quota of places for unaccompanied young people at a local hostel. The presence of on-site staff support, encouragement for education and the relative privacy afforded in the context of a communal setting, made this a satisfactory placement for some young people. Bacia had been living in a hostel for nine months at interview and valued the support available there:

All the staff are there to help us with whatever you want. Anything you need you can just go to them and if they can help you, they are always willing.

Floating support schemes varied considerably, both in organisation and the degree of support provided. Primarily where young people were living within the local authority, floating support was sometimes provided from within asylum teams, using support workers linked to specific houses, or through a contract with a housing support agency responsible for managing most properties on behalf of the local authority and for offering packages of support to young people. In other circumstances, more often (though not exclusively) for young people placed out of authority, teams tended to rely on bespoke contract arrangements with private housing agencies or, especially in Area 3, on community organisations that had brokered placements for young people prior to their referral and about which the local authority appeared to have less control.

Although there was variety within as well as between these approaches to floating support, the available evidence suggests that the former models, by supplying a more dedicated service, tended to work more effectively. They tended to provide for clearer lines of responsibility and channels of communication. The support provided to young people was often more consistent, including more frequent patterns of home visiting and evidence of planning, and tended to address not just placement-related issues but

---

[11] Council tenancies did provide some young people with a greater sense of permanence and stability. However, they could only be accessed where young people had been granted indefinite or exceptional leave to remain for a period of time beyond 18. The potential of permanent tenancies, as one aspect of leaving care provision, is considered further in Chapter 8.

wider aspects of young people's lives, including their education, health and social relationships. Linked workers sometimes adopted a quasi-parental role, as suggested by one social worker referring to a shared house for young females:

It worked really well and I think all the girls benefited from it. There was always a mother figure there they could just sit and talk to. And she was neutral, in that the girls could talk to her confidentially and have a bit of her time without having to share it with the other girls.

Reliance on private housing agencies that provided key worker support to young people was often a major worry for practitioners, especially where young people were placed at some distance from the local authority. This was also the case for those living in unsupervised shared housing of this kind. The quality of accommodation was highly variable, repairs were often not undertaken, young people were sometimes subject to sudden moves at the behest of landlords and key workers were frequently unresponsive or failed to maintain contact with young people. Where they did, their focus was often solely on placement-related issues and the wider needs of young people were more often ignored. It was not uncommon for the only regular contact between young person and key worker to take place through casual office visits as young people collected their money. Although these patterns were not universal and some placements worked well and provided a relatively stable home base, positive assessments by young people usually related to the quality of their homes and of their relationships with other residents, rather than to the support provided by agency workers. In this respect, very few young people were entirely happy and nor often were their social workers:

I wasn't very well supervised by the agency... They didn't come to visit me for a long time. (Abdulkareem)

Staying here is like staying in hell ... You can see how small it is, dusty and cold ... It is not even hygienic. (Ghedi)

I am not happy about the level of work the key worker does. There isn't really the level of continuous visiting that we requested. I think they don't see a key worker for months [and] I am not really happy about that because, although she is a happy person and everything is in place, we at least expected certain monitoring. (Da-xia's social worker)

It is factors like these that help to explain our earlier findings that young people living in supported or unsupervised accommodation were less likely to be engaged in education and to have strong networks of social support when compared to those in care or kinship placements. Although some young people remained settled in one shared housing placement throughout the time they were supported and formed close attachments to their housemates, others did not. Enforced moves were sometimes made by landlords in order to refurbish or re-let properties and, in other circumstances, practitioners unhappy with the standard of accommodation being provided requested moves to better properties with the same or a different agency. Young people often felt they had little choice or control over these events and important relationships they had fostered while in one placement were sometimes ruptured. Moves to areas some distance from young people's social networks or communities of origin, or to areas where they felt unsafe, only tended to increase their feelings of social isolation.

Where placements were monitored by social workers, interventions were usually necessary to broker the relationship between young person and housing agency. This was needed to ensure the contracted key worker role was broadly adhered to and to respond to requests and complaints from young people. However, once young people reached 18, social services were often no longer involved. Essential help of this kind was also much less likely where young people's support workers had been inactive or played only a limited role. In these circumstances, young people were left to negotiate alone, sometimes without being made aware of what they had a right to expect and were disillusioned by the lack of contact and support from social services:

Visit the houses that they give us, see how we are living and then they can judge . . . See what we are going through and then they will understand . . . If they are seeing what I am living in, wouldn't they do something about it then? Knowing that I am not fluent in English and I cannot explain everything that is happening in the house to them, I guess when they see it they could understand. (Meena)

Although Meena had lived in one shared house since her arrival, she was unhappy, she felt unsafe in the local area and was 'trapped in her room' most of the time. Although formally supported by a generic asylum team, she did not receive home visits and her only contact with social services was through a duty-based office service that made it difficult for her to raise her concerns.

From the perspective of social workers, the enforcement of contracts with housing providers was difficult to achieve. In part at least, this was linked to available resources. First, social services had limited financial resources with which to secure better-quality accommodation or to engage more co-operative landlords. In effect, they often had to take what they could get:

> *The problem is we've got limited funds. When you talk about housing in London, how many landlords want to rent to social services for asylum seekers? We pay market rates, probably above, but it's a daily rate. [Young people] can be moved at any time really. We get landlords who take their properties back and [young people] are told they've got to move out that day, which is horrendous.* (Social worker, Area 2)

Second, the effects of this tended to erode or lower practitioners' expectations of what constituted a reasonable standard of accommodation. Third, monitoring young people's placements and liaison with providers were constrained by social work resources. Pressures created by high caseloads and the complexities of resettlement meant that some practitioners reported having to prioritise which cases they maintained closer contact with and which they did not on the basis of perceived need. Fourth, these pressures were compounded by a lack of specialist staff to negotiate service level agreements with housing providers, monitor their performance and develop new accommodation resources. Although there was awareness that providers did not always provide a professional service, individual social workers were expected to perform these time-consuming tasks on a case-by-case basis:

> *It has to be recognised that there are young people we are concerned about that we are unable to monitor, that we are unable to look after properly . . . We are [dependent on] providers who we feel are not as professional as we would like them to be. We don't seem to have*

resources for people to go and find other providers that may be able to give us a better service. We don't have people to monitor the providers . . . It's still [me] who has to keep trying to do that job as well. (Social worker, Area 1)

Out-of-authority placements often increased that sense of dependency. Distance constrained relationships with housing providers, unless contractual requirements to provide reports on young people's welfare were scrupulously observed, and with young people themselves. Infrequency of contact meant that relationships between social workers and young people were more uncertain and less open. Young people appeared less likely to confide in them or complain about their circumstances – and this was evidenced by a lack of correspondence in some interviews between the views of practitioners and young people about the course of recent events or by a lack of awareness amongst some practitioners of young people's circumstances and progress in general. Continuity in these relationships from the point of referral was helpful. Where social workers or support workers changed, or where young people lacked an allocated worker, these difficulties tended to be exacerbated.

Previous studies have pointed to inconsistencies in support arrangements for young people placed with housing agencies (Humphries and Mynott, 2001; Kidane, 2001a; Stanley, 2001). As we have seen, the vast majority of these young people were supported under s17 provisions. It is difficult to escape the conclusion that the limited statutory obligations placed on local authorities when providing s17 accommodation and support have not had a bearing on these patterns and experiences. As previously observed, although packages of support available under these provisions were sometimes quite comprehensive and provided an equivalence to s20 packages of care, these young people as a whole were less likely to have had care plans, regular reviews or allocated social work support. The absence of statutory visiting requirements also helps to explain why patterns of contact with young people were more casual and infrequent. In these circumstances, it was not surprising to find that young people had greater difficulties accessing social work support when placed in these settings.

Developing placement resources

It was also the case that the practice of teams was evolving over the course of the study. The teams had been initiated in response to the influx of high numbers of unaccompanied young people arriving in the UK. As such, their early practice inevitably tended to be reactive and crisis based, lacking clear signposts to guide the development of services. Young people needed to have their basic needs met – for housing, care and finance – and the resources to provide for this were limited. Many young people were grateful for the help that had been provided, even where their circumstances were less than acceptable to the objective eye.

The development of guidance in recent years, combined with the recent fall in numbers arriving, has provided the teams with an opportunity to take stock and review their services to unaccompanied young people. In this regard, steps were taking place to increase the proportion of young people looked after (s20), to improve the range of supported accommodation options, to improve the standards and monitoring of housing agencies and to rationalise and reorganise the social work services provided to young people.

The findings presented here point to the existence of a continuum of placement needs that are likely to require flexible solutions. Many young people settled well in foster care and a small number of young people found a stable base in residential placements. As others have found, there is a need to extend further the range of foster placements available within refugee communities to improve matching (Williamson, 1998; Rutter, 2003a) and to recruit more local authority foster carers to reduce reliance on expensive independent agencies and out-of-authority placements (Stanley, 2001; Dennis, 2002). This is no easy task, since the overall pool of foster carers has tended to remain at a stubbornly consistent level over a number of years.

However, not all young people coped well with family settings and others need to move on as they get older. Investment will therefore be needed in an improved range of supported placement options. These may include supported lodgings, small supported hostels and floating support schemes. Supported accommodation tended to work best when the accommodation was of good quality, when thought had been given to the mix of residents and when housing was located in areas where young people could build positive local connections. It also appeared more effective where young people remained within the authority and where linked support was provided by dedicated social work teams.

These developments are likely to require a considerable investment of time and resources to build partnerships with statutory and voluntary housing providers, including housing associations, and to improve the range of options. Where numbers justify it, specialist staff with a developmental brief may need to be considered to build these links, improve the resources available and monitor enforceable contracts with housing providers. It is not realistic to expect already hard-pressed social workers to provide this function in addition to their casework responsibilities. With respect to these developments, much could be learnt from the experiences of specialist leaving care schemes over recent decades, for whom the development of housing options has been both an area of considerable success and one of enduring frustration (Broad, 2003; Dixon et al, 2004; Hai and Williams, 2004). Sharing expertise and pooling resources may offer a cost-effective way of moving forward. It may also help to reduce the need for young people to move to fully independent settings before they are ready and to reduce the reliance of teams on more unscrupulous landlords in the private sector. While strategic developments of this kind risk being affected by shifts in asylum policy, there was a general recognition amongst practitioners of the limitations of services provided in the past and of the need to develop a more systematic approach to services in the future:

I think there needs to be some consideration of future strategy . . . When I came here you felt you were working in a crisis and always working in a crisis. But we are not working in a crisis any longer. The numbers have slowed up and there is time to plan things properly and get a reasonable structure in place for the services we provide. (Team manager, Area 1)

Summary

Many young people (47 per cent) were placed on the same day as referral. Others had already found informal placements with relatives, adults they had met or through community associations. How placement needs were managed varied according to age, where and how young people were referred, team policies and procedures, the placement resources available and young people's circumstances at the time.

Many older teenagers, especially older males, were routinely placed in unsupported or low-level supported shared housing after only a rudimentary assessment of their needs. Assessments for those already living with responsible adults, relatives or host families were also variable.

Kinship and care placements appeared protective. Young people who mainly lived in these settings were more likely to have had sustained involvement in education, to have developed stronger social networks and to have received a more comprehensive package of professional support than was the case for those who lived predominantly in either supported or unsupported accommodation, usually under s17 arrangements. This tends to reflect the additional responsibilities attached to being looked after (for care plans, reviews and contact).

Foster care was the preferred option for younger looked after children. Residential care was less commonly used and mainly functioned to provide assessment and preparation before moving on. Where foster placements worked well, they provided safety, security and an opportunity to build new attachments. Cultural matching was difficult to achieve and most young people moved into cross-cultural placements. Although many placements lasted quite successfully, cultural tensions were evident and some young people chose to move to semi-independent settings in culturally mixed areas. Little use was being made of provisions for independent visitors that may help to mediate these tensions. Kinship placements often provided young people with stable and familiar attachments and opportunities for cultural integration.

Most young people had a main placement in supported or unsupported housing. Floating support schemes tended to work best when the support was provided directly by a dedicated social work team and linked to comprehensive packages of care. Reliance on private landlords and housing agencies was more problematic, especially where young people were placed out of authority, and resulted in highly variable accommodation and support and greater mobility for young people. Contracts with housing providers were difficult to enforce and housing options were limited by financial constraints.

Further expansion in the pool of foster carers, especially from within refugee communities, and in the range of supported accommodation is necessary. New initiatives were emerging towards the close of the study. These developments require an investment of time and resources to build partnerships with statutory and voluntary housing providers and may require the appointment of specialist staff with a developmental brief.

5 Education and training pathways

If finding a settled home base can offer unaccompanied young people a fundamental building block in their adjustment to life in a new land, then a successful introduction to education or training can also provide an important source of stability, security and reassurance. A placement at school or college is not only essential for English language acquisition and for wider academic or vocational study, it can also provide young people with a sense of everyday normality and offer opportunities for building a network of friendships.

Research about refugee children generally has identified the education system to be the principal mainstream service outside of the family home that provides direct support to these children (Candappa and Egharevba, 2000). For unaccompanied children, predominantly lacking the support of family members, it is likely to be still more significant. Helping young people to find and settle into an appropriate educational placement and providing ongoing encouragement for their education is therefore a crucial aspect of the social work task.

Law and policy

The legal entitlement of asylum seeking and refugee children to mainstream education between five and 16 years is the same as that for other indigenous children. The Education Act 1996 (s14) mandates local education authorities (LEAs) to provide a full-time education to all children resident within their areas, and the role and responsibilities of LEAs towards asylum seeking and refugee children are further codified in recent official guidance issued by Government (Department for Education and Skills, 2004a). An equal right to education is also reinforced through the United Nations Convention on the Rights of the Child 1989 (although the UK Government maintains a reservation with respect to children subject to immigration control), the Human Rights Act 1998 and the Race Relations (Amendment) Act 2000. The latter makes it unlawful to discriminate directly or indirectly against applicants for school places on the basis of their race, colour or nationality, including citizenship (Spencer, 2002).

Local authorities have additional duties with respect to the education of "looked after" children under the Children Act 1989. These requirements provide for collaboration between social services and LEAs to facilitate access to education and information sharing, for young people to have personal education plans and, where a young person is newly arrived or a placement disrupts, for an education placement to be provided within 20 school days (Department of Health, 2000a; Department of Health/Department for Education and Skills, 2000). Additional responsibilities relate to provision of free school meals, school uniforms, travel arrangements, home–school liaison and provision of essential equipment for study. Local authorities are also required to report annually on the educational attainment of looked after children (including unaccompanied children) as part of the Government's Performance Assessment Framework.

The Children (Leaving Care) Act 2000 requires local authorities to provide "eligible", "relevant" and "former relevant" young people with a pathway plan and personal adviser that, as part of overall transition planning, should include planning and support arrangements for education, employment or training for young people leaving care (Department of Health, 2001).

With these points in mind, this chapter focuses on the education and training careers of young people participating in the study. It considers how young people's educational needs were assessed, describes the range of education and training placements accessed by young people, including patterns of mobility and non-participation, and considers young people's experiences of participation. It also assesses how these experiences related to other key aspects of young people's past and present lives, and how the support they received (whether professional or informal) may have mediated these experiences and it identifies constraints that tend to inhibit the social work role.

Assessment

Research on the education of asylum seeking and refugee children has pointed to the diversity of their social and educational backgrounds (Candappa and Egharevba, 2000; Rutter, 2003a). Young people from within the same national group will often have different social class, linguistic, political and religious affiliations. Some young people may not have attended school at all, while others may have consistently attended English language schools in their home countries. Many may have had their educational experiences disrupted by war, persecution or conflict. Flight may well have brought about a profound lowering of economic circumstances or left an emotional legacy that makes concentration and learning more difficult.

Once young people arrive in the UK, therefore, this pattern of heterogeneity points to the need for a careful assessment of young people's educational backgrounds, capabilities and interests as a prelude to identifying appropriate education and training opportunities. It is important that these initial assessments are well managed and that education is not overlooked, not least since many education professionals feel they receive insufficient information about young people's educational histories or needs when they are referred to school (Ofsted, 2003; Remsbery, 2003).

Information about education assessment was mainly drawn from case file recordings. It suggests that, for the vast majority of young people (80 per cent), some initial assessment of their educational needs was undertaken. However, there was considerable variation in the level of recorded information about young people's educational histories, current needs and interests. In many instances, files pointed to assessments that appeared perfunctory, with little evidence of any attempt to collect historical information about the young person, and recording little more than the need for an education placement to be identified. In many others, however, there was evidence of more detailed assessments that highlighted the diversity of young people's educational backgrounds and the disruption to schooling that had been experienced.

Some young people had a continuous history of schooling whilst living in their home countries. At the other end of the spectrum, some had received no formal education at all, often having had to work to supplement the family income from a very early age. Disruption to schooling figured prominently in the lives of the majority and a variety of factors were at play. Most commonly the onset or acceleration of war, conflict or family persecution brought schooling to an end. Either schools closed altogether or young people were forced to leave, often to go into hiding or to adopt a more nomadic life going from place to place in search of sanctuary. Radical changes in family circumstances also brought schooling to a close. The death or disappearance of one or both parents often required young people to work in the family business, to find other ways to supplement family income, to remain at home to care for younger siblings or, if left alone, to seek casual forms of work to survive.

Recording of assessment outcomes was also highly variable. For almost one-half of the young people (48 per cent), no outcome or proposed action was recorded on case files. Where there was evidence that some education assessment had taken place (169 cases), in 60 per cent of these cases there was some record of proposed action, but in 37 per cent of cases no outcome was recorded at all.

Where some record of a decision had been made, there was a continuum of proposed action. At one extreme, the action appeared minimal, perhaps simply handing young people information to take away about courses or a generalised note to "offer support" with education. Recordings also quite commonly noted that the need for an education placement had been identified, without any further note clarifying how this was to be achieved. In some cases, workers undertook to arrange a school or college placement directly. In others, this task was delegated to a refugee support agency, to carers or to relatives. Referrals to specialist education services were also common, including referrals to Ethnic Minority Achievement Services (EMAS), to representatives at the LEA, to Education Welfare Officers or to Connexions.

There were also several instances where young people had arranged their own education placement without much assistance from social services. Furthermore, what often came through the case file recordings was the frequency with which young people, although by no means all, appeared eager and motivated to attend school or college and learn English as a platform to opening up further opportunities. However, it was not always the case that planned action at the assessment stage necessarily facilitated a smooth transition into education or training.

"C" arrived in the UK from Kosovo aged 14. He had attended school from age seven and had most enjoyed history and maths. It was noted on file that he was able to read and write well in his own language, but had little knowledge of English. He was keen to continue his education and the need for a school placement was identified. This was not forthcoming for more than two months, despite continuing liaison by his social worker, foster carer and solicitor with the Education Co-ordinator at the LEA. The reasons for this delay were not clear from the file.

In overall terms, better assessments tended to collect information about young people's past record of schooling – identifying the number of years they had attended, qualifications they may have attained and, at a basic level, the range of languages spoken and their proficiency in using them. In some instances, information was also collected on the types of subject studied, young people's interests and on their aspirations for the future. Although information of this kind is not always easy to collect at an early stage, it is likely to be helpful when considering appropriate placement options and to be appreciated by education professionals when young people are referred to them.

Patterns of education, training and work

The case files were used to construct an overview of young people's participation in education, training and employment for the period of time they had been supported by social services – a period ranging from approximately four to 30 months across the sample. This was inevitably an imprecise process. Records of changes in education or training placements were not always accompanied by dates and they often had to be estimated from other associated information on file. Furthermore, for 18 per cent of the young people, there was no information recorded at all about their education or training careers.

First and last education placement

Table 5.1 shows the first and last known education placement for the sample as a whole. The first placement relates to the first known placement once referral and initial assessment were completed, although in a minority of cases the placement had started before referral to social services. Final placement relates to the last known placement either at the point of case closure or, for those cases remaining open, at the point of data collection.

Table 5.1
First and last "education" placement (n = 212)

	First placement	Last placement
	Per cent	
School	13	19
Further education	25	32
Other education	20	3
Training placement	7	6
Work	0	1
Non-participation	10	10
No clear evidence	26	28

Table 5.1 illustrates that, at both time points, a majority of young people were participating in full-time or part-time education. One in ten young people were not participating in education, training or employment at one or other time point and, for more than one-quarter of the young people, it was impossible to discern from the file exactly what they were doing at either point.[1] It also points to some patterns of movement over time. In particular it highlights movement from "other" education, usually part-time alternative English language provision, to school or college placements. Finally, it emphasises the restricted opportunities that existed for employment and training.

---

[1] "No clear evidence" includes cases where there was no recorded evidence of careers on file at all. It also includes cases where there was evidence that young people had at some time participated in education or training but it was not clear when these placements had started or whether or when they had ended. This lack of clarity accounted for 11 per cent of cases at final placement.

Relatively few young people participated in training schemes. Although recorded information on the content of young people's activities was extremely sketchy, it appeared that most of those engaged in training were participating in community-based training provision – incorporating elements of English as a Second Other Language (ESOL) or English as an Additional Language (EAL) courses, combined with information technology (IT) and perhaps some periods of work experience. Access to accredited employment-based training schemes appeared rare. In only one case was there a record of a young person studying for National Vocational Qualifications (NVQs) in Business Administration linked to a training placement. There was also evidence of some young people feeling unhappy with training schemes, of attendance problems and attempts to transfer to mainstream college courses.

Employment was simply not an option for most young people. Opportunities for work were limited and, for many young people, their status as asylum seekers prevented them from working (see Rutter, 2003b). The files suggested that only two young people were working at data collection and neither file specified the nature of the employment. A few practitioners suspected that some other young people, mostly male, might be working casually, although they were unable to substantiate this. In some instances, it was felt that there could be pressure to send money home from families whose existence young people may not have disclosed. In others, there was a feeling that young people coming from backgrounds where they had experienced little schooling and where work at an early age was expected might have less commitment to education and view employment as a more desired option:

I think for a lot of young people, education is not the priority. For some young people it is, but if you have never been to school before or you have had only limited schooling in your country, there is probably more of an emphasis on going to work to make money. (Social worker, Area 2)

For the majority of young people, however, education was the main activity. Increased participation in post-compulsory education for all young people reflects, at least in part, the restructuring that has taken place in the school to work transition over recent decades and the expansion of education and training opportunities for this age group which has been associated with it (Coles, 1995; Furlong and Cartmel, 1997). With respect to asylum seeking and refugee young people in particular, it also reflects the emergence of specific funding streams to encourage courses and services targeted to their needs, especially in relation to language support and in areas where higher numbers are resident (Ofsted, 2003; Rutter, 2003b). However, as the quote above suggests, it may also reflect the lack of alternatives available to unaccompanied young people where education is not the most desired option.

Levels of education attainment and post-16 economic participation for looked after young people as a whole have been a long standing concern (Stein and Carey, 1986; Raychuba, 1987; Aldgate *et al*, 1993; Jackson, 1994; Broad, 1998; Pinkerton and McCrea, 1999). The need to improve attainment and participation by care leavers has been a central commitment underpinning the Government's Quality Protects initiative and the Children (Leaving Care) Act 2000. Recent evidence points to some improvement in the level of participation in post-compulsory education amongst care leavers (Broad, 2003; Dixon *et al*, 2004) and national statistics also identify some differences between unaccompanied young people formerly accommodated under s20 and other young people leaving care. For example, figures for the year 2002–2003 suggest that unaccompanied young people were more likely to be participating in education at their 19th birthday (including higher education) – 50 per cent were doing so compared to just 21 per cent of care leavers as a whole (Department for Education and Skills, 2003a).

Children and young people who were at school were mostly studying or preparing to study for GCSE, AS or A level qualifications. No young people had yet entered higher education, although a small number were preparing to do so. Those who had accessed colleges were participating in a range of courses. Discrete pathways for young people depended on the particular provision available at individual colleges and on young people's knowledge of spoken and written English. Provision included: enrolment on full-time or part-time ESOL courses, perhaps also including elements of IT and other subjects; enrolment on mainstream/ESOL link courses, where young people studying mainstream subjects received separate intensive language support; and enrolment on mainstream academic and vocational courses (see also Stanley, 2001). While most young people in this sample were engaged in

ESOL or ESOL-linked courses – and the part-time nature of some of this provision was often a source of frustration – others had progressed on to GCSE, GNVQ or A level courses.

In Table 5.1, "other education" identifies young people who were participating in community-based or alternative educational provision, mostly ESOL courses that were often part time, ranging from a few hours to four days per week. This type of provision tended to be arranged on a temporary basis to help young people prepare for mainstream education, to get them started while they were waiting for a school or college placement or, if a course ended, acted as a bridge until a new placement could be found. However, for some young people, this was the main type of provision accessed, perhaps interspersed with periods of non-participation or time spent on other courses. Provision of this kind was provided by a range of agencies, including residential units, independent fostering providers, housing and refugee projects and local youth, community and adult education centres.

Education and training pathways

Looking only at first and last placement, however, masks the degree of change in young people's early education and training careers. While well over one-quarter of the young people (28 per cent) had remained in the same education or training placement throughout the time they were supported, just over one in five (21 per cent) had experienced three or more changes of placement (including periods of non-participation).

Table 5.2 shows the main type of activity in which young people were engaged over the period of time they had been supported by social services (or by agencies on their behalf). This was constructed from a chronology of all known placements for each young person and the "main" type of activity was calculated where it was possible to discern from case files the type of placement in which young people had spent the majority of their time.[2] For more than two-fifths of the sample it was not possible to calculate this accurately due to limitations in case file recording.

---

[2] The "main" type of placement does not equate to young people being in the *same* placement for the majority of their time in the care of social services. Young people may have experienced more than one placement of the same type, sometimes interspersed with placements of a different kind.

Table 5.2
Main type of education or training placement (n = 212)

	Per cent
Mainly school	18
Mainly college/community education	23
Mainly training	4
Mainly non-participation	10
No clear evidence	45

Further analysis was carried out to identify factors in young people's characteristics and experiences that were associated with being "mainly" in education (combining school, college and alternative education) or with being "mainly" non-participating (out of education, training or employment).[3]

Young people referred at an older age were more likely to have spent the majority of their time out of education than were those who were younger (p = 0.01; n = 109).[4] There was also an association between participation and young people's regions of origin (p<0.01; n = 108). Around one-third (34 per cent) of young people originating from European countries (predominantly from the former Republic of Yugoslavia) and over one-third (37 per cent) from Middle Eastern countries were mainly non-participating compared to just 9 per cent from African countries and no young people from Asian countries.[5] Some caution should be exercised with respect to these findings, since the numbers of young people in specific regional groups were quite low. At the very

---

[3] "Training" had to be excluded from this analysis as the numbers were too small to permit reliable statistical tests. Given the reduced sample size (n = 109) and the relatively low numbers "mainly" non-participating (22), Exact tests were used. Findings in this section should, therefore, be considered as indicative.

[4] Only 8 per cent of those aged under 15 at referral were mainly non-participating, compared to 23 per cent of those aged 15, 25 per cent of those referred at 16 and 35 per cent of those aged 17.

[5] In relation to Africa the main national groups were Somali, Congolese, Eritrean and Ethiopian. Asia included young people from Afghanistan and China. The two main countries in the Middle East have not been described to preserve the anonymity of our local authorities.

least, it is indicative of diversity and points to the need for further research to develop a deeper understanding of differences in patterns of educational participation for unaccompanied young people from different national and ethnic backgrounds.[6]

Non-participation also varied according to type of placement ($p<0.01$; $n = 102$). At one end of the spectrum, no young people who had mainly lived in foster or residential placements and just 6 per cent of those mainly placed with "kin" had spent most of their time out of education or training, compared to 32 per cent of those mainly living in supported accommodation and 33 per cent of those in unsupported accommodation. This suggests that being in care or kinship placements was protective and that the additional support often available in such placements helped young people continue with their education.[7]

These findings highlight the additional difficulties young people are likely to experience in sustaining participation when living in semi-independent or independent settings and/or in environments that offer lower levels of support and encouragement. They are also consistent with other research findings. Stanley (2001) suggested that unaccompanied children looked after under s20 appeared to be better able to access education than were those living in semi-independent or independent accommodation and attributed this to the additional support provided by carers and social workers. Research on care leavers has also found that young people who are more successful in starting their careers tend to be those doing so from the shelter of supported settings – with foster carers, supported lodgings providers or in small supported hostels (Biehal et al, 1995; Wade, 1997). It also reinforces the value of providing s20 accommodation and support to unaccompanied young people, since the vast majority of those living in less

---

[6] Evidence concerning the under-achievement of some groups of asylum seeking and refugee children in schools is also beginning to emerge, including Somali young people, Turkish/Kurdish boys and European Roma children (Ali and Jones, 2000; Rutter, 2003c; Department for Education and Skills, 2004a).

[7] Age factors also influenced these patterns, since those in care and kinship placements tended to be younger at referral and were more likely to have been of statutory school age ($p<0.001$; $n = 180$). However, log linear modelling indicated that age and education participation were each separately associated with type of placement.

supported environments were those assisted under s17 (p<0.001; n = 168).

Changes in placement often involve changes in school for looked after young people. High levels of placement mobility are associated with damaging discontinuities for young people's educational progress and for their relationships with teachers and friends (Jackson, 2002). With respect to this study, it was therefore not surprising to find a clear association between placement movement and non-participation (p<0.01; n = 109). Those with higher levels of mobility were much less likely to establish a secure foothold in education. When thinking about placements, therefore, the implications for continuity in young people's education needs to have a high priority.

Analysis of patterns inevitably tends to flatten out the contours of young people's lives and cannot adequately capture the complexity of their education and training careers. In order to draw these findings together and provide a more holistic picture, some brief illustrations of differing types of career are provided below:

Stable (mainly education)

"G" arrived in the UK from China aged 14. At referral he was living with a family friend. This was supported by social services as a private fostering arrangement and he was still living there over three years later. At initial assessment, the need for a school placement was identified and his case was referred to an Education Welfare Officer. Although it took six weeks to secure a school place, once identified, he settled quite well and continued to make good progress. Case file notes record that he received additional language support and that the school had linked him with other Chinese pupils locally. At data collection, he was continuing his studies at the same school.

Unsettled (mainly education)

"J" arrived in the UK from Iraq aged 14. His subsequent progress was very unsettled. He had six different placements over a period of 18 months, including a mix of children's homes and foster placements. These moves were driven, in large part, by his challenging behaviour.

In consequence, he had several education placements. He attended in-house provision at a residential unit, had a placement at school (from which he was eventually excluded), alternative education at a community centre (which he failed to attend regularly) and a period non-participating. At data collection, he was living in semi-independent accommodation, but closely supervised by two key workers, and had recently started attending college.

Mainly non-participation

"K" arrived in the UK from Kosovo aged 15. He was placed in an unsupported private house shared with other unaccompanied minors. This proved stable and he was still there some 13 months later. However, there is no recorded evidence of any involvement in education or training on file. At referral, it was identified that support to access education was needed. There appears to have been very little follow-up until, seven months later, a letter from a local college indicated that ESOL courses were full and that they would notify him when a vacancy occurred. The only other note on file, some six months later, recorded a referral to Connexions as the young person was eligible for Job-seeker's Allowance and was not in education or training.

The experience of education

Interviews with young people and practitioners provided insight into a range of issues affecting the educational experiences and progress of young people. Most of these issues interplay closely with the support available to young people from social workers, support workers, educational professionals, family and friends. Broader aspects of the support dimension – and its interaction with young people's experiences of participation – form the substance of the concluding part of this chapter.

Commitment and motivation

It was quite commonplace for practitioners to refer to the commitment and resourcefulness of young people when discussing their participation and progress in education. It was also often apparent in the voices of young people themselves. Some, even when they had no consistent pattern of past schooling and had difficulty communicating in English, found the means to organise their own education, relying on only minimal support to get them started or by conjuring up the support they needed from a variety of sources. For these young people education provided a sense of purpose and direction:

I thought that if I got to school and if I could learn English, I could be something. I could be something in the future. I did work hard for myself. I did work hard for myself as well. (Kamuran)

Where education was highly valued, sacrifices were sometimes required and difficult choices had to be faced. Kamuran, for example, was placed with a white British foster family in an area that meant he was socially isolated from other Kurdish people. Although he was lonely, the family was supportive of him and his education. On reflection, he felt it was a price that had been worth paying. He had learnt English quickly, with their assistance, the placement had proved stable and he had successfully completed his GCSEs at school and was now studying mechanics at college. With respect to his unhappiness, he had kept his own counsel and not shared his feelings with his social worker.

Practitioners could find some young people's exclusive focus upon education troubling, even though most recognised the desire in young people to make something of themselves while they were here, to "be something" in the future. In a few cases, it led practitioners to question from where this singular determination originated, it being substantially different to the impulses in other groups of young people with whom they had contact. Was it a principal reason for their journey to the UK? Were there subtle or overt pressures from families at home about which workers knew little? Were they genuinely doing this for themselves or, in the longer term, to earn money to send home? In other cases, workers found this preoccupation could function as a barrier, excluding them from engagement with other aspects of young people's lives about which they remained silent:

He won't talk about anything, he is a very quiet boy. It seems that while he is here, he has got an ambition to get an education . . . That's his main focus, his education, and that's about it. I try to engage him with other activities and try to get to know him a bit better but he just doesn't want to know. (Amir's social worker)

Where support from social services for education was low key or perhaps non-existent, young people's self-reliance was borne of some necessity, or support from other sources needed to be engineered. Where this support was lacking, however, successful engagement with education was much less likely.

Hassan moved from his home authority when aged 15 to live with an older cousin and his friends in London. Planning for this move appeared minimal, no links were established with the receiving authority and, as a result, Hassan spent several months without professional support of any kind. He was financially dependent on his cousin and, lacking the language skills or confidence to negotiate access to education, remained out of school for almost a year until he finally approached a local social services office for help.

Successful engagement occurred more readily when support was available to help young people harness their own determination.

Abdulkareem had no past experience of schooling when he arrived aged 14. He was placed by a refugee support agency with a carer from the same ethnic background in an unregulated placement. He lived there for one year before being referred to social services. He was highly critical of the lack of support from this agency, although his carer was supportive and helped him to access school. Despite a disadvantaged starting point, he was highly motivated and excelled at school. He attained good GCSEs and was studying A levels with a plan to go university. He valued highly the support he received from the school careers adviser, whom he 'used to annoy . . . nearly every week' and from two teachers, in particular, who were supportive. He also managed to develop a strong peer network and he studied with his friends. Once involved, social services played a relatively minor role in relation to his education, but provided practical assistance (a bus pass, clothing grants and a computer).

Not all young people manifested such commitment to education and difficulties with motivation were a preoccupying concern for many practitioners. A number of factors influenced young people's engagement with education or affected patterns of attendance. Lengthy delays in accessing education or prolonged periods of non-participation could lead to boredom, frustration, a loss of structure to young people's lives and, ultimately, to disillusionment. Where young people were moved around frequently or placed in unsupported housing with other unaccompanied young people lacking a strong commitment to education, their participation was more likely to suffer. In a few instances, these factors could come together to create a broader disaffection:

He has got no set structure, I think that's the biggest problem. I just think he interacts with boys during his spare time. He finds things to do . . . That is why I think his behaviour goes up and down so radically, because he has got nothing to look forward to . . . He mixes with the wrong crowd and therefore gets into trouble. (Joseph's social worker)

Other young people became increasingly frustrated with the limited educational options presented to them, especially where they were caught up in a cycle of casual or part-time courses that failed to stretch them or to offer a sense of direction. In these circumstances young people sometimes voted with their feet. Some young people simply wanted to work, had little desire to study and were frustrated by the lack of opportunities. Others who had engaged with education found it impossible to sustain due to difficulties associated with their mental health and well-being:

He was supposed to be going to college but it was difficult to get him to go . . . He has got high anxiety and he got really depressed and he found it really difficult to cope . . . When he was feeling great he would go to college, and he would be so impressed with himself . . . and then the next thing he would just stop and that would be it. (Walid's social worker)

Most workers were disquieted by young people's non-participation and tried hard, though sometimes unsuccessfully, to promote their re-engagement. In some instances, the seeds of disillusionment had been sown before they became involved. In others, they were hindered by the resource and policy environment that tends to constrain the educational and employment opportunities available to unaccompanied young people. Where support was lacking, young people were more likely to drift and support appeared harder to muster when young people were placed at some distance from the responsible authority. In these circumstances, workers found it more difficult to assist young people into education, to monitor their progress and tended to be heavily reliant on housing agencies contracted to provide key work support, much of which was highly variable (see also Stanley, 2001).

Access to education

Despite the clear entitlement of asylum seeking and refugee children to places in mainstream education, reports have pointed to delays in accessing places and to variations in the degree of co-operation between social services and LEAs to resolve such problems (Audit Commission, 2000; Candappa, 2000; Children's Legal Centre, 2003; Rutter, 2003b). Access to schools and colleges was influenced by a number of factors.

In some cases, a shortage of school places or the availability of places on particular courses at college precipitated periods of non-participation as young people waited for spaces to open up. Time of arrival was also influential. Where young people arrived in mid-term, especially between April and June, finding an immediate placement proved extremely difficult. Workers who tried to respond to this situation (and not all did) would attempt to get young people involved in temporary ESOL provision or on short summer courses to help them through this period.

The age of young people at referral could also be a factor requiring similar creative solutions. A number of young people arriving mid-year and aged 15 were unable to access a school placement and several practitioners identified this as a common problem:

We come across that again and again. It is a real loophole. Because they are not over 16 they cannot access colleges, but trying to get them into the last year of a school placement . . . when it is ending in May is just impossible. That's why we use [alternative educational provision].
(Desta's social worker)

Access issues also arose in a few cases where a young person's age was either disputed by social services or by a school. Where there was a perceived discrepancy between a young person's physical appearance or behaviour and their stated (and formally accepted) age, they could be caught in the gap between school and college as neither would accept them. In a similar vein, one or two young people were pressured to move on from a school placement for this reason.

Extended delays, for any reason, brought frustration and disillusionment to young people. Desta only later realised the "loophole" she had been caught in for five months. At the time she just felt angry and unsupported:

> Yeah, I had support [from social services] but they couldn't do nothing. I was between the age that I couldn't go to college and I couldn't go to school. So now I understand the system I know it wasn't their fault. But at the time I felt angry . . . I wasn't enrolled in ESOL . . . It felt quite boring. I didn't have anywhere to go, I just stayed at home.

Adjusting to school

Most children and young people found the initial transition to school or college difficult. Almost all had either had little previous experience of schooling or had experienced significant disruption to their education and most had very limited, if any, knowledge of English. Young people also spoke about their feelings of cultural disorientation, where school cultures were profoundly different to those they had experienced previously, and of feeling friendless and isolated. The act of going took considerable courage and it would not be surprising to find that some were reluctant. Others, though profoundly unhappy, maintained a stoic silence, preferring to carry a private burden rather than trouble others about their feelings. Albert, when asked why he had not shared his feelings with his social worker, answered in the following way:

> No, I didn't tell my social worker. I told them I was happy and didn't tell them I was unhappy and felt alone . . . because I felt they have a lot to do for me. I didn't want to tell them more problems.

This is clearly a time when children and young people need considerable support and reassurance from carers, social workers and other significant adults in their lives. Practitioners need to be vigilant, given the reluctance of some young people to share their feelings, and try to ensure that young people are linked into pastoral support at school or college. Clear lines of communication will also be helpful so that, where children are seen to be struggling, information can be exchanged and support be adjusted accordingly.

Schools also have important responsibilities and there is evidence of an emerging consensus about what helps refugee children to settle and prosper at school. These include providing a welcoming atmosphere, sensitive admission and induction policies, providing a designated teacher for refugee children, the use of special funds (the Ethnic Minority Achievement Grant [EMAG]) to provide adequate EAL (English as an Additional Language) support, encouragement for young people's home languages and policies to promote multicultural education and to tackle racism and bullying in schools (Refugee Council, 2000; Rutter, 2003b; Department for Education and Skills, 2004a). There was also some evidence in this study of schools operating "buddy" systems that paired new arrivals with more established children in school, and of mentoring being used to assist children's progress. Given the social isolation often experienced, these would appear to be positive strategies to help children to adjust (see Philip *et al*, 2004).

Language support

Most young people felt that the acquisition of English language skills was crucial to their future education, their self-confidence and for their social interaction with others. Some young people, like Kamuran, introduced earlier, gave this the highest priority, sacrificing other aspects of their identities and social lives in the process. Others actively sought out friendships with English speakers to accelerate their learning or, when placed with other unaccompanied young people from different national-ities, entered pacts to speak only English at home. In contrast, where young people mixed predominantly with young people from their own national or ethnic background – and especially where they were less engaged with formal education – the acquisition of language skills was often delayed. Young people (mainly non-participating) who had primarily communicated in their own language at home and with peers often had a very limited knowledge of English some two to three years after arriving in the UK.

Many children and young people who entered school had received EAL support, although there is evidence of variations in the provision of this support within and between areas – and especially in areas where the numbers of refugee children are relatively low (Audit Commission, 2000; Ofsted, 2003). Where this was provided effectively, it was often highly valued by young people. While there is a need for intensive help at first, needs may also be quite long term. One young person studying A levels still felt keenly the need for additional help and resented the fact that it was not available to him. There was also evidence that some young people lacked the confidence to seek help when they needed it, and this was a wider issue than just one of language. Some young people at school or college struggled by themselves through a fear of showing that they were not managing or due to concerns that the difficulties they were experiencing were theirs alone and not shared by others.

Attainment and progress

Although the poor educational attainment of looked after young people generally has been the subject of great concern, it should not be surprising to find that unaccompanied children accommodated under s20 tend to have fewer qualifications than other young people in the care system. Local authority returns for 2002–2003 show that, whereas 44 per cent of all care leavers attained at least one GCSE at any grade, only 30 per cent of unaccompanied young people did so (Department for Education and Skills, 2003a). Unfortunately, it was impossible to assess the qualifications gained by young people in this sample from social work case files, since there was no recording at all about their achievements in the files of 189 of the 212 young people.

It is also the case, as we have already seen, that many young people make positive and speedy educational progress relative to their starting points on entry to the education system (Ofsted, 2003). While their determination and resilience often saw them through, there were other factors that tended to have a more negative influence on their progress and educational welfare. Evidence from case files suggested that only 5 per cent of young people had engaged in truancy and that only 3 per cent had been excluded from school at some point. However, given patterns of case file recording on educational issues, this may be an under-estimate.

Of greater significance to young people's well-being were experiences of bullying and harassment at school or college, some of which were racially motivated. As other studies have found, these experiences ranged from verbal abuse to physical assaults and from one-off incidents to a persistent pattern of harassment over time. They could also include conflicts between different groups of refugee children (Stanley, 2001). Wider racist attitudes towards asylum seekers inevitably formed part of the background canvass:

If people know you are an asylum seeker in this country or a refugee, immediately it is like discrimination, they are racist towards you. (Meena)

There were variations in the responses made by social services and schools to young people's experiences of racism and bullying and in the willingness of young people to speak about these experiences to teachers or social workers. Direct action by young people in the playground or on college campuses could bring sanctions – and this occurred in one or two cases where suspensions followed episodes of fighting. Some young people, however, opted to suffer in silence, either through a desire not to burden staff or a fear that disclosure might prejudice their own progress. Meena, for example, ultimately chose to keep her status as an asylum seeker a secret from the outside world and only confided in her personal tutor at college. In some instances, responses appeared speedy and appropriate and, as others have suggested, these are likely to be enhanced where schools and colleges have effective anti-racist and anti-bullying policies, good links with behaviour support services and clear accessible channels through which young people can make complaints (Stanley, 2001; Dennis, 2002).

Immigration status

Many young people experienced high levels of anxiety and uncertainty as they approached 18, especially where they lacked a settled asylum status. Although the intersection of social services and Home Office responsibilities for unaccompanied young people at 18 and its effects on transition planning will be considered later, some points in relation to education planning and financial support are relevant here.[8]

Where young people on reaching 18 were still seeking asylum or appealing against an earlier negative asylum decision – and one-third of those aged 18 or over (34 per cent) were doing so – responsibility for their accommodation and/or financial support generally transferred to the National Asylum Support Service (NASS). Where young people had been accommodated under s20, the local authority had a continuing responsibility to provide leaving care support. Those previously supported under s17, however, faced a risk of dispersal and, in the vast majority of cases, the formal ending of social services involvement at 18. Uncertainty was also evident for those who had been granted "exceptional leave to remain" (ELR), as was the case for 55 per cent of those aged 17 or over. Many had only been granted this status until they reached 18 and therefore needed to apply for an extension, the outcome of which could affect their right to stay.

Although NASS procedures may exempt young people from dispersal where they are in the final year of a course leading to a public examination, the effect of a transfer in support arrangements was nonetheless disruptive to young people's education. The weekly allowance provided by NASS tended to be lower than that provided by social services and created additional financial hardship. Furthermore, NASS was less likely to provide funds for travel, books and equipment or for childcare costs where young parents were attempting to return to study. Educational Maintenance Awards were not available to asylum seeking young people and, at least for those formerly supported under s17, practitioners had little option but to direct young people to charities or student hardship funds to help alleviate their financial difficulties.

Uncertainty around immigration status also affected planning for the future. Although many practitioners tried to work flexibly, taking account of the range of possible outcomes for young people, it inhibited the

---

[8] See Chapter 8 for a more detailed discussion of variations in support arrangements for unaccompanied young people at 18.

potential for pathway planning. Young people were frustrated at the lack of employment opportunities available to them. Where they were studying, they were not always sure they would be able to complete their current course or continue to pursue their education at a higher level. Young people in such circumstances often felt disempowered, lacking a genuine sense of control over their lives:

She's been here so long and she doesn't yet know which direction she's going in. There's still that worry that she's going to get sent back and about what's going to happen to her. (Diane's social worker)

Waiting for a final decision, in Diane's case for more than two years, could affect young people's ability to focus on their current studies, as the fear of ultimate removal gradually took a toll on their sense of mental well-being or on their commitment to education.

Supporting education and training careers

We have seen that young people's participation in education and training was subject to a broad range of influences, both positive and negative. Variations in their careers were associated with age, region of origin, the types of places they lived in and the degree of support that was attached to them. Their progress was also influenced by their motivation to succeed, by events in their lives that may have served to corrode that determination and by the degree to which support was available from within their social network (including key professionals) to help them overcome barriers to participation. This final section provides a brief overview of social services support for young people's education and training careers and considers broader factors that may facilitate or constrain social work practice in this area.

Support overview

Information from young people's case files was used to make an assessment of whether the support provided by professionals and from within young people's own social networks was associated with the progress of their educational careers. In order to assess the professional support provided by social services staff, we constructed a measure of the

119

adequacy of the overall support package provided to each young person. Judgements were reached about the adequacy of support provided in ten separate life areas and was then summed to provide an overall score per case on a scale of 0–10 (see Chapter 2 for further details). This analysis showed that young people's participation in education was significantly associated with a broader or more comprehensive package of care ($p < 0.001$; n = 109). Young people were much more likely to have had a continuous pattern of education if the support that was provided for education formed part of a comprehensive package of support that addressed most aspects of their lives.

In contrast, young people were more likely to spend significant amounts of time out of education and training, without a formal structure to their days, if the overall support provided by social workers, support workers and carers was weak. We have already seen that sustained participation was made more likely where young people lived in "care" or "kinship" placements and that this was likely to reflect the additional support and encouragement available in these settings. Taken together, these findings reinforce the value of placing unaccompanied young people, especially those who are younger, in more highly supported settings, of giving education a high priority when considering placements in more independent settings and of placing support for education in the context of young people's wider needs (including support for placement, health and well-being and life and social skills).

Research on looked after young people and on care leavers has high-lighted the reciprocity between different aspects of young people's lives. While adverse events in one sphere of a young person's life may have a negative impact on other life areas, the reverse is also true. Strategies that attempt, in often quite small ways, to build young people's self-confidence and sense of self-efficacy in one aspect of their life may then have positive knock-on effects in other areas and can help to build their overall resilience to adversity (Daniel *et al*, 1999; Gilligan, 2001; Dixon *et al*, 2004). Providing support for education in isolation from other life areas, while better than nothing, is therefore likely to be insufficient and needs to form part of a package of support that addresses the needs of unaccompanied young people as a whole.

Participation in education was also associated with young people having stronger networks of informal support (p = 0.03; n = 109). Where young people had contact with family members or other significant adults and friends, this was positively associated with their educational careers. We have seen that where young people had a supportive network of friends linked to school or college, it could help to reduce social isolation and provide opportunities for joint study and co-operation. Similar effects could accrue through links with older siblings or adult extended family members, such as aunts, uncles or cousins, whether or not young people resided with them. The range of significant adults that young people identified as playing an important role in their lives was quite broad, including adult members from their own communities, workers from refugee agencies, mentors, solicitors, members of the clergy and education professionals (careers advisers, Connexions staff and teachers). Young people often needed advocacy and support to help guide their steps in the context of an unfamiliar education system. The wider pastoral role played by some education professionals was of great value to young people, especially where support from social services for education was less forthcoming:

I asked my tutor what I could do and she was the one who helped me out a lot, more than even the social workers . . . I got a lot of advice from her. . . She sent me to Connexions . . . and, after that, they helped me. They gave me the application form to fill. There it says reference and when I came to social services they were not helpful, they could not give me a reference. So I went to her and she gave me a good reference and I posted it off. . . Ever since then I have been in that college. (Meena)

Strategies that help to strengthen young people's social networks are therefore also likely to be helpful in creating a more supportive environment for education and training. Mentoring initiatives may offer one avenue for unaccompanied young people to receive additional advocacy and support. Recent evaluations of mentoring projects suggest that, while they cannot remedy all ills facing vulnerable young people and they require careful negotiation between mentor and mentee, the informal "professional friendship" that underpins successful mentoring relationships can be successful in contributing to young people's sense of confidence, their skills and development (Philip *et al*, 2004).

Career planning and monitoring

Responsibility for helping young people to plan their education and training careers and monitor their progress rests primarily with social workers and support workers working in tandem with carers and other professionals. Planning and monitoring were rarely straightforward processes and plans were often buffeted by events in young people's lives or by wider external constraints. Effective planning appeared more likely where young people were placed within the responsible authority. Statutory requirements for visiting, care planning and regular review for looked after children helped to ensure that education was not overlooked.

In overall terms, planning and monitoring were highly variable. In some instances, young people who were newly arrived in the UK and spoke very little English were simply handed a referral letter to college and were told to go and enrol themselves. Besnik, for example, remained out of education for about one year after failing to negotiate the hurdles that were involved for him in doing this. Amongst some workers there appeared to be an expectation that young people should do these things for themselves and that direct support would only be provided if they encountered difficulties. Strategies that help to empower young people are undoubtedly helpful, although they need to ensure that the expectations made of young people are both realistic and timely, and they also require careful follow-up. In other cases, the monitoring of young people's attendance appeared to take the form of financial regulation. In these cases, young people's attendance at college was monitored periodically to ensure that their entitlement to bus passes and other associated allowances was still valid, but there was little evidence of further planning and review. In contrast, as we have seen, many practitioners did work diligently to support young people's educational careers and to review their progress.

Albert had arrived in the UK aged 15 and had been living in the same shared house, arranged by a refugee agency (under s17), with other unaccompanied minors since his arrival some 18 months previously. After a period of time at school where he felt isolated and unhappy, he moved to college and was studying to be a chef alongside learning English. He valued the support provided by his social worker. She had helped him to consider different course options (in conjunction with the college EAL unit), helped him enrol and make an Education Maintenance Allowance (EMA) application, and had organised the financial assistance he would need (including bus pass, clothing allowances and equipment for the chef's course). She now saw her role as supporting his progress through regular visits and planning meetings, providing help with motivation and liaison with college staff.

There is a requirement for all looked after young people to be provided with Personal Education Plans (PEPs – Department of Health, 2000a). These should be constructed by social workers in collaboration with young people and teachers, cover the main aspects of a young person's education and their extra-curricular activities and be subject to regular review. Taken together with other aspects of care planning, PEPs should help to ensure a rounded appreciation of young people's educational activities and progress and identify areas where further support is required. Evidence of their use, however, is mixed (Social Exclusion Unit, 2003).

The case files indicated that a PEP had been completed for only a small minority (6 per cent) of the sample, although this accounted for just over one in four of those accommodated under s20. Without a statutory obligation, PEPs were not being used for young people supported under s17. Where they had been used, social workers tended to find them helpful, although engaging over-stretched education professionals in the process was sometimes difficult. PEP meetings provided opportunities to obtain feedback from schools or colleges about how young people were faring, consider educational issues from the young person's point of view and open up channels of communication.

Planning was also impeded where important details of young people's educational history were not recorded on case files. Where pre-exile educational experiences were not discovered or not recorded or where their patterns of participation (and achievement) in the UK were not properly documented, workers relatively new to a case often had difficulty reconstructing young people's stories or understanding how issues affecting their attendance or motivation may have linked to previous experiences. This was the case with Jetmir's support worker, when trying to explain his lack of engagement with education:

> *Everything links with the background information. It makes it so difficult sometimes because you don't know what experiences he had in school, what schools he went to, how long he was in school for... I don't know... Maybe he attended a school with a [small] number of students and here colleges are big institutions, so when he goes it is kind of scary.*

Information of this kind is not always easy to discover. Where it is known, careful documentation can provide greater continuity for workers who may become involved at a later point. In doing so, it may prevent young people having to re-tell their stories, which may be difficult for them, and reduce the need for workers to rely on guesswork and speculation.

Liaison and resources

While planning and monitoring are important, other factors also serve to structure young people's opportunities. These include financial assistance and links with education and training providers to share information and to broaden young people's options.

Most young people, irrespective of whether they were supported under s20 or s17, were entitled to a weekly allowance (or pocket money if in a care placement), clothing grants and, if they were in education or training, a travel pass and leisure card. While the majority appeared to receive these entitlements, this was not always the case. Some young people in further education, especially if they were living with kin in situations that were arranged informally or in unsupported accommodation settings, failed to receive some of these things at all or at least for significant periods of time. Some had never been made aware of all their entitlements at the outset and only gradually learnt of them as they became more aware of the system. In such circumstances, young people had little choice but to fund their travel to college and other necessary items from their weekly allowance, which was usually set at around £35 per week at this time.

Beyond these basics, arrangements for financial assistance were often highly discretionary. Assistance for pens, paper or books was not always forthcoming and specialist items for particular courses or for computer access often depended on the willingness and ability of individual workers to plead a young person's case to managers. These were sometimes allowed as special cases, to avoid setting a precedent for other applicants. Such a situation would seem unsatisfactory and highly discriminatory. While it is the case that, for looked after young people generally, there is variation in the level of assistance to support learning, the situation is improving with the introduction of clearer baseline procedures and guidance (Department of Health, 2001; Social Exclusion Unit, 2003). Guidance to the Children (Leaving Care) Act 2000 encourages use of financial assistance in this way and, in response, leaving care services have been developing financial incentive schemes to promote post-16 participation in education, by topping up young people's allowances accordingly (Broad, 2003; Dixon *et al*, 2004). However, only in one Area was there clear evidence of provision of financial incentives for unaccompanied young people and only in relation to those who had been looked after (s20). Although, as we have seen, funding for education is also affected by young people's immigration status and the role of NASS, there is a case for reviewing unaccompanied young people's financial entitlements, including those supported under s17, in line with those now available to young people in the care system, whose situation is often very similar.

Opportunities are also affected by the links that workers build with education and training providers and by the time they have available to undertake this work. In most of our Areas, formal links with education services were more clearly defined for children of school age. Although, as we have seen, there were considerable difficulties in accessing school places for young people who arrived in Year 11, younger children could be referred to specialist "looked after" education teams, Education Welfare Officers or EMAS to co-ordinate access to placements and arrange additional learning support. In many cases, however, responsibility for finding placements was devolved to carers, relatives or refugee agencies that were supporting children, sometimes with mixed success.

Liaison arrangements for young people accessing further education or training appeared less certain. In two of our Areas, Connexions workers were attached to the asylum teams and they could offer a similar role, by helping young people to become aware of the range of options, offering assistance with access and providing ongoing advice and advocacy. Whether or not formal arrangements existed, there was evidence of individual workers developing informal links with teachers, college tutors and agencies providing education or support services to refugees. Links with young people's tutors, where these were sought, brought considerable benefits. It permitted workers to monitor young people's progress more effectively, identify issues where support might be needed and pick up on emotional issues that might be affecting them.

Links were also made in an effort to find more appropriate education or training options for young people. However, there was a pervasive sense of chance surrounding these *ad hoc* developments. The extent to which liaison took place tended to depend on the individual commitment of workers, making time within an already crowded work schedule, rather than from clear corporate and strategic leadership. Where workers lacked this commitment or the time to seek out options, young people were more likely to remain on courses that failed to meet their aspirations or remain out of education and training altogether. Individual liaison is essential to ensure young people get the best out of their education or training experience. However, there is a wider strategic role that needs to be performed to open up opportunities for young people in education, training and work experience. This role requires an overview of available resources within the local authority and a developmental brief to create new opportunities for asylum seeking and refugee young people locally and, as such, may be best performed by clearly designated officers within the local authority. Developments of this kind may prove resource efficient and limit the need for frontline workers to plough their own individual furrows.

Summary

Most young people received some assessment of their educational needs. Better assessments gathered details of young people's past educational experiences, language skills and attainments and placed them in the context of their current needs and interests. In many cases, however, no written plan of action resulted from these assessments.

Most young people were participating in full- or part-time education. Limited use was made of accredited training schemes and opportunities for employment were highly restricted. However, at least one in ten young people failed to establish a foothold in education, training or work. Patterns of participation were not always continuous and non-participation varied according to age at referral, region of origin, placement stability and type of placement. Stable care and kinship placements were protective and provided greater support and encouragement for education. Those placed in more independent settings (often under s17) found it more difficult to sustain participation. This reinforces the importance of place-ment stability and of giving education a high priority when considering placement changes or placements in independent settings.

Access to schools or colleges was frequently difficult, especially for those arriving in mid term or at age 15 and young people's adjustment to new educational environments also took time – anxiety and fears about raising concerns were not uncommon. This is a time when young people need considerable support from teachers, carers and social workers. Practitioners need to watch for signs of distress and establish good liaison to ensure prompt access and that young people can benefit from pastoral support or mentoring services available in some schools and colleges.

Most young people were resourceful and committed, although some lost motivation. Sustained participation was more likely where pro-fessional support for education formed part of a broader, more compre-hensive support package that addressed young people's needs as a whole and where young people had strong networks of support from family, other adults and friends. Strategies to strengthen these networks may assist the progress of young people's educational careers. Little use was being made of Personal Education Plans to help plan these careers.

Most young people did receive some basic financial assistance associa-ted with education and training expenses. However, not all were made aware of their entitlements and most assistance was discretionary. Greater transparency is needed and there is a case for reviewing these entitlements to bring them into line with those for citizen young people in the care system, including provision for financial incentives.

Liaison arrangements for young people accessing further education, in particular, were often uncertain. Connexions staff linked to asylum teams were helpful and many workers had informal links with schools and colleges. However, a broader strategic role is needed to widen opportunities and establish formal links with schools, colleges, training providers and employers. This role will require use of dedicated lead officers.

6 Health and well-being

The Children Act 1989 places a responsibility upon local authorities to promote the health and well-being of vulnerable children and young people within their locality, whether they are looked after or being assisted within the community in other ways. The physical, emotional and mental health of unaccompanied children and young people who come to the attention of social services should therefore be of particular concern, given the kinds of experiences that may foreshadow their arrival in the UK.

Research into the health needs of refugee and asylum seeking children is limited (Mather and Kerac, 2002). What there is suggests that young people themselves view their health in a broad way, linking separation from their families and worries about their welfare, poverty, social isolation, language barriers, and access to health care and school difficulties as factors affecting their health and well-being (Gosling, 2000). This chapter adopts a similar approach and considers how young people's health needs were assessed by social services. It describes experiences in young people's past and present lives that connect with their physical, emotional and mental well-being, identifies risks and some factors that appear protective, and assesses the strategies adopted by young people and practitioners to promote overall well-being.

Policy and guidance

Unaccompanied children and young people, irrespective of immigration status, are entitled to access all public health services, including medical and dental treatment, eyesight tests, family planning and mental health services (Save the Children, 2003). Access to health services also features in international agreements. Article 39 of the UN Convention on the Rights of the Child provides for appropriate care for physical and psychological recovery and social reintegration. In addition, an EU Directive on the reception of asylum seekers states that governments must ensure that minors who have been victims of inhumane or degrading treatment, including suffering from armed conflict, have access to rehabilitation services and appropriate mental health care.[1] Some guidance on meeting the health needs of refugees and asylum seekers has also recently emerged, including a Government-endorsed information and resource pack (Burnett and Fassil, 2002), a review of health care requirements by the British Medical Association (BMA, 2002) and, specifically related to refugee children, guidance issued by the King's Fund and the Royal College of Paediatrics and Child Health (Levenson and Sharma, 1999).

Local authorities also have particular responsibilities aimed at improving the health and well-being of looked after children. Official guidance emphasises the importance of regular assessments of children's health and for individual health plans that are regularly reviewed. It also stresses the need for local authorities to develop protocols to facilitate information-sharing, for Primary Care Trusts to have a designated nurse or doctor for looked after children and for local drugs and teenage pregnancy strategies to take account of their needs (Department of Health, 2002). Quality Protects (QP) also requires local authorities to report on three performance indicators linked to improving health outcomes, including immunisations and the proportion of children receiving annual health assessments and dental checks. Although performance varies across authorities, these indicators have tended to point to a steady improvement (Social Exclusion Unit, 2003). Finally, guidance to the Children (Leaving Care) Act 2000 states that pathway plans should provide a vehicle for assessing and monitoring the health needs of young people leaving care and for promoting healthy lifestyles (Department of Health, 2001).

The assessment of health needs

Several reports have pointed to the potential health needs of refugee and asylum seeking children and young people on arrival in the UK (Kidane, 2001b; BMA, 2002; Rutter, 2003b). Young people may come from areas where communicable diseases, such as TB, malaria or HIV/AIDS, are relatively common. They may come from areas where a breakdown in health systems has occurred, resulting in lower levels of immunisations

---

[1] Council Directive 2003/9/EC of 27 January 2003 laying down minimum standards for the reception of asylum seekers.

and undiagnosed conditions, or may have a physical legacy arising from war or inhumane treatment. They may also arrive malnourished and in a relatively weak physical state. The adverse effects of these experiences of conflict, disruption, of separation from family and the familiar may also have a negative impact on young people's mental well-being, one that may be compounded by the confusion and disorientation of their early post-arrival experiences.

While some of these health difficulties may be present, it is equally important not to portray unaccompanied young people as passive figures in an unfolding tragedy. Migration is a courageous act and studies also point to the resilience of young people in overcoming these adversities (Richman, 1998a; Ahearn, 2000). As young people, they have similar capacities to other groups of vulnerable youth. As young people, they also have a need for care and protection, for a safe environment in which they can recuperate and start to recover the lost or broken narrative threads of their lives (Kohli and Mather, 2003). This is not to gainsay the importance of making a careful assessment of young people's health needs when they come into contact with social services. Responding sensitively to young people's health concerns can be a valuable step towards this process of recovery.

Information about the assessments made of young people's health and well-being was gathered from case files in relation to three broad areas: physical health, emotional well-being and risk factors (including substance use, offences, risk of exploitation). Where there was recorded evidence that an initial assessment of young people's needs had taken place, some assessment of their health was almost always included.[2] Sometimes recordings were minimal and just included phrases such as: 'no major health problems', 'appears in good health'; or 'need to register with GP'. In other cases, more detailed recording enabled some understanding of the range of physical health issues that young people presented.

Many young people were assessed as being fit and healthy. However, for others, the physical legacy of past violence was often apparent. A few

---

[2] There was evidence of an initial needs assessment in 85 per cent of cases and in 94 per cent of these cases some assessment of health needs was included.

young people were found to have fractures that had not healed properly, while others reported painful scarring, burns, swellings or wounds caused by firearms, or difficulties with eyesight or hearing that originated in beatings they had received. In some instances, assessments picked up on long-standing issues (such as joint or back complaints, chest pains, heart problems, asthma or skin infections) that had not been diagnosed previously. It was also not uncommon for young people to be described as being thin, pale, tired or generally in a poor physical state, often derived from periods spent hiding indoors in their countries of origin, to limited food supplies or to the rigours of their journeys to the UK. Efforts were also commonly made to identify young people's family medical histories and to ascertain whether they had received appropriate immunisations. However, it was often difficult to obtain this information from young people, since many could not remember or simply did not know.

Depending on what was discovered through assessment, the proposed action that was recorded appeared to vary considerably. The need for young people to register with a local GP, dentist or optician was often recorded. In some instances, young people were given referral letters and expected to make their own arrangements. In others, especially with younger children, it was expected that carers or support workers would accompany children to appointments. Referrals to GPs were also made in response to concerns about potential medical conditions or where it was likely that young people would require x-rays or access to more specialist health care. Where the assessment of young people's physical health was undertaken by children's teams, referrals were often made for medical examinations or health screening as a matter of procedure. These tended to be conducted by medical officers for looked after children or, in Area 3 where more young people were supported under s17, through formal arrangements with a Primary Care Team that operated a "walk in" clinic.

Although young people's basic physical health needs were quite routinely assessed, coverage of emotional well-being or risk was subject to more variation, occurring in 66 per cent and 34 per cent of cases respectively. Whether or not these areas were included in health assessments varied according to the age of a young person, the team conducting the assessment and to the presence of a qualified social worker during assessment.[3] This suggests that, where young people were referred below the age of 16, where they were referred to a children's team and where the assessment was conducted by a qualified social worker, they were more likely to receive a well-rounded assessment of their health needs.

Recordings about risk tended to centre on the appropriateness of young people's living situations or on the potential for reunification with other family members or family-related adults in the UK, for which risk assessments would be required. Where teams used health checklists to conduct assessments, these would routinely provide for some information to be collected on lifestyle issues, such as whether young people smoked or used alcohol. Where there was concern about a young person's correct age, there could be some consideration of risk factors before placing them in children's homes or in the community with other unaccompanied minors. Concerns were also recorded where there was a perceived risk that young females had been trafficked for sexual exploitation. In these circumstances, young people were usually placed in foster care and liaison was often initiated with immigration services and the police in order to provide for their protection.

Efforts were also often made during assessment to gauge a young person's emotional state by listening to their experiences and by assessing their self-presentation and mood during the assessment interviews. In some instances, the harrowing nature of young people's stories raised immediate concerns. Recordings showed that some young people reported symptoms of anxiety or trauma linked to their past experiences, including sleep loss, nightmares, flashbacks or depressive thoughts about the fate of their families. Others raised indirect or non-verbal concerns where social workers reported worries that young people appeared withdrawn, sad, distressed, fearful or tearful through these encounters, or where they did respond, that their tone was particularly neutral or measured. In other cases, practitioners were able to pick up on issues associated with loneliness and isolation as young people struggled to come to terms with their new environments.

---

[3] Associations for emotional well-being: social work team ($p<0.001$; n = 212); age at referral ($p<0.001$; n = 212); qualified or unqualified social worker conducting the assessment ($p<0.001$; n = 166). Associations for risk: social work team ($p<0.001$; n = 212); age at referral ($p<0.01$; n = 212); assessor ($p<0.001$; n = 166).

An immediate response to these concerns was difficult to achieve. Although practitioners sometimes suggested the possibility of counselling or made young people aware of the existence of specialist services, young people did not always feel ready or want to take advantage of them. In most instances, these issues were noted as a marker that could be returned to once young people had become more settled – although such a return did not always take place. As a strategy, this may be helpful for the majority of young people not requiring psychiatric intervention as a matter of urgency. Listening to young people's stories and bearing witness to their experiences tends to create in us a desire to intervene or to be helpful. However, interventions of this kind may be ill judged and based on partial understanding. They may have more to do with making us, the listener, feel purposeful and better about ourselves and have less to do with young people's actual emotional and practical concerns (Blackwell, 1997). Provided young people are placed in a supportive environment, it may be helpful for them to have time to collect their thoughts and feelings. It takes time for a more trusting relationship to develop, one that will allow for a more rounded appreciation of a young person's personality and for their emotional needs to be understood in the context of their day-to-day interactions. In a number of cases, a deferral of intervention was planned, allowing time for carers or support workers to monitor the progress made by young people in placement.

Disability

Disability amongst refugees and asylum seekers tends to be a hidden issue. There is no official source of data on the prevalence of impairments or chronic illness amongst refugee groups in Britain. Within refugee communities, lack of official data may also be compounded by the stigma associated with disability in many cultures, concerns that revealing impairments may jeopardise asylum claims or to limited knowledge or expectations of the support that may be available (Burnett and Fassil, 2002). However, one of the few studies in this area found many different kinds of impairment stemming from accidents, torture, war-related injuries, amputations, congenital disabilities and sensory impairments (Roberts and Harris, 2002). This study found evidence of unmet personal care needs, of unsuitable housing, a lack of aids and personal equipment and of acute social isolation amongst some disabled refugees. It also highlighted the need for closer co-operation between immigration, social care and health services in planning to meet these needs.

Evidence from case files also pointed to the existence of physical, sensory or learning impairments affecting the daily lives of a small number of young people in this study. However, variability in recording practices suggests this is likely to be an underestimate of the incidence of disabilities amongst this group of young people as a whole. Six young people were considered to have sensory impairments, including deterioration or loss of vision or significant difficulties with hearing that affected their ability to study and interact with others. Three young people had been assessed as having learning disabilities. As with hearing problems, learning disabilities were less likely to be identified at initial assessment. Difficulties in these areas were more often identified over time as young people struggled to cope in classroom settings. Two young people were assessed as having physical impairments. However, a number of others had physical conditions that affected their day-to-day functioning, including persistent back pains, joint problems, migraines and persistent stomach complaints.

In general terms, the involvement of social work services seemed helpful to these young people and facilitated their access to appropriate health care. In most cases, once young people's needs had been identified, the practical responses made by social workers were considered and relatively prompt. Young people were usually referred on to primary health care services for further assessment and to gain access to specialist services where this was needed. There was also evidence of practitioners monitoring young people's progress through review and planning meetings and through liaison with health care providers. However, this was not always the case. There were occasions where emotional and behavioural difficulties associated with some forms of disability were not picked up quickly enough and resulted in placement breakdowns and further disruption to young people's lives. There were also scenarios where health assessments had not taken place and subsequent contact with support workers was minimal, resulting in physical conditions that affected young people not being responded to in an appropriate manner. This appeared less likely to occur where formal policies existed to provide health screening at the point of initial assessment and where joint working arrangements with health providers were well established.

Physical health, health monitoring and lifestyles

As practice guidance suggests, local authorities have a responsibility to facilitate young people's access to primary health care services, to monitor their health and to promote healthy lifestyles.

Access to primary health care

Registration with a doctor and dentist is a basic requirement for accessing services in the health system. These details should therefore be recorded and kept up to date on case files as a matter of procedure. However, it was impossible to discern from case files with any degree of accuracy the proportion of young people who were registered. In almost one-third of cases (31 per cent) there was no evidence on file concerning registration with a doctor and in almost one-half (48 per cent) there were no details of a dentist. While it may have been the case that, where young people were placed out of authority or where they were living semi-independently and supported primarily by housing agencies, these details may have been kept locally, it is surprising that this information appeared not to have been passed on to workers in the responsible authority and/or recorded by them.

Although a majority of young people appeared to have access to a doctor and dentist and were supported to do so, access problems were not uncommon. Where problems existed, most teams approached the local health authority to arrange a doctor:

He couldn't get a GP to start with. I think a lot of them turned him down ... [and] ... I think we wrote to the Primary Health Care and got him allocated a doctor. (Besnik's social worker)

However, this process was not always straightforward. Official letters offering an allocation tended to be sent direct to the young person – '... they send the letter to the client, not to you, who has to respond within two days or the allocation is cancelled'. Where young people failed to respond, for whatever reason, the whole process had to be re-started. This could also be the case where young people changed placements, especially if they did so repeatedly or moved out of the local authority area. In some instances, where support from housing agencies or key workers was not forthcoming, young people found themselves adrift without access to health care for periods of time or had to resort to their own devices. Sirvan, for example, was living in a hotel with other unaccompanied minors and had to ask them for advice about how to proceed:

> He [his key worker] didn't arrange any appointment for him regarding health issues. Once he realised he needed to go to a doctor, he was just watching the other residents and asked them how to do it. (Reported through an interpreter)

Health monitoring

The majority of the young people did not have serious physical health problems during the time they were supported by social services. Although almost one-half of the young people (49 per cent) had some health problems that may have required one-off or more prolonged treatment, around one in eight (13 per cent) were experiencing what might be termed chronic or longer-term health problems. There was also evidence of variations in the support provided by social services (or by agencies acting on their behalf) in relation to monitoring young people's health and responding to health issues.

Department of Health guidance on the health of looked after children promotes the need for regular health assessments and for health planning in the context of the wider child care planning and review system (Department of Health, 2002). Evidence from this study tends to reinforce the value of such arrangements for unaccompanied young people. In general terms, health monitoring and support tended to be more adequate where young people were looked after under s20 (p<0.001; n = 198). Health monitoring therefore tended to be linked to the additional statutory responsibilities that are associated with being looked after or, where supported under s17, to the provision of an equivalent package of care.

Qualitative data from case files pointed to a number of shared features in cases where health planning had taken place, irrespective of care status, which may have helped to facilitate health monitoring and support. Most of these young people had managed to find a settled placement. The majority had been living in foster or residential care, although a smaller number were living in shared supported housing, with kin or in independent tenancies. In most cases, these young people had either remained in the same placement throughout or, after an unsettled start, had been assisted to find a settled home base. In addition, the day-to-day role of foster carers or support workers in responding to young people's health concerns appeared important. Responsibility was usually devolved to them to arrange medical appointments, to support young people through treatments and to inform social workers of emerging health needs. In most of these cases, health planning and monitoring were also facilitated by the active engagement of social workers. Regular assessments of young people's health tended to occur where social workers were in regular contact with young people and where there was evidence that arrangements for child care planning, such as reviews or planning meetings, were in place. As such, health monitoring usually formed part of a well-organised and wider package of care. Even where young people had unsettled placement careers, were placed out of authority or led more chaotic lives, this combination of informal and formal monitoring helped to ensure that their health needs were not overlooked:

"M" was Kurdish and arrived in the UK aged 14. He was accommodated under s20 and placed in an out-of-authority foster placement. He had lived there for two years and had a positive relationship with his foster carer. His carer had a key role in registering him with a local GP and dentist, arranging an optician and accompanying him to health check-ups, including two statutory medicals. Although direct contact from his social worker was sporadic, due to the distance involved, liaison was maintained with his carer and the fostering agency, and health concerns, of which there were few, formed part of the agenda at statutory reviews.

"R" arrived from Iraq aged 16 and was supported under s17. After living in a shared flat, he moved to his own tenancy supported by a refugee agency and a support worker from social services. Concerns about his deteriorating mental health led to more active involvement by qualified social workers (child care and mental health). He was referred for psychiatric assessment and placed on medication to control his symptoms. His progress was good and the psychiatrist and mental health social worker withdrew. However, acute anxieties about the progress of his asylum claim brought a further deterioration and his social worker re-engaged mental health services to monitor his progress. Although his situation remained difficult, the management of these concerns was marked by consistent support, regular planning meetings to share concerns and constructive engagement/advocacy with health services. Health monitoring was also part of a broader package of care that addressed his placement needs, education and legal circumstances.

In circumstances where health monitoring was not part of a support package based on formal planning and review, social services responses were more varied. In many cases, only minimal information was recorded on case files about health issues. Some files indicated that only limited priority had been given to young people's health concerns and pointed to delays in identifying needs and to a lack of follow-up once issues had been identified. In one case, for example, a young person who reported that he was suffering from abdominal pains at the point of initial assessment was just handed a standard referral letter for a GP and given directions. He was still unregistered some four months later. In another, a young woman with a long-standing heart complaint and continuing chest pains appeared to have received minimal support from social services. Although her GP referred her to hospital for treatment, she appeared to have negotiated this for herself and the only other health-related recording in the case file related to provision of a leisure pass.

Although a lack of formal arrangements for health monitoring tended to increase the risk that health needs would be overlooked, it was by no means always synonymous with a lack of support for young people's health. Where concerned practitioners were in regular contact with young people, their health concerns were often responded to effectively in a more informal way, as the following illustration suggests:

"S" arrived, aged 17, and was supported under s17. Health screening at referral identified scarring associated with torture and it emerged during initial assessment that she had witnessed the death of family members and, while detained, that she had been sexually and physically abused. Her support worker arranged and supported her through various health checks associated with this (including tests for HIV and hepatitis B) and arranged for an assessment at the Medical Foundation in London in relation to these experiences. At 18, her outstanding asylum claim led to a transfer to NASS and (at data collection) her support worker was attempting to negotiate a transfer to London to facilitate longer-term counselling.

Promoting healthy lifestyles

Official guidance also places a responsibility on local authorities to promote healthy lifestyles amongst young people supported by them, including support in relation to diet and nutrition, use of drugs and alcohol, sport, leisure and sexual health. Evidence drawn from best practice in leaving care points to the value of partnerships with health professionals to provide accessible information and training to social services staff and young people in these areas (Stein and Wade, 2000; Wade, 2003). Recent reviews of QP Management Action Plans in the leaving care field, while acknowledging the limited nature of health initiatives in many local authorities, point to the emergence of helpful developments. These include partnerships with health promotion teams to audit needs and to provide training and information, peer education initiatives to offer advice on healthy living to looked after young people and initiatives around sexual health and teenage pregnancy (Department of Health, 2000b; Robbins, 2001).

Where there was evidence from case files of health promotion work, it tended to occur largely as part of one-to-one casework with young people, and formal links with agencies engaged in health promotion initiatives appeared rare. However, where some teams offered young people an induction period, there was evidence of young people being provided with health information in their home languages, of efforts to make young people aware of how health systems operated and to provide advice on health promotion issues. Some teams also provided general or gender-specific groups. These were designed to reduce social isolation, provide a range of outside activities and were also sometimes used to address basic life skills and related health issues. Young people often valued their involvement in groups, especially in the early stages of resettlement before they had established more secure social networks of their own:

> *I'm not going to that [group] any more. Before I was going because I was bored at home, so I was going to meet other people . . . There was some food and drink . . . We were playing games with social workers. It was a very good place to go when you are bored at home.* (Zola)

In many cases, advice about nutrition and help with domestic skills formed part of the core work undertaken by carers and support workers. Young people often needed help to familiarise themselves with shopping, with the safe use of cooking appliances, to develop their cooking skills and to identify places where foodstuffs familiar to them could be obtained. However, it was also not uncommon, especially where young people were living in more independent settings, for monitoring to amount to little more than checking the contents of the fridge periodically. In addition, the pressure of managing on low income (usually around £35 per week) tended to stretch young people's skills and inventiveness to the limit.

Some help was often available to support young people's sport and leisure interests. Some teams provided young people with a leisure pass to access swimming or a gym as a matter of procedure or provided a small monthly grant to allow young people to pursue leisure interests. In other teams, however, support of this kind appeared more discretionary and requests for particular items or pieces of equipment had to be negotiated on an individual basis. Furthermore, young people were not always made aware of their entitlements and some reported that no one had ever asked them about their interests, as was the case with one young man who expressed bemusement when asked if he had received help – 'no, why would they do that?'

There was also limited evidence about use of drugs and alcohol by young people. What there was suggested that, while some young people desisted altogether for religious or cultural reasons, most use was recreational and problematic usage was only noted or raised by workers in relation to a very small minority. However, many practitioners lacked knowledge about young people's pattern of substance use and some felt that placing young people together in shared housing in the same area created a social milieu in which exposure to risks from drugs and alcohol was higher:

Whenever you place 16-year-olds together in a house, there is always some risk. Kids don't move out normally at that age. (Zani's support worker)

A few workers also raised concerns about young people's exposure to sexual risk in such settings. In some instances this concerned young males who displayed inappropriate sexual behaviour. In others it related to a small number of females who were thought vulnerable as a result of past experiences of sexual abuse or enforced prostitution or where there were fears that they had been trafficked for sexual exploitation. Once these young women moved on to semi-independent living, perhaps in a different area, and ties with social services were loosened, anxieties amongst practitioners responsible for their welfare were sometimes increased:

I would imagine those elements of risk are always there, once you are moving young people into the community. Well, you don't even have to move them . . . If people want to abuse young people, manipulate them in any way, they have ways of contacting them . . . I think there is always an element of risk if young people have been involved with criminals or traffickers, that risk is always there. And I suppose especially if they move to [another] area where you are not able to monitor them on the same basis as if they were living with a family. (Miremba's social worker)

There were also one or two instances where young women experienced domestic violence from partners or boyfriends or where they were involved with or surrounded by a shadowy circle of older males about whom social workers worried much, but knew little about, and found difficulty in disentangling their client from them. Although (at least for females) advice about sexual health and strategies for keeping oneself safe were quite commonplace, especially once concerns were raised, the limits of the social work role (or perhaps of parenting more generally) made it difficult to provide adequate protection against risk.

Young people's health and welfare could also be affected or placed at risk by going missing or through victimisation associated with crime or racism. Limited evidence was available from case files about incidents of young people going missing from placements, although there were notes made in relation to 14 young people (7 per cent of the sample). It is difficult to determine how accurate this representation of missing incidents for unaccompanied young people may be. In practice, it is likely to underestimate the scale of the problem, since there is evidence that recording practices when young people go missing have tended to be highly variable (Wade *et al*, 1998).

Virtually all of these young people (14) had gone missing overnight, including a female who spent one month away and a male who had disappeared completely, and at least one-half had gone missing more than once. Although the majority were male, recordings tended to centre on the small number of females who were considered to be at risk of sexual exploitation. In these circumstances, incidents of going missing raised clear child protection concerns and responses to them appeared reasonably appropriate. There was evidence of close liaison between social services, the police and immigration services, and procedures were put in place with carers to prevent access to the placement by suspicious males or to divert telephone calls to social services. In each of these cases, at least at the point of data collection, the worst fears of practitioners had not been realised and the young women appeared to be leading relatively safe lives in the community.

Case file records only clearly identified six young people, all male, as having been cautioned or convicted of a crime. In some instances these were for what seemed relatively minor or one-off incidents, such as shoplifting, criminal damage or driving a borrowed car without a licence. Others, however, were far more serious, including two males charged with the sexual assault of younger girls, or formed part of a cycle of assaults and damage to the property of others. In other cases, irrespective of whether a criminal charge resulted, fighting was sparked by inter-ethnic conflict between groups of unaccompanied minors in residential units or in the local community. Young people who were innocent bystanders to, or who risked becoming embroiled in, such scenes, often found the experience extremely unsettling.

Records also showed that at least 20 young people (9 per cent of the sample) had been the victims of crime, including theft of their possessions, burglary, street robbery and physical assaults that were sometimes aggravated by racism. One young man, for example, had been attacked and severely injured on two separate occasions by large groups of white British youth in his locality. He lived in a shared house and, on several occasions, their home had sustained broken windows and been broken into by this group. Although an offer of alternative accommodation had been made and the police had been involved, the young people were reluctant to leave the area they knew and preferred to wait for accommodation in the locality. A number of others living in mainly white areas also reported experiences of racially motivated harassment. Although many practitioners were generally mindful of safety issues when trying to place young people, limited housing resources contributed to difficulties in adequately meeting their health and welfare needs.

Emotional and mental health

The mental health needs of young people looked after and leaving care have, until recently, been relatively neglected in research and practice. However, there is growing evidence of need. Studies have pointed to a high incidence of emotional and behavioural disturbance amongst young people referred to social services (Sinclair *et al*, 1995; Triseliotis *et al*, 1995) and, in comparison with non-care peers, to far higher levels of psychiatric disorders amongst looked after children (McCann *et al*, 1996; Meltzer *et al*, 2003). Small-scale surveys of care leavers have also highlighted the existence of mental health problems, including self-harming and attempted suicides (Saunders and Broad, 1997). The response to these health needs has tended to be patchy with evidence of limited opportunities for young people to access counselling or other specialist health services (Berridge and Brodie, 1998; Farmer and Pollock, 1998).

While this growing concern about the mental health of looked after young people is relatively recent, this is also likely to be the case for unaccompanied young people, for whom features of their past and present lives may create risks for their emotional and mental well-being. They are quite likely to have experienced traumatic events, may continue to be haunted by them and may be troubled by repetitive and intrusive thoughts, flashbacks, sleep disturbance or nightmares. They may also experience some loss of control over their lives and find difficulty in planning for the future (Kohli and Mather, 2003). They may have experienced several periods of disruption, their loved ones may be dead or missing, they may have experienced torture or been forced to engage in violence themselves and they are very likely to carry feelings of worry, loss and perhaps guilt at their own survival or escape. Once they arrive in the UK, the challenges of resettlement and uncertainty about the future may create further stressors that can affect their emotional and mental well-being.

However, there is also evidence of the fortitude and resilience of young people in overcoming these challenges (Richman, 1998a; Ahearn, 2000). It is suggested that, while a minority may be sufficiently troubled to require psychiatric treatment, the majority may be helped through consistent care and through strategies that help young people to re-centre their lives, promote their resilience and strengthen their capacity to cope in adverse circumstances (Burnett and Fassil, 2002; Kohli and Mather, 2003).

Factors influencing emotional well-being

Although young people's adjustment to life in the UK was invariably difficult, many had settled well and appeared positive and purposeful in their outlook. This seemed more likely to occur where young people had found a settled placement, were engaged in education and where they had developed supportive relationships with carers, significant adults and friends. In these circumstances young people were less likely to be visited by loneliness and isolation. Some had experienced a sense of relief to be free of troubles in their home countries and feelings of greater safety and security were linked to a belief that events at home would not be replicated here. Others had found a new sense of purpose and direction, often linked to their studies, to homebuilding and to making plans for the future. As was the case with Zola, this was more likely where young people had received a positive asylum decision.

Zola, who had recently moved into her own council flat, felt quite contented about her life: 'I feel safe. I've got what I want to do.' She discussed her plans for the future. She was going to college and wanted to study accountancy and talked about her desire to start her own family:

I will feel happy when I finish my studies . . . and then start my own family because I feel like I am alone – no brothers, no sisters, no father, no mother. . . Life is very complicated for me.

Her security and forward thinking was helped by having been granted "exceptional leave" to remain for a further four years. Although isolated at first, she attended groups run by the asylum team until she had developed her own social circle. She valued the regular practical support provided by her social worker, especially in relation to accommodation, education and finance. Her worker felt that, despite spending a considerable amount of time with Zola, she was unable to get emotionally close or get a real purchase on Zola's sense of well-being. She felt that Zola preferred it that way, kept an emotional distance and looked to her primarily for practical help.

From case file recordings there was evidence that almost one-third of the young people (31 per cent) had experienced or were continuing to experience some emotional turbulence that affected their overall well-being, although usually not their day-to-day functioning. In relation to almost one in seven cases (15 per cent), however, there were recorded concerns about young people's mental health.[4] Information from interviews with young people and practitioners pointed to the range of factors that could strain young people's emotional and psychological resources; factors that often connected to the past, the present and the future and that interacted together in quite complex ways.

Many young people continued to be troubled by thoughts of their own past mistreatment or by worries about what was occurring at home. Some were struggling to come to terms with bereavement, resulting from the death of parents or other family members that may have been witnessed

---

[4] These data should be treated with considerable caution. First, they may well underestimate the proportion of young people with significant emotional concerns. Second, they derive from a reading of case files by the research team rather than from the use of more scientific measures and, in consequence, should only be seen as broadly indicative.

or have occurred subsequent to their leaving. Many were dealing with the emotional effects of separation from their families and with continuing uncertainty about the welfare of family members. Not knowing often had particularly corrosive effects on young people's sense of well-being:

> *It wasn't my choice to be here at all. Most of all, my family, I really miss so much and I don't know where they are or what is happening to them . . . At least if I knew they're safe, then it would help me a lot . . . Sometimes I can't sleep . . . I have had many relatives that have died in the war [or been] detained. All I want to know is that they are fine.* (Meena)

Continuing anxieties of this kind may articulate with resettlement difficulties in the present in a manner that threatens young people's emotional resources. This was proving to be the case for Meena at the time of interview. At face value she appeared to be managing well. She had been living in the same shared house since her arrival in the UK, although it was in poor condition, was at college studying A levels and was highly committed to her work. However, the strain of coping alone (she had received only minimal support from social services and had few friends) combined with her fears for her family were affecting her ability to focus on her studies. In addition, her repeated requests for family tracing and for counselling had gone unheeded:

> *I tried to do everything by myself, to stand on my own feet, but I'm not coping now. I don't think I've done bad considering the fact that I don't have my parents here to help me.*

Resettlement required all young people to make major cultural adjustments – to new carers, new customs and practices, new environments and systems for doing things. Some were nonplussed at first and many experienced difficulties communicating across cultures. Where young people lacked consistent support and guidance or where they were placed in settings that isolated them from their own cultures or where they felt unsafe, these difficulties tended to be exacerbated.

Young people's well-being was also affected by other interrelated difficulties. Concerns were expressed by both young people and practitioners about the effects of not participating in education and training and of living on low incomes. Involvement in school (or college) can promote the psychosocial well-being of refugee children, not just through language and learning, but through the pastoral support provided by teachers and the access to friendships it affords (Melzak and Kasabova, 1999). Prolonged periods of non-participation removed the structure from young people's days and often increased their sense of social isolation. Several young people living alone expressed a reluctance to return home where their minds would be crowded by morbid thoughts. Others expressed frustration at the limitations placed on their social lives by the level of income they received. Difficult decisions often had to be made about who they saw and whether or when they would go out socially and sometimes added to feelings of depression and loneliness.

Uncertainty about the future was an overriding concern for many young people. Although Zola's asylum decision meant that it was possible for her to think into the future and make plans for her life, many young people had no idea whether their claims for citizenship would ultimately succeed. Inevitably, these anxieties increased as young people approached 18 amidst fears that everything they had worked hard to achieve would be snatched away. Drita, a young mother, when asked what the best thing in her life would be, responded:

> *To know that I'll be here and, when [my baby] grows up a bit, I'll be able to go back to college, to have a job, to get on with my life properly.*

The effects of a negative decision could be devastating for young people, causing some to disappear into a transient world reliant on support from friends or acquaintances or, where young people had a history of previous mental health difficulties, it could lead to a further or a renewed deterioration, as occurred with Abdulaziz:

> *When I received the decision of the HO and they refused my application for asylum, I was almost mental and I was admitted to the hospital. I am on tablets to help me cool down. I stopped going to college for four months.* (via interpreter)

From a social work perspective, these events lie beyond the control of practitioners, although efforts to provide advocacy, support and counselling and to develop clear plans that took account of the range of possible outcomes were generally appreciated by young people and could help to mitigate some of the worst aspects of uncertainty. In general terms, the messages that derive from the brief discussion above suggest that, where young people are provided with a stable and positive placement, where they are encouraged and supported to pursue education and where efforts are made to strengthen their social networks, these are likely to be protective of young people's emotional and mental well-being. This is consistent with findings from other studies on refugees that suggest that recovery from trauma over time is linked to the reconstruction of social networks, economic activity and independence and to contact with 'own community' individuals and organisations (Burnett and Peel, 2001).

Helping strategies

Where support of this kind was provided, time often proved healing and provided opportunities for young people to make use of their own personal resources for self-recovery:

> *It is really good now. But before I used to think a lot, back, remembering what happened and that. But now I just – I do think about it but not as before. So I don't know, we'll see what happens.* (Abdi)

Abdi's comments point to the length of journey many young people had to make, re-visiting past events continuously in an effort to reconcile these experiences and move forward. As was the case with other young people, the comments were also provisional, relating to the here and now and pointing to a future that remained uncertain. Opportunities to talk and to be listened to were helpful on this journey. Abdi had a good relationship with his support worker, lived with his younger sister and a male friend and had positive links with his own community locally. These sources of support were important to him, although his studies were the most important aspect of his life.

Young people exhibited different coping strategies to deal with the emotional effects of displacement and resettlement. Many, like Abdi, tried to keep busy, filling their days with purposeful study and reducing the time available to think or in an effort to forget past traumatic events – 'I try to forget, I make myself busy' (Amir). Others relied heavily on comfort and support from friends – 'The best thing is I've got friends, I can talk to

149

them' (Miremba). In contrast, some young people tended to withdraw and were variously described by practitioners as shy, quiet, self-contained or as having few outside interests or connections. Where concerned practitioners tried gently to explore young people's feelings, they were sometimes met with denials that difficulties existed or were faced by young people who felt unable or unwilling to make emotional disclosures.

Practitioners were often most disquieted by these responses. There was a tendency for some young people to keep their support workers at arms length, to maintain an emotional distance from them. In these circumstances, practitioners often felt they had little choice but to retreat, accept the young person's decision and focus on more practical issues, as had been the case with Zola:

I spent loads and loads of time with her when she moved into the house and got absolutely nowhere. (Zola's social worker)

Offers were quite commonly made to help young people access external counselling or specialist therapy. Where there was evidence that young people had experienced traumatic events, counselling was sometimes raised at the point of initial assessment or, in other scenarios, was suggested at a later point as emotional or mental health issues emerged over time. Looking just at the case file data, over one-quarter of the young people (28 per cent) who had experienced emotional difficulties that affected their overall well-being had received or were continuing to receive specialist services. Receipt of these services was also significantly more likely for young people accommodated under s20 rather than for those assisted under s17 (p <0.001; n = 198).

However, professional counselling raised complex questions for young people and practitioners. Not all unaccompanied young people want, feel ready for or trust therapeutic encounters. Some may lack understanding of what it means, others may harbour suspicions about disclosing in the context of their asylum claims or may be preoccupied with the pressures of day-to-day life or lack sufficient stability to be able to participate meaningfully (Stanley, 2001; Kohli and Mather, 2003). Counselling also has a cultural meaning. There may be no equivalent concept in the home cultures of many young people and different coping mechanisms, including "active forgetting", may be deployed to deal with psychological distress (British Medical Association, 2002). While some young people will be willing to share their stories, others will not and may find such a process distressing. In this sense, one size will not fit all and responses need to be tailored individually through a grounded understanding of each young person. The ambivalence experienced by some young people was reflected in the comments of their workers:

She could have had the counselling here. There's never been a problem and I'll always push for counselling if people need it. But she wasn't ready and there's no point putting forward people who are not ready. (Diane's social worker)

I did explain to him about counselling. It might do some good although he doesn't feel like he wants it now, he wants to forget. I think he's a bit proud and maybe he didn't understand what counselling was. He thinks it's not cool or it's a bit strange for him to do that. (Besnik's support worker)

Where young people did feel ready and able to confide in someone, therapeutic counselling was often highly valued. Miremba, for example, felt that her weekly sessions had made the biggest difference to her life here and that the opportunity to share her worries in this way had significantly improved her overall quality of life. Others, however, did not get this opportunity and there were many cases where, as we saw with Meena, repeated requests for counselling never met with an adequate response or issues that had been identified at an early stage were only picked up once a new social worker had become involved, often a long time later.

While professional counselling will be appropriate for some young people – and all who may need it ought to at least be offered this opportunity – it is unlikely to work for all and, given the scarcity of therapeutic resources, not all will be able to access it. There may therefore be a need to consider more flexible and imaginative strategies for meeting these emotional needs, at least for the majority not experiencing more acute mental health problems that may require psychiatric assessment or treatment. Recent work on psychotherapeutic engagement with refugees points to the potential value of forms of "therapeutic care", rather than just formal therapy, as a means of weaving therapeutic support into the daily lives of refugees (Papadopoulos, 2002; Kohli and Mather, 2003). This approach entails continuing engagement with young people in their home setting by carers, support workers and social workers, provision of a safe environment in which young people may feel able to speak about their experiences and time, space and understanding to enable young people to tell and re-tell their stories at their own pace and in their own way. It is hoped that, through this process of bearing witness to young people's experience, rather than attempting to rescue them from it (Blackwell, 1997), young people may gradually be able to use their own agency to promote self-recovery by re-weaving the threads of their past and present lives that may have been fractured by experiences of trauma and displacement.

Inevitably, such an approach has implications for social work time and resources, and lack of time was a preoccupying concern for many practitioners that often led to the prioritisation of practical over emotional concerns:

I just don't think we the social workers have the time, given the caseloads we have, to do what we would like to do with these children.

It is also likely to require training and back-up from psychotherapeutic services to provide consultancy to practitioners, since many workers felt they lacked the confidence and expertise to engage in work of this kind. These are not new issues for social services. Concerns about the mental health needs of care leavers more generally have led some specialist leaving care schemes to develop formal links with mental health clinicians to provide this role or to offer a direct service to young people *in situ*, where necessary, and initiatives of this kind may prove helpful (see Dixon *et al*, 2004).

Our findings also reinforce the need for support for young people's emotional and mental welfare to be placed in a broader context. How young people felt was closely interrelated to how they were faring in other aspects of their lives – in their placements, in relation to education and training and in their social lives. Where young people felt safe, where they had positive attachments to those whom they lived with, where they had a sense of purpose and some control over the course of events and where they had a broader base of social support, the effects on emotional well-being were generally positive.

Recent work on promoting the resilience of looked after young people (Daniel *et al*, 1999; Gilligan, 2001) and of those leaving care (Stein, 2004) is of relevance here. This work points to the value of strategies that help to build young people's feelings of self-esteem and self-efficacy, a sense that events are within their control, and which help to develop young people's social competencies. Building on young people's strengths and creating opportunities for them to experience success, perhaps in quite small ways, may therefore lead to them having a more positive feeling of well-being. Whether these opportunities occur in relation to life skills or through study, involvement in youth activities, leisure pursuits or hobbies that they value or through social groups provided by asylum teams, constructive engagement of this kind can help to improve overall quality of life. Although, as we have seen, unaccompanied young people of necessity tend to be quite resilient, strategies of this kind may nonetheless prove helpful.

Summary

Where initial assessments took place, physical health was nearly always included, but this was less often the case for emotional well-being and risk issues. Comprehensive health assessments were more likely for younger children supported by children's teams. In some teams, though not all, arrangements for health screening were routine.

Although a majority of young people were physically healthy, around one in eight were experiencing chronic health problems. Health monitoring and support tended to be better for those who were looked after (s20), linked to the statutory responsibilities for health assessments and planning, and for those supported under s17 who were provided with an equivalent package of care. Monitoring was facilitated where young people were in stable placements, where priority was given to health concerns and where patterns of social work contact, planning and review were regular.

Most health promotion work occurred through one-to-one casework; links with health promotion agencies appeared rare. Help with nutrition, shopping and cooking was often undermined by the low level of income young people received. Finance to pursue sport and leisure interests was often discretionary, although some teams funded access as a matter of procedure. Problematic use of drugs or alcohol only appeared to be an issue for a very small minority, although there were instances of young people going missing and of victimisation through crime and racism.

Many young people had settled well and were purposeful in their outlook, especially where they had a stable placement, were involved in education and had supportive relationships. However, almost one-third were continuing to experience some emotional turbulence connected with the past, present and future. Anxieties about the past often articulated with resettlement difficulties and concerns about an uncertain future to stretch young people's ability to cope.

Offers to access counselling were commonly made, although not all young people wanted or felt ready for these encounters. Others never got the opportunity, as their needs went unmet. More flexible and imaginative strategies for meeting these emotional needs may also be necessary, strategies that seek to weave therapeutic support into the daily lives of young people utilising the skills of social workers and carers. Such an approach, however, has implications for social work time and resources, for training and for back-up from psychotherapeutic services.

7 Social networks: family, friends and community

Irrespective of other differences in their lives, separation from parents or primary caregivers is common to all unaccompanied children and young people. From the young person's perspective, it has usually been an enforced separation caused by the death, imprisonment or disappearance of these caregivers or by young people being sent away by their relatives, either for their own safety or to escape other forms of hardship. To varying degrees, the process of leaving creates social and cultural dislocation. Commonly, young people experience a loss of connection with family, friends and community. Their arrival in a new and strange land carries a distinct risk of social isolation and means that they bring with them a range of psychosocial needs associated with separation and settlement.

Social care professionals are faced with the complex tasks associated with helping to minimise the disconnection between young people's past and present lives. In part, these are about helping to promote important continuities that can provide a bridge between old and new – discovering information about young people's family histories, building links with extended family members in the UK or at home or links with communities resident here from young people's countries of origin. In part, these involve making new connections through placement or school, with supportive peer networks or through mainstream community or leisure activities. It is with these fundamental considerations that this chapter is concerned.

Policy and guidance

Although the concept of partnership is not a term that is used explicitly in the Children Act 1989, it is one of the underlying principles of the Act and is used repeatedly in the guidance and regulations associated with it (Packman, 1993). The partnership principle is expressed through the belief that children should be raised within families and that, where young people do need to be looked after, those adults with an interest in the child should be involved in decisions about their care, wherever this is consistent with their welfare.

Practice guidance in relation to unaccompanied young people stresses that, in the absence of parents, it is important that those who may have an interest in the young person's welfare (whether relatives, friends of the family, independent advocates or caring agencies) are involved in the assessment and care planning process (Department of Health, 1995; Kidane, 2001b). The guidance provides a number of pointers to help practitioners when thinking about the arena of family and social relationships, including the importance of:[1]

- gathering information on young people's family histories, on their experiences of being parented and on any contact with family members or significant adults;
- maintaining and promoting contact with interested relatives and friends in the community (or overseas), provided it is considered safe to do so and young people want this, and monitoring these relationships to gauge the effect of contact on young people;
- providing young people with an option to trace missing relatives, taking care not to raise unrealistic expectations and being mindful of the ambivalence this may create in young people;
- keeping sibling groups together and providing support to maintain and enhance these relationships;
- supporting young people's involvement with their own communities of origin, with cultural and religious practices that may be important to them and with broader hobbies and leisure interests that may help to strengthen their social networks.

Previous chapters have also highlighted the resilience of unaccompanied young people when faced with the challenges of settlement. Practice guidance on the health of refugees and asylum seekers has also pointed to factors relating to the social world that appear protective to overall health

---

[1] These should be read in conjunction with guidance presented in Chapter 4 on placement, especially with regard to placement with friends or relatives in the community and placement of sibling groups.

and well-being. Factors that overlap with those identified above (Burnett and Fassil 2002) are:[2]

* developing a feeling of belonging – enabling young people to develop an attachment to at least one involved adult carer;
* encouraging a sense of agency – enabling young people to be involved in decision making and make active choices that help to increase feelings of self-efficacy and control over the course of events;
* providing time for young people to think and express their feelings in a safe environment with adults and peers and through activities, such as art, drama, music and story telling;
* promoting community participation – through involvement with own community activities and cultural events and through mainstream community links, including youth groups, after-school and leisure activities.

Thinking about the "social" therefore connects up the main dimensions of young people's lives (placement, education, health and social relationships) and the main stages of social work involvement from initial assessment onwards. This chapter therefore looks first at the knowledge gained by practitioners about young people's families, friends and community links during the assessment process.

Assessment

Information on the assessment of young people's existing social networks was derived from social work case files and related primarily to the phase of initial assessment. As the above guidance implies, this is sensitive ground for young people and practitioners. Asking questions, especially about family, may be met with silence or suspicion or with emotions that are too raw to be expressed in words. Practitioners were generally aware of the need to balance their need to enquire with an understanding that young people often needed time to feel sufficiently secure to speak about events that were painful to them.

---

[2] These pointers are also broadly consistent with research evidence on factors that may help refugee children to overcome distressing experiences and to maintain continuities with their own cultures while finding a place within new ones (Blackwell and Melzak, 2000; Kohli and Mather, 2003).

Some information was collected in relation to social networks for the majority of young people (81 per cent). However, in 45 per cent of these cases this process of assessment did not result in a recorded outcome or plan of action. In these cases, therefore, the assessment was confined to basic information gathering, perhaps providing a marker for further consideration at a later date. The extent and nature of recordings varied considerably. In some instances there was very little indication that any discussion had taken place. In a few files, for example, the appropriate section of the assessment form had simply been crossed out, had the word "nil" inserted within it or simply noted one or two names of family members. In others, quite detailed consideration was given to young people's family backgrounds, the whereabouts of relatives, to links young people had in the UK and to identifying needs that should be addressed.

Most recordings centred on young people's families. Efforts were often made to identify young people's pre-exile family structures, to find out with whom they had lived, how they had become separated and what had happened to their relatives, if this was known. It was quite common for this recorded information to be basic – the names of relatives, the number of siblings and contact details if these were available or young people were willing to provide them. However, practitioners were often also trying to get a feel for the kinds of thoughts, worries and memories that young people may have brought with them. In some cases, negative family experiences were uncovered, including instances of rejection, abandonment or abuse. Some files mentioned young people's acute worries for their families whose whereabouts were unknown or noted the traumatic implications for young people of witnessing family members being killed or taken away. In these cases, the potential value of counselling and family tracing services was sometimes mentioned during the assessment process.

Consideration was also often given to potential family links in the UK. As we saw in Chapter 4, some young people were already living informally with relatives prior to referral or arrived as part of a sibling group. Others arrived with contact details of relatives in the hope that they would be able to stay with them. These included older siblings, aunts, uncles, older cousins or more distant relatives/friends of the family. Precise relationships were sometimes difficult to discern and some practitioners had concerns about the degree of trust and optimism that young people placed in relatives whom they barely knew or had never even met. The task of assessing the potential of these relatives to provide adequate care was challenging and, as we have seen, the degree of care taken in these assessments appeared to vary quite considerably. Where older young people living with distant relatives or family friends were referred to adult asylum teams, there were also instances where the potential of these placements was ignored. These young people were often placed in shared housing without consideration of how these placements could have been supported and, in some cases, the fragile links young people had established seemed to have been lost altogether.

There was evidence of a strong commitment to keep siblings groups together, whether in foster care or shared supported housing, and to develop plans for reunification where older siblings were already living in the UK. However, where these groups were placed together in more independent settings, usually in the care of the eldest sibling, it was not always clear that an adequate assessment had been made of their ability to take on a caring role for the family or of the personal impact this might have on them.

It was not surprising to find that initial assessments involved less coverage of young people's links with friends and community, since networks of this kind were often lacking at this stage. In a small number of cases, mention of friendships occurred where young people had travelled to the UK with another young person from their homeland or with someone they had met during the journey. Where young people expressed a wish to remain together, consideration was often given to a joint placement in supported or independent shared housing.

In other scenarios, there was acknowledgement of young people's lack of social links and of the potential for isolation. This was often reflected in decisions about placement locations and the mix of residents, in plans to encourage young people's participation in in-house social groups or to promote community links, and to encourage early involvement in education. While some young people already had links with refugee agencies or community associations at the point of referral (and may have been placed by them), there was a broad recognition of the need to help young people forge links with their own communities.

Although at the assessment stage recordings that provided information about young people's hobbies or leisure interests were uncommon, issues of culture and community were addressed through some consideration of young people's religion and the cultural practices associated with it. As we saw in Chapter 3, references to religion were made in 72 per cent of cases. These references ranged from the merest note to more detailed explorations of the place religion had in young people's lives, whether and how they chose to practice, and whether there were other cultural practices that were important to them. In these cases, plans were sometimes made to introduce young people to local mosques or churches, to provide Korans, prayer mats, bibles and cookery books, or to make links with other unaccompanied young people or known members of the community who shared similar interests. In so doing, space was opened up that could provide young people with connecting threads back to their homelands and with opportunities to re-integrate these practical and symbolic links into their present lives (Kohli, 2001).

However, in most cases, assessments tended to be practical and focused on the most pressing needs – for placement, education, finance and health. Most assessments of social networks tended to be restricted to gathering factual information about young people's family backgrounds and links, not least, in some instances, because these helped to determine young people's eligibility for services and the possibilities for future reunification. In itself, this overall focus should not be surprising, given the urgency of young people's practical needs at referral and the opportunity this provided for practitioners to carry out tasks that were immediately helpful. Consideration of wider social and cultural connections were features of more comprehensive and well-rounded assessments that attempted to place these needs in a more grounded understanding of young people's lives. It also depended on young people's willingness to share sensitive and personal information of this kind. Information often only emerged in drips over time as young people felt more reassured about those who were working with them and, as we shall see below, some chose or felt it necessary to maintain a relative silence or distance in relation to these relationships throughout the time they were supported by social services.

Family

This section explores the extent to which practitioners were able to gain an understanding of young people's family histories, how and when this tended to occur, and the obstacles that limited this knowledge. It also considers the links young people were able to make with immediate and extended family members in the UK and overseas and the strategies that practitioners employed to help promote these links.

Knowledge of family histories

Guidance has suggested that it is important for practitioners to gather information about the family histories of unaccompanied young people (Kidane, 2001b). Some understanding of family background, past parenting patterns and of the reasons for separation may help in gauging young people's emotional well-being and in assessing the potential for life history work, contact or eventual reunification. Gathering information of this kind, however, can be difficult. In this study, younger children did not always remember the chronology of events. Confusion and language barriers also made conversations about family and past events more difficult during young people's early encounters with social workers. Uncertainty about the motives that underlay these questions, about the role of social services and about the implications of providing information for their families at home were also not uncommon. Some also found the traumatic nature of past events too painful to relive and the promptings of social workers were met with silence.

The interview data suggested that some young people were more "open" and others more "guarded" in their responses to these questions and in their relationships with practitioners over time (see also Okitikpi and Aymer, 2003). Where young people were guarded or silent, practitioners tended to feel greater uncertainty and ambivalence about the authenticity of the stories they did present (see also Kohli, 2001). Awareness that some young people were told to present "formal" stories by their families or by agents to aid their claim for asylum meant that some ambivalence was ever present. This was the case for Desta's social worker, when asked what she knew of Desta's family background and reasons for coming to the UK:

Like a lot of our young people, not that much really . . . Quite often they can't tell us everything anyway or they have been told to give us a different story to the reality of their situations . . . But you kind of pick things up over time . . . But the circumstances as to why she is actually here, I don't know the reality and I don't know we ever will.

Practitioners were generally aware of the range of factors that could constrain young people from talking openly about their families. Patience, time and greater trust were needed before young people's stories could properly emerge, allowing workers to 'pick things up over time'. Workers often tried to avoid being overly intrusive and confined themselves to the factual information that was initially needed, preferring to wait for the young person to make a further move:

In the very beginning she was quite traumatised, so it's not something we delve into. We like to build up the relationship first. It was through me building that relationship with her that she opened up. (Diane's social worker)

As the relationship and information grew, the possibilities for counselling or family tracing could be discussed or re-visited.

However, reticence in broaching past family issues also related to other, sometimes more pragmatic concerns. Where assessments were undertaken hastily or where continuing support from workers was limited, young people were sometimes never asked these questions or information that was gleaned appeared not to have been followed up. In this respect, it was ironic that Desta had – and continued to have – overriding concerns about the welfare of her missing father. In her account, she suggested that her feelings about him had not been discussed during assessment and that she had been too nervous and unconfident to raise them herself, but that she continued to worry in private. Lack of continuity also affected young people's willingness to confide. Where there had been changes of worker and where past information was poorly recorded, it was more likely that the past would remain a closed chapter in favour of the more pressing concerns of the present. This order of priorities was also reinforced by resource constraints. In these circumstances, time spent reviewing the past was unlikely unless workers had concerns about a young person's mental health:

> Given the timescales of our work, we often don't have the opportunity to have real in-depth conversations with them about the past. Particularly with cases that have been around for a while and you inherit them. You are so focused on sorting things out now . . . The only time we do work on the past is if there are some problems for the young person and they are struggling. You know, if there is trauma or something. (Social worker, Area 2)

Some young people continued to resist discussions about the past. Focusing on the present and managing the practicalities of day-to-day living may have required them to close off or control their emotions about separation and loss (Richman 1998b). Closure and keeping busy were sometimes employed as coping mechanisms:

> He keeps to himself quite a lot. He doesn't want to talk about lots of stuff, like previous history, his background, his family and stuff. He is quite closed, in the sense of understanding where he comes from, his culture and identity and his history as a child. It is quite hard to get at that. (Jetmir's support worker)

> When I have said little things like, 'you must miss your family a great deal', he would acknowledge that and then . . . the body language would say, I don't really want to go there. I think that is part of their coping mechanism. They have each other, which I think is a great help to them . . . I think they cope as best they can. (Abdi's social worker – Abdi lived with his younger sister)

This lack of knowledge and the experience of being kept at arms length was a matter of considerable concern to many practitioners and bore heavily on the help they could provide. Workers were often aware that these young people continued to be troubled by their pasts but felt powerless to intervene and had little choice but to focus on more practical issues in the present. Providing young people with openings to re-visit the past, however, remains important. Time brings changes. Although young people may not feel ready or able to respond to cues at one point in time, at another they may feel the need to talk about their families or about events that have taken place. It is important that this option is kept open. It is also important that where information is gathered it is carefully recorded. Where this was not done, it was sometimes the case that subsequent changes of worker led to important information about young people's histories being lost. Asking young people to re-tell distressing experiences from the past can, in itself, represent a form of abuse and, in these circumstances, it was more likely that the past would remain locked away.

Family tracing

Where young people were willing or able to share information about missing relatives at home or in third countries, offers were often made to explore the possibilities provided by family tracing services, such as the British Red Cross or International Social Service. This can be sensitive territory for young people. Enquiries can carry or be perceived to carry risks for family members. It can also arouse suspicions, since some young people may previously have had experiences of being used as informers to the detriment of their families (Kidane, 2001b). The outcomes of these enquiries are uncertain, may not bring welcome news and are often dependent upon the accuracy of information available and the political climate in young people's country of origins. It is also an area of practice in which comprehensive guidelines to assist practitioners have been lacking (Ayotte and Williamson, 2001).

Although there was no clear evidence that attempts at tracing had yielded positive outcomes, at least within the timeframe of the study, a number of young people welcomed the opportunity to try. In these cases, practitioners generally tried to proceed with caution and to ensure that the young person's consent was informed and based on a fairly balanced understanding of the potential benefits and risks that might be involved:

I think some people are just scared that their family is going to be jeopardised or get into trouble if someone goes and finds out where they are. Before, we tried to explain to people that that is not going to happen . . . Now I give them the facts and [then it's] their choice. (Social worker, Area 1)

However, some young people would have appreciated help of this kind but were never asked and were unaware of it as a possibility. In other cases, although young people received initial offers of help and the appropriate forms were completed, there was a subsequent drift that left them feeling confused, dispirited and alone:

I have just lost hope . . . [Would you have liked help to trace your father?] . . . I would love to, yes. But I don't know how to find him, that's the thing. (Abdulkareem)

I said to my support worker, 'What has happened about my Red Cross?' I have not been contacted. It has been approximately two years now . . . She says, 'Haven't the Red Cross called you?' I really don't know what is happening . . . Has it actually been done? Has my information been sent off? (Meena)

Caution was not uncommon amongst young people and some decided not to accept offers of help. In some instances, the reasons for refusal were clear and were linked to negative past experiences of birth or adoptive families or to past rejection by them. For example, Besnik's mother had walked out on him to start a new family some time previously, leaving him to fend for himself. After his arrival in the UK, he refused further offers of help to re-establish these links, even though he may have known where she was:

That's why he doesn't want to find his family, because he knows where they are and he knows they're not interested. (Besnik's social worker)

In other scenarios, refusal was rooted in concerns about the impact tracing may have for family members or in suspicions about the motivations of the agencies concerned. Considerable trust in the ethos and practice of tracing agencies was needed and, in these cases, where young people had some informal link to their homelands, they preferred the option of making discreet enquiries through these contacts:

I didn't like it. I don't like the Red Cross. I want to do it my way. I told [my family friend] if there is something he could do. I don't want the Red Cross . . . I don't trust them. Things [happen]. (Amir)

Where young people's reasons for refusal were unexplained, it could arouse feelings of ambivalence in workers about young people's motivations for being here. In the absence of firm information, speculation sometimes took over about whether families had arranged for a young person's arrival, whether or not young people maintained contact with their homelands and who this may be with and whether their silence was linked to their concerns about asylum or to other factors in their past or present lives and relationships. In most instances, this speculation was benign, borne out of frustration and a desire to be helpful. In others, however, it may have reflected a lack of engagement with the young person, an overly low-key social work role in which the relationship necessary for a young person to share sensitive information of this kind had not been effectively built.

The attempt to re-connect young people to relatives at home was generally perceived to be a good thing, one that could provide important practical and symbolic reassurance. It was also an aspect of planning that took account of the possibility that young people might have to return at some point in the future. If this were to be the case, links that could be established now might prove important to young people in the future and might lessen the likelihood that they would find themselves alone and exposed.

Family contact

Partnership and contact with birth families for looked after children are important threads underpinning the Children Act 1989. Recognition of the value of contact has led to it being much more common and more frequent than was the case in the past for young people in foster care (Cleaver, 2000; Farmer et al, 2004; Sinclair et al, 2004), although the need for contact with siblings is perhaps still less appreciated than it might be (Rushton et al, 2001; Selwyn et al, 2003). Contact enables birth parents to give "permission" for parenting to take place, prevents children constructing idealised fantasies about their families, is important for identity formation and provides a resource for later support after care (Cleaver, 2000). Research on leaving care has also pointed to the potential role of the wider kin network in providing support and to the limited use made of such networks by social workers (Marsh and Peel, 1999).

In contrast to these patterns of greater contact, the majority of un-accompanied young people have no relatives to whom they can turn for support. Information from case files suggested that only just over one-third of the young people (36 per cent) were known to have relatives resident within the UK, but not all of these young people were in direct contact with them.[3] A small proportion of young people (11 per cent) were also known to have links with relatives in other countries, although some of these young people also had contact with relatives in the UK. This suggests that, in overall terms, around three in five young people (62 per cent) had no family contact of any kind.

The nature of this contact varied considerably. A significant minority of young people mainly lived with members of their extended family. Other young people, although they lived in different placement settings, maintained contact with family members. Forms of contact were various and included frequent or irregular patterns of visiting, telephone contact or, more rarely, letter writing. In some instances, these young people had lived for a period of time with their relatives, either before or soon after referral, but were unable to stay. In others, plans for reunification were made but either the assessment process led to a negative conclusion or the young people changed their minds and wanted to live elsewhere. Despite this, young people generally wanted and valued continuing contact and, in this regard, placing young people close to relatives (or to friends and community links) was genuinely helpful in promoting continuity in these relationships.

A small number of young people had links with family members outside the UK. Contact was usually, though not exclusively, with people in their country of origin and ranged from one-off "safe and well" calls, to enquiries about the welfare of missing family members or patterns of regular telephone or letter contact. Where workers were aware of these links, contact was often brokered or supported by them through provision

---

[3] This may, however, underestimate the extent of young people's links with family. Uncertainty about young people's relationships was not uncommon and, in these circumstances, links may not have been known or recorded by social workers. The files suggested that 92 per cent of those with family in the UK appeared to have been in touch with them in some way.

of international phone cards or help with letter writing and faxes. In other cases, young people chose to operate independently or felt unable to seek help and workers only became aware of these connections by chance. However, there were also cases where these links were factually recorded but there was little evidence of any action having been taken to promote further contact. In the context of young lives affected by displacement, separation and loss, it is difficult to overstate the importance of encouraging these connections to home and family. Although contact may bring bad news as well as good, it may offer reassurance and help young people's adjustment in the present.

The primary source of family support for young people came from siblings. One in five young people (20 per cent) had links with one or more siblings, amounting to 57 per cent of those with known family contact in the UK. Most siblings lived together, often as family groups, and the presence of brothers and sisters provided a critical reservoir of emotional and practical support. These were usually *the* primary relationships for young people and a main source of family identification and solidarity.

Placement together in the care of the eldest sibling required subtle social adjustments. Younger children had to negotiate a space within the family unit that was reasonably comfortable for them and had to adjust to the authority of older brothers and sisters. For those with a primary care role, the assumption of these responsibilities was a considerable burden. Their individual needs often came second to those of the family group and, in some cases, affected their pursuit of education and their ability to socialise, make friends and access wider community resources. The willingness to provide this care to keep the family group together was universal. However, the making of these placements was often based on an assumption about the needs of the sibling group as a whole rather than on a careful assessment of the particular needs of each individual within it and their capacity to care and thrive. Continuing support also tended to be based on whole-group needs, carrying the risk that the voices of individual children within the group would be less likely to be heard. While keeping siblings together should be a priority and is strongly desired by young people themselves, it should not be at the expense of the needs of each individual within the family unit.

It is important for practitioners to keep a close eye on dynamics within the family, to be mindful of those who appear to be thriving and those who are not and for them to adjust the support they provide accordingly. This did not always happen and some sibling groups, especially where they had together made a transition to independent accommodation, found life difficult. Coping with transition, the burden of family responsibilities, limited financial resources and a reduction in professional support meant that young people's capacity to manage was severely tested. Where monitoring did take place, as was the case with Abdi and his younger sister, it was possible to help offset some of the burden of responsibility. His sister suffered from a degenerative illness and Abdi's social worker kept a close eye on their progress and made links to the health and counselling services she might need in an effort to prevent Abdi becoming overwhelmed:

I felt that was too much responsibility to put on [Abdi]. You need to be careful. You need to watch. If you think she is slowly becoming ill and she doesn't recognise it, you need to do something about it. I didn't think it was fair to put that responsibility on to him.

In general terms, assessment and monitoring of young people's contact with relatives were necessary to establish the credentials of these relationships, to ensure the safety and protection of young people and to gauge the effects of contact for their well-being. This was especially the case where young people arrived with contact details for relatives they had never met or where relatives suddenly appeared at a later point. The status of these relationships was sometimes difficult to determine and careful assessment took time, was intrusive and was often a source of immense frustration to young people who were waiting for the requisite checks to be completed before they could visit relatives or for overnight stays to be sanctioned:

It's a bit rude, I think. It's not nice . . . to say that my social worker wants . . . to look at your passport, see your house, things like that. I talked to [my social worker] once about it but he said he had to do it, so I left it. (Amir)

Most young people who had contact with known relatives had received some support from their workers to promote these links.[4] Apart from activities related to assessment, placement and monitoring, support was also provided for visiting (provision of travel warrants or cash), to stay in touch (phone cards, fax or letters) and to help locate relatives (through tracing or through links to young people in other local authorities). In addition, counselling was sometimes provided to or accessed on behalf of young people who needed help to come to terms with loss, the death of family members, the negative effects of contact or news that arrived from abroad.

Support services with respect to family issues were, however, uneven. As we have seen, many young people would have appreciated support but never received it or were unaware that services to help them re-connect with family members were even available. Support was also harder to provide where uncertainty about young people's family relationships predominated. Where young people were secretive about their contact with family, their workers were largely restricted to the role of interested onlookers, as the following comments suggest:

I have got the impression he has got relatives here. (Ghedi's social worker)

I don't know . . . about the family . . . It is difficult because a lot of the kids won't tell us about contact with their family because they are worried that if they tell us, we will tell the solicitors and they'll be sent back. (Walid's support worker)

I know they have an uncle in London, who they have quite regular contact with and visit quite frequently . . . They have never approached for financial assistance . . . so I am assuming that he pays for that . . . So I think they have quite a lot of contact with their uncle, although I've never met the gentleman. (Social worker for Abdi and his sister)

---

[4] Some support was provided to 79 per cent of those in touch with relatives in the UK and to 71 per cent of those with links overseas. The nature and quality of the support provided were variable and included those living with kin as well as those living elsewhere but in touch with relatives.

Other significant adults

A sizeable minority of young people (at least 16 per cent of the sample) had also formed connections with other significant adults who, to varying degrees, had played an important role in their lives.[5] Where young people lacked a connection to family or where social work support had proved unreliable, the presence of these figures and their potential for practical support and emotional reassurance assumed greater significance. The range of people involved was quite extensive and included present or past carers or support workers, representatives of refugee agencies and community associations. There were links with refugee families or families of friends, teachers, solicitors and links established through churches or mosques. Although not all of these people were central, each had some contribution to make to the overall fabric of young people's lives.

Evidence from the interviews suggested that practitioners were not always aware of the connections young people had made nor of their potential significance for young people's overall well-being. Support to promote these links was also less common than was the case for known contact with family. In only 41 per cent of the cases where there was documentary evidence of contact with significant adults had young people received help from practitioners to strengthen these relationships. Where support was provided, it took a similar form to that offered for families, including assessment and monitoring of contacts, provision of travel or telephone cards to facilitate contact and encouragement for young people to stay in touch, especially with past carers, host families or known family friends.

The pastoral support role provided by other professionals, such as teachers, careers advisers and solicitors, was commonly cited by young people and often under-appreciated by practitioners. In some instances, these relationships appeared to be relatively instrumental, linked to a young person's desire to learn or remain within the country:

---

[5] This is a minimum percentage based on documented evidence from case files. Other young people may of course have had undocumented links of this kind. At interview, young people were asked to draw up a social network map of all the people who they felt were important to them. The information presented here is based on both sources of data.

She helped me with my English . . . She gave me extra books and [advice] about how to learn better. . . and talked to me about many things. She was friendly. (Drita)

He is my teacher; he is a nice man. (Hassan)

Because my solicitor can appeal and help me, maybe help my future. (Da-xia)

These desires for education and for permanence are fundamental and, in this respect, the role of professionals working in these arenas can be quite pivotal to the ambitions of young people. However, sometimes these relationships took on the qualities of a "befriending" role and touched the need in some young people for a broader or deeper pool of emotional support:

He knows everything about my story in this country. He knows about my benefits and everything . . . He can see that I haven't got any family and no-one to help me for my studying. He said, any time you need help, just phone me. (Diane, talking about her college tutor)

Young people often needed advocacy and support to help guide their steps in the context of unfamiliar education, immigration and benefits systems. However, as Diane's comments suggest, these needs may overlap with a desire to have someone understand important aspects of their story, to comprehend the context in which their particular struggles were being acted out. Whatever label is given to this role – befriender, mentor or independent visitor – its potential was not being greatly exploited for young people in this study. One or two had accessed befrienders linked to refugee agencies or therapeutic services and some young people benefited from having support workers from their own countries of origin. However, the vast majority (as was the case with Diane) had to seek out their own advocates or sources of emotional support beyond that provided directly or indirectly by social services.

Practice guidance on unaccompanied children has highlighted the duty conferred on local authorities to provide looked after children with access to independent visitors if this would help to safeguard their welfare. Since many unaccompanied young people have no close or special adult in their lives, it suggests that the use of independent visitors to befriend young people may be advisable and that it would be helpful for these to be drawn from within the refugee communities (Department of Health, 1995). The Special Guardianship provisions of the Adoption and Children Act 2002 may offer another avenue to provide unaccompanied young people with the substitute attachments that may accrue from more legally secure, permanent placements without affecting the bonds they may have with their families abroad (Department for Education and Skills, 2004b). Mentoring and befriending initiatives may also help to provide a pool of adult figures to help young people on their journey to adulthood. Although initiatives of this kind have significant resource implications, they may go some way to supplementing and reinforcing the formal support provided by social services.

Friends and community

Research on refugee children has highlighted a tendency for their lives to be marked by isolation and loneliness. They may have fewer friends than other groups of young people (Candappa and Egharevba, 2000) and their access to community, leisure or youth services is often constrained by lack of money, limited engagement in education, language barriers and by the racism commonly experienced by asylum seekers (Cunningham and Lynch, 2000; Gosling, 2000; Stanley, 2001). Mainstream youth services have also not always taken adequate account of the specific needs of refugee children and young people (Norton and Cohen, 2000). These factors create social distance and refugee children themselves have identified the effects of poverty, bullying, loneliness and cultural isolation as factors that negatively affect their well-being (Gosling, 2000).

These experiences were shared by many young people in this study, especially in the early stages of settlement, and many practitioners were mindful of the need to help young people connect with friends, with aspects of their own culture and community and with mainstream youth and leisure activities. Good friendships helped young people to re-orient their lives and provided an important source of company, solidarity and emotional support:

They are very special to me actually. They have supported me and gave me help whenever I have needed it. They are there all the time if you need them. They will come and visit me and give me a bit of company if I want it. (Abdulkareem)

Friendships with young people from similar cultural backgrounds were generally valued for ease of communication, for cultural identification and for the bridge they often provided between young people's past and present lives. Friendships with citizen young people were generally harder to make. More explanations were needed, language barriers made communication more difficult and negative encounters linked to racism and bullying made some young people reticent to engage. For some, the cultural divide was too large to cross:

It's a bit difficult [to make friends] because English people don't like making friends. I wouldn't understand what they're talking about because it's a different culture . . . What I look for they don't look for, what they look for I don't have a clue. (Amir)

This sense of being in separate worlds was made more likely where young people were living exclusively in shared housing with other unaccompanied minors and where they were out of education for considerable periods of time.

School or college are critical arenas in which young people can re-establish their education, recover a sense of everyday normality to their lives and forge new relationships (Richman, 1998a; Melzak and Kasabova, 1999). Involvement in education provided a major source of new friendships and a broadening of young people's social networks, often to include citizen young people. Some young people sought out these friendships to broaden their outlook and to improve their language skills. Extra curricular activities and homework clubs also provided opportunities for further study and for socialisation. Where young people lacked family links or other significant adults in their lives, the friends they made through these means sometimes represented the sole source of informal support that was available to them.

Placements were a second main arena for meeting young people's needs for stable attachments, friendships and community. Of particular importance were the types and locations of placements and the degree to which they helped to minimise young people's initial sense of cultural dislocation. Placements in kinship settings, in same-culture foster placements and, to a more varying extent, in placements arranged through refugee agencies or community associations, tended to provide greater opportunities for young people to connect with their communities of origin. Although the direct support provided by refugee agencies was variable, these placements were usually located in areas with established refugee populations. In some instances, young people felt embraced by these communities:

> *Sometimes it makes me feel that I'm in Somalia really, because people always talk Somali and eat Somali food. They do Somali practices.* (Abdi)

Finding a cultural place and developing a sense of belonging were important ingredients in helping young people's adjustment to life in the UK and most concerned practitioners were keen to encourage these connections. However, it is important to keep a close eye on young people's welfare in this regard. In some cases, where young people appeared to have positive "own" community links, the social work gaze turned elsewhere. In these circumstances, young people were sometimes left overly reliant on sources of support that were in reality quite fragile or were exposed to situations that carried a risk of exploitation.

Cross-cultural foster placements presented more challenges to young people and carers, although many did prove stable and worked well. Even where foster carers worked hard to respond to young people's cultural needs (for diet, religion and cultural practices), tensions sometimes led to a breakdown or to young people eventually making a decision to move away. These difficulties appeared to be exacerbated where placements were located in more isolated areas, away from young people's communities of origin. Miremba, for example, eventually chose to relocate to supported accommodation in a more culturally mixed area:

> *It is very very important to be with people from my own country . . . I felt depressed because there were not so many black people around. It made it very difficult.*

Location was also important for young people living in more independent settings. Where placements were situated close to their family, friendship or community network, the benefits for young people's sense of social integration were considerable. Where young people were placed in areas that were potentially unsafe or that were distant from these networks, their social lives were inevitably much more constricted. Although practitioners were generally sensitive to these factors when thinking about placements, as we have seen previously, placement decision-making was heavily circumscribed by available resources and satisfactory solutions could not always be found.

Shared living arrangements, especially where residents were carefully matched, provided a major source of friendships. In some scenarios, friendships made while young people were in care placements enabled them to make planned moves together to supported housing. In others, however, where young people were more routinely placed in shared housing at referral, perhaps out of authority, and were reliant on inconsistent support from social services or from housing agencies acting on their behalf, relationships made with flatmates were often pivotal. These friendships sometimes constituted young people's sole reference point in an uncertain world, especially if wider links to school, college or community were lacking.

Many young people found comfort and companionship through membership of churches and mosques. Attendance not only met their religious needs, it provided a symbolic connection with home and opened up a social space in which new social relationships could grow. As one social worker commented: 'there is a real sort of community feeling around the church'. Members of churches or mosques often embraced young people, offered advice, guidance and a listening ear and the social activities attached to membership provided opportunities to swap stories about home and to learn new skills (cooking, recipes and so on). Practitioners were generally conscious of the benefits that could accrue to young people from this type of involvement and were often willing to assist them to locate places of worship or to provide bibles, Korans, prayer mats or other items they needed.

Although there was very little evidence of young people accessing mainstream youth services, help was often provided for young people to access sports and leisure facilities by providing basic leisure passes. Financial assistance to support particular hobbies or interests was, however, discretionary and, based on the case file data, often required a concerted effort on the part of practitioners for requests to prove successful. In this respect, money to support dance, gymnastics, music lessons or other more expensive pastimes often appeared difficult to obtain. Where asylum teams organised social groups and other linked activities or trips, these did help to reduce the worst effects of social isolation, especially for those newly arrived and lacking networks of their own. Once young people had found their feet or became heavily involved in their studies, they tended to move away:

He doesn't really need us, the team, in that sort of way. I think the [group] is very good for new arrivals who don't know many people and need something to anchor to. He's past that. (Albert's social worker)

However, lack of money was something that few young people were able to get past. Poverty was an overriding factor that constrained the potential for young people to lead active social lives, especially where they were living in more independent settings and had to manage on very low personal allowances (usually around £35 per week at the time of the study). Young people often spent their leisure time playing football with friends, walking in the park, window shopping or socialising at home. The decision to go out with friends often had to be carefully balanced against other expenses and was especially difficult where the group might include citizen young people who were working or living with their families. Young people were often dependent on their friends when money was particularly short, some refused to invite friends back through a sense of shame at the condition of their homes, while others spent much of their time at home, alone with their thoughts:

It's not enough, but they say they can't do anything about it . . . Sometimes I'm sitting here without nothing . . . If I go to college, I need to buy my lunch there. Sometimes I don't have enough money to buy my lunch. I have to wait until I come back home and eat my food here. (Diane)

Overall social networks

Information from case files also afforded an opportunity to identify factors associated with young people having stronger or weaker overall social networks. A measure of the strength of this network was constructed for each young person, based on whether there was evidence of contact with relatives, significant adults, friends or with members of a young person's own community of origin. These were then summed to provide an overall measure of the social network available to each individual (on a 0–4 scale).[6] Table 7.1 shows how this breaks down for the sample as a whole.

Table 7.1
Strength of overall social network (n = 212)

Sources of support	Per cent
None	25
One	20
Two	31
Three	24
Four	1

In general terms, Table 7.1 highlights the relative social isolation experienced by many unaccompanied young people and, for a sizeable minority, their almost compete dependence on the support provided by social services and other allied professionals. For one-quarter of the young people there was no documented evidence of any informal support beyond that provided by professionals and for a further one in five there was only one source of support identified. At the other end of the spectrum, one-quarter of the young people appeared to have quite strong networks of support from family, other adults, friends or community.

---

[6] This measure should be treated with caution. It is restricted to information recorded on case files and may therefore underestimate the contact young people had in practice with family, significant adults, friends and community – about which there was often some uncertainty. Nonetheless, it does provide a useful indication of these overall networks.

Some aspects of young people's personal characteristics were associated with having stronger or weaker social networks. Although there was no variation according to physical health, mental health or disability, there were differences by sex. Females tended to have stronger networks, while males were more prone to social isolation (p<0.01; n = 212).

However, the main findings repeat and consolidate those presented in previous chapters. Where young people were referred below the age of 16, their cases were more likely to have been managed by children's teams and to have subsequently followed an s20 pathway. These factors were all associated with young people subsequently developing stronger networks of support when compared to older teenagers supported under s17.[7] Stronger networks were also evident where young people spent the majority of their time living in care or kinship settings when compared to those who mainly lived in supported or unsupported accommodation, the majority of whom were supported under s17 (p<0.001; n = 180). This was also more likely where young people were placed within the local authority area, since out-of-authority placement carried a greater risk that young people would have weaker networks of support (p = 0.01; n = 153).

As we saw in Chapter 4, the additional support available to young people in care or kinship placements tended to offer greater protection against the risk of social isolation and also tended to provide greater encouragement for young people to pursue their education. It was not surprising to find, therefore, as the qualitative material in this chapter has suggested, that access to education was associated with a broadening of young people's social networks (p = 0.03; n = 109). In Chapter 5, we highlighted the additional difficulties that might affect motivation and continuity in education for young people living in semi-independent or independent settings, especially where social work support was limited. However, non-participation also had social costs, by restricting the opportunities available to young people to broaden their social support base.

As research and practice guidance has indicated, the investment of social work time in helping young people to strengthen their social networks (through placement, education, family, friends and community)

---

[7] Associations for these variables were as follows: age at referral (p<0.001; n = 212); social work team (p<0.001; n = 212); care status (p<0.001; n = 212).

may bring benefits to young people's overall health and well-being. It may also reinforce factors associated with greater resilience – feelings of belonging, of agency, self-efficacy and control (Burnett and Fassil, 2002; Kohli and Mather, 2003). As we have seen, social participation also provided opportunities for young people to rediscover a sense of ordinariness through everyday activities and to find ways of minimising the disconnection between their past and present lives. These are all important features of successful settlement.

Early investment in social networks may also help to reduce young people's longer-term dependency on social work support. This, for example, was the case with Desta. When she first arrived, Desta was heavily dependent on the support provided by her social worker. She felt very alone, unhappy and was frequently tearful. At this time, the emotional support provided by her social worker was both critical and intensive. Over time, however, the support provided by her foster carer and her participation in college and at the local church meant that she began to feel more confident and was able to build a wider circle of friends. Although she still valued her social worker for the practical help she provided, she no longer needed her in the same way and their relationship was therefore less demanding and more relaxed.

Support to strengthen young people's informal networks also constitutes an essential part of young people's preparation for adulthood. As we shall see in our next chapter, formal social services involvement frequently ended once young people reached 18 or relatively soon after. Even where young people were eligible for continuing support under the provisions of the Children (Leaving Care) Act 2000, the support available was finite and time limited. Once social services involvement ceases, young people are inevitably heavily reliant on other networks of support. If young people are not to be left in an isolated and vulnerable position in early adulthood, it is essential that the social dimension of their lives is placed at the forefront of care planning from the point that young people are first referred. If planning is left to the leaving care stage, there is a risk that it may be too late to make a substantial difference.

Summary

Most assessments addressed the area of family and social relationships, although they were mostly restricted to gathering basic information about family constitution and the whereabouts of family members. Where acute anxieties were revealed, offers of counselling or family tracing were sometimes raised. Less attention was given to young people's friendships or community links.

Some young people were guarded about their relationships with family. Patience, time and trust were needed for young people's stories to emerge. However, just over one-third (36 per cent) were known to have relatives in the UK and 11 per cent had known links overseas. Over three-fifths (62 per cent) had no known family links. A majority of those with known links had received help from social services to maintain them.

Most family links were with siblings and these relationships were often *the* primary source of family identification and solidarity. Priority was given to keeping sibling groups together, although some strains were evident for those in a primary care role and support was often based on whole-group needs rather those of individuals within it.

Around 16 per cent of young people had links with a range of other significant adults. Workers were not always aware of these links or the potential significance of them for young people's well-being. Support to promote these links was less common than it was for families. Initiatives to connect young people to mentors, befrienders or independent visitors were not sufficiently exploited.

Education and placements were the main arenas for broadening young people's friendship networks. Finding a sense of belonging was important in helping young people's adjustment to their new lives and many workers were keen to encourage connections to young people's communities of origin. Limitations in the supply of foster and independent placements often constrained these links and, where social work support was limited, relationships made with peers in shared housing were often young people's only anchor in an uncertain world.

Comfort and companionship was also found through contact with churches or mosques and workers were generally willing to assist young people in this area. Young people's involvement in leisure activities and in their social lives was heavily circumscribed by lack of money.

Many young people were socially isolated and dependent on support from professionals. Those whose careers followed an s20 pathway, who were mainly placed in care or kinship placements, preferably within the local authority, and who were consistently involved in education tended to have stronger informal networks of support than did those living more independently under s17 arrangements.

An *early* investment in strengthening young people's social networks (through placement, education, family, friends and community) may help to improve young people's overall well-being, strengthen their resilience and help to reduce their longer-term dependency on social services.

8 The transition to adulthood

Most unaccompanied young people come to the UK in their mid-teen years. Preparation, planning and guidance to help young people negotiate the transition to adult life once they reach 18 years of age should therefore be at the heart of social work practice. The timescales for doing so are often relatively short, perhaps one or two years in many cases. Looking to the future is also crowded by the emotional and practical demands of the present. Young people invariably arrive in a confused and vulnerable state. Their primary needs are for settlement – for a period of stability, an opportunity to build new and meaningful attachments, to gain a foothold in education and to construct new networks of support. These are also fundamental prerequisites for successful transition at a later stage and form part of the process of preparation for adult life. Activities in the present may therefore help to lay a more secure foundation for the future and feed into a process of transition planning.

However, the majority of unaccompanied young people face futures in the UK that are often clouded with uncertainty and that may be foreshortened by asylum policies and procedures. If it is the case, as this chapter will contend, that transition planning and "after care" support for unaccompanied young people has been an area of considerable weakness for social services, then part of the explanation for this (though by no means all) derives from the tensions inherent in the interface between child care and immigration policies. On the one hand, differences (according to age) in the level of Home Office Special Grant paid to local authorities to support unaccompanied minors has been identified as one factor that has driven policies of supporting older teenagers in the community under s17 of the Children Act 1989, policies which have weakened their entitlement to leaving care services (Stanley, 2001). On the other, the central thrust of leaving care legislation in recent years has been centred on social inclusion and forward planning into adulthood, policies that are difficult to enact when young people's right to remain in the longer term is uncertain. Transition planning, therefore, has to take account of a range of possible outcomes, including the possibility of return.

It is also the case, however, that these weaknesses have related to factors specific to social services. In particular, and in a context of limited resources, they have stemmed from social services delimiting its responsibilities to a relatively new and rapidly growing client group and to factors associated with the nascent development of new services to meet these responsibilities. As earlier chapters have indicated, specialist services for unaccompanied children emerged from confused beginnings, in circumstances that were at times overwhelming and where clear guidance and procedures were lacking. More recently, significant policy developments have coincided with a drop in the numbers of young people arriving to create conditions in which some restructuring or realignment of services is possible, including possibilities for the further development of leaving care services and in the numbers of young people eligible to receive them.[1] How these developments will eventually play out in practice and what they will mean for the lives of young people, however, largely lie beyond the scope of the present study.

Law, policy and leaving care services

From a research perspective, we know very little about how unaccompanied young people have negotiated these stages of transition nor about how social workers and allied professionals have attempted to guide young people through them (Stanley, 2001). However, long-standing concerns about the problems faced by citizen young people leaving care have fuelled both legislative changes and the development of specialist services to assist them, changes that form part of the context for thinking about transitions made by unaccompanied young people.

The development of leaving care services

Over the past two decades, research on leaving care has consistently highlighted the problems faced by young people. Despite their disadvantaged backgrounds, young people have left care at a much earlier age than

---

[1] In particular, LAC(2003)13 and the Hillingdon judicial review (see p. 188).

other young people in the population have left home (Stein and Carey, 1986; Garnett, 1992; Jones, 1995). Not only do they leave early, but the main elements of the transition to adulthood have also tended to be compressed. Learning to manage a home, finding a foothold in education and employment and starting a family have tended to overlap in the period after leaving care (Biehal *et al*, 1995; Corlyon and McGuire, 1997; Stein, 2004).

It is not surprising to find, therefore, that while some young people went on to do well, others continued to struggle. Evidence has pointed to young people facing a heightened risk of unemployment and homelessness (Cheung and Heath, 1994; Broad, 1998) and of social isolation, as support from families often proved inconsistent (Biehal and Wade, 1996; Marsh and Peel, 1999) and sources of professional support tended to fall away soon after leaving care (Biehal *et al*, 1992; Garnett, 1992).

Growing awareness of these problems fostered the growth of specialist leaving care services from the early 1980s. The leaving care provisions of the Children Act 1989 (s24) provided a further stimulus to service developments in the 1990s (Stein and Wade, 2000). The gradual development of these services led to improvements in the support provided to young people and in the outcomes achieved by them, especially in relation to accommodation, life skills and financial support (Biehal *et al*, 1995). However, service developments were markedly uneven and were associated with considerable variation in the services provided to young people within and between local authorities (Department of Health, 1997; Broad, 1998; Stein and Wade, 2000).

Implementation of the Children (Leaving Care) Act 2000 (CLCA 2000) in October 2001 was intended to tackle these inconsistencies. The objectives were to delay transitions, improve preparation, planning and support for leaving care and create more consistent arrangements for financial support. New duties were placed on local authorities to assess and meet the needs of "eligible" young people, including the financial needs of those aged 16 or 17, to provide each young person (at age 16) with a pathway plan and a personal adviser to co-ordinate a support package through to the age of 21, or beyond if continuing in education (Department of Health, 2001). Early evidence on implementation of this legislation suggests that the CLCA 2000 has been broadly welcomed in the social work field and that it is leading to some improvement in consistency, planning and support for young people leaving care (Broad, 2003; Dixon *et al*, 2004; Hai and Williams, 2004).

Policy relating to unaccompanied young people

Policies affecting transition at 18 for unaccompanied young people are both complex and continuously shifting. Entitlements and transition pathways differ, *inter alia*, according to asylum status, date of arrival in the UK and to the support arrangements provided by social services. Given this complexity, just a brief outline will be provided here to provide context to the substantive material that follows.[2]

For young people accommodated under s20, all duties and powers associated with preparation, planning and after care support apply in the same way as for citizen young people. Where young people have been granted "indefinite leave to remain" (ILR) or "discretionary/exceptional leave or remain" (DL/ELR) or where they have made an "in time" application to extend their leave beyond 18, they are entitled to work and study, claim benefits (at age 18) and access social housing.[3] Where young people are still seeking asylum at age 18 or have an outstanding appeal against a negative decision, primary responsibility for financial support transfers to the National Asylum Support Service (NASS). However, responsibility for day-to-day accommodation and support remains with the local authority, with NASS providing some financial recompense to local authorities for services provided. These young people are not at risk of dispersal, may continue to study and are covered by the provisions of the CLCA 2000 until the point that all appeal rights have been exhausted and they

---

[2] Sources of up-to-date information include: the Children's Legal centre (www.childrenslegalcentre.com), the Refugee Council (www.refugeecouncil.org.uk) and the Immigration and Nationality Directorate (www.ind.homeoffice.gov.uk).

[3] The research period broadly covered mid-2001 to late 2003. From 1 April 2003 new asylum classifications were introduced. In particular, "exceptional leave" to remain (ELR) was replaced by "discretionary leave" (DL) and a new category of "humanitarian protection" (HP) was introduced. This change post-dates our sample and all young people in this study granted leave for a specified period, usually until their 18th birthday, had been granted ELR.

refuse to comply with removal directions (Children's Legal Centre, 2004; Home Office, 2004a).

Local authorities have fewer legal duties with respect to unaccompanied young people supported under s17. The Children Act 1989 confers a general duty to safeguard and promote the welfare of children "in need" and this would include a general duty to make adequate plans for their transition at 18. However, there is no specific duty to provide leaving care services, although local authorities may make provisions of this kind, and in most instances formal responsibility ends at 18. Where these young people have been granted leave to remain (ILR, DL/ELR or HP) or where an "in time" application to extend their leave has been made, they may be able to claim benefits (from age 16) and have the same social rights (for work, study and housing) as other young people. Where they are still seeking asylum at age 18 or have an outstanding appeal, they are likely to transfer to NASS, may face dispersal to another area, but may continue to study.[4] However, NASS has discretion, in exceptional circumstances, to defer dispersal and young people can apply for just a financial support package if they have accommodation of their own. Where these young people receive a final negative decision and have exhausted all appeal rights at age 18, they are likely to have no entitlement to support from NASS or social services.[5]

With respect to these differing scenarios, Home Office guidance stresses the importance of social services planning ahead to ensure that young people experience a relatively smooth transition (Home Office, 2004a). In particular, there is a need to ensure that applications to extend young people's leave to remain are timely (made before the previous period of leave ends) and that applications for NASS support are made four to six weeks before young people reach 18.

As previously indicated, other developments may be effecting a change in the numbers of unaccompanied young people accommodated under

---

[4] Eligibility for NASS support may also apply if a young person has made an application for further leave "out of time" (after their leave to remain has expired) and the Home Office decides to treat this application as a fresh asylum claim.

[5] In the context of the Hillingdon judgment, however, it may be possible for those previously supported under s17 to mount a legal challenge against a denial of leaving care support.

s20 and in the proportion entitled to leaving care services. In June 2003, the Department of Health issued guidance on the appropriate use of s17 accommodation (LAC(2003)13, Department of Health, 2003). The guidance was issued in response to s116 of the Adoption and Children Act 2002, which had the effect of amending the Children Act 1989 to expressly permit the use of accommodation for children and families under s17. The guidance clarified that, in the case of lone children, there should be a *presumption* for the use of s20 unless there were clear contraindications uncovered during assessment and, as such, clearly questioned the routine placement of unaccompanied young people aged 16 or 17 under s17. Although the likely impact of this guidance on local authority practice lies outside the scope of this study, early evidence based on a survey of 19 local authorities suggests that, while the overall response has been patchy, some progress towards the use of s20 accommodation for older teenagers is being made (Refugee Council, 2005).

A second development affecting entitlement to leaving care services concerns the findings from the Hillingdon judicial review (August 2003), a case brought against Hillingdon Social Services by former unaccompanied minors previously supported under s17 and denied access to a leaving care service.[6] The judgment held that there was an equivalence in the accommodation and support services provided to these young people, irrespective of formal care status, and that they therefore had a common entitlement to leaving care services beyond 18. Although the legal judgment only applied to cases before November 7 2002 (the date at which the Children and Adoption Act 2002 was implemented), it may, together with LAC(2003)13, have wider resonance. The likely increase in demand for leaving care services has also been recognised by Government through provision of additional financial support to those local authorities most affected (Department for Education and Skills, 2004c).

Pathway patterns at data collection

Differences relating to age and the service pathways of young people at the point fieldwork ended have a bearing on what can be said about

---

[6] R *(Behr and others)* v *Hillingdon London Borough Council (2003)* EWHC 2075 (Admin)

transition at 18. Only a small minority of the sample (n = 38) were looked after (s20) and the vast majority of these young people were still below the age of 18 at data collection, although just over two-thirds (68 per cent) were aged 16 or 17 at this point. For those on an s20 pathway, therefore, the findings relate primarily to those processes associated with preparation and planning for transition at 18.

However, where young people moved on from s20 accommodation before the age of 18 this almost invariably involved a change of care status. This relates to the voluntary nature of this provision. In effect, three formal choices are presented if a young person's new placement is not to be considered as a continuation of *care* (s20): (a) to treat those moving on aged 16 or 17 as "relevant" young people under the CLCA 2000 and provide leaving care services; (b) to re-designate these cases as s17 (before or after age 16); or (c) to cease to provide formal services. Around one-third of those who started out on an s20 pathway (32 per cent; n = 12) were re-designated as s17 cases during the course of the fieldwork cycle, all before reaching the age of 18. Analysis of case file data identified three broad scenarios that led to this re-designation and that had some implications for young people's later entitlement to leaving care support.

First, re-designation occurred in some cases where young people were reunified with extended family members after a stay in foster or residential care. Once young people appeared to be settled, their status was changed and social work support tended to withdraw or be substantially reduced. Second, re-designation sometimes applied to sibling groups where the eldest reached 18 and was required to leave foster care for independent living. Where the family group wanted to stay together, which was usually the case, the care status of the whole group (including those under 16) was changed. These moves were primarily systems rather than needs led and, although often well planned and supported, tended to weaken in practice the entitlements of younger family members to later support. Third, re-designation also frequently occurred when young people moved on from foster care to semi-independent living before reaching 18. This could occur after a brief period of assessment and recuperation in an s20 placement or at a later point when young people were perceived to be ready for or wanted greater independence.

Although the majority of these young people remained "eligible" for services under the CLCA 2000, there was little evidence that such services were being envisaged beyond the age of 18. In most cases, social work activity had tailed off and greater reliance was placed on the support provided by extended kin, older siblings or, for those living semi-independently, on the more variable support provided by housing agencies. Where activity remained high, it tended to focus on getting the foundation stones in place (finance, housing, education, social networks) before the likelihood of case closure at 18 (or relatively soon after) became a reality.

The majority of young people (76 per cent), however, had been supported under s17 from the point of referral. Not surprisingly, these young people were older at data collection. Over one-half (56 per cent) were aged 18 or over at this time and the vast majority in this age group (77 per cent) had ceased to receive support from social services past their 18th birthday, as their cases had been closed. This reflects the lack of formal duties attached to s17 support generally and, in particular, at the leaving care stage.

Only 23 per cent of these young people continued to receive some support beyond this point, often not for very long. Although the reasons for this were not always clear from case files, two main issues were apparent. First, continuing support was provided, to varying degrees, while arrangements were being finalised for a young person's transition to independence before case closure. This tended to occur in some cases where young people's accommodation or their application for Housing Benefit or Income Support had proved complicated to arrange. Second, continuing support occurred in some cases where confusion reigned over young people's transfer to NASS or where difficulties existed in the asylum application or appeals process. Where the transfer process was delayed or the progress of an asylum claim was confused or subject to administrative errors, support tended to continue until these issues were resolved. However, for the vast majority of young people supported under s17, case closure at the 18th birthday was routine and they were expected to make their own way in the world.

Immigration status at data collection

Immigration and transition planning are integrally related. Where unaccompanied young people lack a positive final decision on their asylum applications, the approach of adulthood can be a time of great uncertainty. Table 8.1 shows the asylum status for the whole sample and for those aged 18 or over at the close of the study.

Table 8.1
Immigration status at close of study

	All ages (n = 212)	Age 18 plus (n = 99)
	Per cent	
Awaiting a decision	28	34
Exceptional leave (ELR)	53	41
Indefinite leave (ILR)	10	14
No asylum status	2	4
Unclear	7	6

It is evident that only a relatively small minority of young people had been granted a right to remain in the UK indefinitely. Amongst those aged 18 or over at the point of data collection, around one-third were either still seeking asylum or were awaiting the outcome of an appeal against an earlier negative decision. Three-quarters of this group (74 per cent) had transferred to NASS support at age 18. Although the Home Office attempts to give priority to asylum applications from unaccompanied children, waiting times for a final decision have been unacceptably lengthy (Stanley, 2001). With respect to young people still awaiting a final decision, the average length of time since they had been first referred to social services was 19.7 months and one in five had been resident in the UK for over two years.

Across all ages, just over one-half of the sample had been granted ELR, the majority until their 18th birthday (60 per cent). However, around two-fifths of the young people aged 18 or over at data collection had either been granted ELR for a longer period (usually for four years) or were awaiting the outcome of an application to extend their leave. These patterns tend to reflect a *de facto* change in Home Office policies with respect to granting leave for restricted periods over the course of the study. Those granted four years' leave tended to be older and were therefore more likely to have been referred to social services in the first half of the sampling period (in 2001). In almost one-half of these cases (46 per cent) their right to remain would extend until the age of 20 or 21. In contrast, the period of leave granted to the majority (76 per cent) of those who were under 18 at data collection (and therefore were likely to have been referred in 2002) was only up to their 18th birthday. Only 8 per cent had been granted ELR for a period substantially beyond this age. This tends to reflect a hardening of the Home Office stance on granting leave for restricted periods and on the perceived potential for these young people to be returned as young adults.[7]

The small minority of young people with "no asylum status" at 18 were in the most difficult circumstances of all. This group had all been supported under s17 and their cases had been or were about to be closed at data collection. Their asylum applications had failed and they had either exhausted their rights to appeal or had failed to make one. At age 18, they were faced with the twin prospect of return or of a genuine risk of homelessness and destitution. If they chose not to return, they were likely to become dependent for their survival on the informal networks they had managed to accrue while they were supported by social services.[8]

Careful monitoring and recording of the progress of young people's asylum applications are critical. Although the progress of claims is effectively outside the control of social work practitioners, up-to-date information about the current state of claims and about what steps need to be taken at what times is important for the present and future well-being of young people. Detailed recordings are also necessary in circumstances where social workers change. The level of detail held on case files was, however, quite highly variable. As Table 8.1 suggests, in 7 per cent of cases it was not possible to discern from case files the asylum status of young people at data collection and, in a similar proportion of cases, there was no written detail provided on the progress of young people's asylum claims. Furthermore, in 25 per cent of case files the details of

---

[7] See: Home Office information note on asylum applications for unaccompanied asylum seeking children (pp. 4–5). Available at: http://www.ind.homeoffice.gov.uk/ind/en/home/applying/asylum_applications/unaccompanied_asylum.html

[8] Although, by the close of study, one or two young people had become dependent on these informal networks, none had yet been issued with removal directions.

young people's solicitors were not recorded. Given the central importance of asylum to young people's lives, improvements in the consistency of recording practices are necessary.

The remaining sections of this chapter will explore issues arising from young people's experiences and the support provided to them in relation to preparation, transition planning and transition at 18, taking account of their interrelationship with immigration issues.

Preparation

Although local authorities have a duty to prepare looked after young people for adult life, research has consistently pointed to inadequacies in the preparation young people receive. Care arrangements have tended to be over-protective, have provided young people with limited opportunities for decision-making and preparation has tended to be unsystematic, often dependent on the quality of relationship with particular caregivers (Stein and Carey, 1986; Who Cares? Trust, 1993; Biehal et al, 1995). What makes for effective preparation is less certain. Evidence suggests that preparation should occur gradually over the time young people are looked after and may best be achieved in the context of a stable placement, where continuity in important links and relationships is provided, where education is encouraged and where it is formally integrated into child care planning (Clayden and Stein, 1996; Stein and Wade, 2000). Guidance to the CLCA 2000 emphasises the importance of providing balanced attention to practical and financial skills, interpersonal skills and relationships (Department of Health, 2001). Previous chapters have focused in detail on some of these key areas – placement, education, health and well-being and social networks. In this section attention will be given to the acquisition of practical and financial skills.

Preparation for adult life should be a central feature of social work practice with unaccompanied young people. Given the age profile of this population, preparation should be planned from the point young people are first referred to social services. It has been suggested in previous chapters that some of the conditions necessary for effective preparation were more likely to occur for young people placed in care settings (s20) or when placed with extended kin. The support provided in these placements encouraged more consistent engagement with education and the development of stronger networks of support with family, friends and community. The statutory duties associated with being looked after were also important. Young people in care placements and, to a lesser extent, in kinship placements were more likely to have had care plans, regular reviews, regular contact with allocated social workers and broader overall packages of support than were those either living in supported or unsupported accommodation, mostly under s17 arrangements. Although preparation was variable within all groups, the structure of the planning and review system for looked after children tended to provide a more solid platform for preparation than was the case for young people supported under s17.

Responsibility for providing life skills support tended to be devolved to prime caregivers (foster carers, residential workers, relatives or support workers). Where social workers were active in addressing these issues, they tended to have greater responsibility for assessment, planning and review. During the early phases of resettlement, considerable attention was needed. Many young people were unfamiliar with the operation of domestic appliances. The currency was strange to them and young people often lacked previous experience of managing money. Where young people had limited English language skills, everyday activities like travelling and shopping were challenging. Placements in care, with kin or in adequately supported accommodation often provided young people with the time and guidance that was needed to acquire essential skills and develop confidence.

There was also evidence of *planned* preparation, utilising the review system to identify areas of weakness and developing strategies to strengthen skills. This was more likely for looked after children and was dependent on the quality of communication and contact between social workers, caregivers and support workers. In most cases, however, preparation appeared more *informal* and strategic planning was less evident, especially where young people were supported under s17. This carried risks that young people's specific needs would be overlooked. Informal practical support appeared to work quite well for some young people living in supported shared accommodation where support workers made regular home visits. Regular visits provided opportunities to assess how well young people were faring and there was evidence of advice and guidance being provided in relation to cooking, cleaning, shopping and finance. However, this was not always the case and many young people in these settings said they had received no practical help with life skills.

Reports of insufficient support were most common amongst young people who were routinely placed in unsupported shared housing at referral. Indeed, many young people were placed in these settings without any assessment having been undertaken of their ability to manage in the first place. The quality of accommodation itself was highly variable and some young people were living in circumstances where essential domestic appliances were broken for lengthy periods of time and where landlords were unresponsive to requests for help. Patterns of home visiting from social services were often irregular, sometimes non-existent, and young people often had no allocated worker to approach. In these circumstances, young people often felt bereft of professional support and, in relation to life skills, commonly spoke of a shared process of learning with their peers. Where relationships between residents were positive, sharing resources to make ends meet and learning from each other provided some compensation for a lack of consistent adult support.

Practitioners often worried about the ability of young people to manage financially at transition. The expectations made of young people were high and, for many practitioners, quite unrealistic. Even while supported by social services, allowances were very low for young people living in more independent settings (on average around £35 per week at this time). However, for many young people (though by no means all) these allowances were supplemented by travel expenses, free leisure passes, clothing and birthday allowances. Practitioners were therefore mindful that the transition to benefits or to the NASS system in particular (around £30 per week), would involve a harsh financial adjustment:

I think the biggest change that most of the young people have to get used to is the financial change ... I struggle with that ... I think it's very hard to say one day you are entitled to a bus pass, leisure money and a clothing allowance ... and then suddenly all that stops. Even though they know they are building up to that, I think it is even harder for those that move into the NASS system, because that's a different system altogether ... I look, and I think, I don't know how you cope. I don't know how they manage physically... to keep themselves on such limited funding. (Social worker, Area 3)

Many practitioners felt equally nonplussed about their ability to prepare young people for such a change and develop a financial plan for transition within which young people could realistically live. Although efforts were made to provide some young people in foster placements with trial periods that might replicate the reality to come and to help young people to reconcile income and expenditure, it was nevertheless the case that the objective situation they found themselves in stretched their financial skills to the limit.

Transition planning

Transition or pathway planning for unaccompanied young people is a complex, often confusing and challenging area of work. Although the needs of all young people for consistent information, support and guidance are similar, the specific duties of local authorities vary according to the section of the Children Act 1989 under which young people are supported (s20 or s17). Where young people have been looked after (s20), all the provisions of the Children (Leaving Care) Act 2000 (CLCA 2000) apply until the point that an individual refuses to comply with Home Office removal directions.[9] Although these duties do not specifically apply to young people supported under s17, their need for effective pathway planning to assist them to negotiate the transition to adulthood is no less pressing and, arguably, forms part of the general duty to "safeguard and promote" their welfare.

---

[9] A recent Home Office information note, however, suggests that this position may harden in the future. The note reinterprets Schedule 3 of the Immigration and Asylum Act 2002 relating to withdrawal of social services support. It suggests that former unaccompanied children (who have received a final negative asylum decision and exhausted any appeal rights) may not just fall into the category of "failed asylum seekers" (eligible for continuing social services support) but into the category of those "unlawfully in the UK". If this were to become an established policy, social services could withdraw support before a failure to comply with removal directions, unless to do so would contravene Article 3 of the European Convention on Human Rights, or face taking full financial responsibility for services (see Children's Legal Centre, 2005; Howarth, 2005).

The intersection of immigration with child care policies calls for a "multi-dimensional" approach to planning. The concept of "parallel planning", of concurrently planning for different eventualities, has been present in social work discourse and practice for some time (Monck *et al*, 2004). A recent guide to transition planning for unaccompanied young people refers to "triple planning" to embrace the forms of support that may be necessary to prepare young people for a range of possible outcomes at 18 (Howarth, 2005). "Multi-dimensional planning" suggests a need for discrete but overlapping strategies of planning and support for several distinctive groups of young people who, although they may have common core needs, may face quite different futures. These include: a) those with long-term futures in the UK; b) those seeking a longer-term future; c) those who have been refused permission to stay; and d) those who may choose to return to their country of origin. Pathway planning for these groups has to take account of different rights and entitlements (to work and study, to housing and financial support) and, with respect to groups (c) and (d), of the need to prepare and support young people's return. Multi-dimensional planning, therefore, needs to be flexible and realistic, taking account of these likely scenarios for each young person, and to develop individual support packages that maximise young people's choices and options.

Pathway planning

The duty to provide written pathway plans for young people "eligible" under the CLCA 2000 was rarely exercised. Across the sample as a whole, only 3 per cent of young people had a copy of a pathway plan on file, amounting to just 12 per cent of those who had been accommodated under s20 and who were aged 16 or over at the point of data collection (n = 26). In addition, the need to provide a pathway plan was envisaged in a further three cases, although two of these young people were already aged 17.

Pathway planning is intended to bring greater clarity and transparency to the planning and review process. Although early evidence on implementation has pointed to variations in the use of pathway planning by local authorities (Broad, 2003), it provides an opportunity to think into the future with young people, to envisage their life beyond care and to prepare for different eventualities. The requirement for six-monthly reviews also allows plans to be adjusted in the light of changing circumstances, an important factor for unaccompanied young people. Where this process worked well, young people felt better informed about their future options and reassured about the support that would be available. Desta, aged 17, was preparing to move on from foster care when she reached 18. Pathway planning had enabled her to explore options for the future, including where she might live, her continuation at college, the finance and support that would be available and, since she had ELR to age 18, how this might affect her future plans. Realistic information, advice and guidance proved reassuring:

> She [her social worker] does everything that I want . . . and I can talk to her if I have problems . . . I know that when I see her I'm going to find something new, or there is something that she will tell me, some information about something I can do . . . They give you advice, they give you information, they tell you . . . what you need.

Given the complex situation of many unaccompanied young people, access to clear, reliable and accessible information that takes proper account of different future scenarios may help to enhance their sense of control and well-being in the present (Stanley, 2001; Howarth, 2005). For Desta's social worker, pathway planning had also helped to bring focus to her work:

> Over the next few months [we will be] looking at moving on and how that is going to happen . . . We are already thinking about it now . . . We have a pathway plan that we do and that helps us to think about it. We will be talking to her, explaining the options . . . We will support her through it really.

However, the timescales for leaving care planning have often been short, compressed into the last few months of care (Dixon et al, 2004), and this was evident for young people in this study. Guidance suggests that pathway planning should begin early (at least at the age of 16), take place at the young person's pace, include all those with an interest in the support of a young person and a well rounded appreciation of their needs (Stein and Wade, 2000; Department of Health, 2001). This was not always the case. Planning often appeared truncated and, perhaps especially for those who moved to supported housing at 16 or 17 and were re-designated under s17, tended to take the form of a basic "exit plan" for young people at 18.

Evidence of pathway planning was also less likely for "eligible" young people living with relatives or in more informal fostering arrangements. In these situations, the role of social services had tended to be more circumspect and, in some cases, was restricted to a distant monitoring role. Although there was often an assumption that young people would stay until 18 or beyond, evidence of detailed pathway or contingency planning was often difficult to discern from these case files. In some instances, practitioners appeared confused about how these young people's entitlements to leaving care services would be managed, perhaps reflecting a lack of co-ordinated links with mainstream services in the authority:

He will be [eligible] now, when that's sorted. I don't know what they're going to do about that as well. I don't know whether we're going to do it or whether (the leaving care team) are going to do it. (about Abdoul, who was living with his aunt under s20)

Effective pathway planning builds on what has gone before. In this context, irrespective of young people's formal service pathways (s20 or s17), evidence of planning and practical support was more likely where young people had previously experienced a regular pattern of contact with social workers or support workers. For some young people supported under s17, there was evidence of children "in need" planning meetings being used to assess, plan and monitor their progress towards transition. However, for this group as a whole, evidence of planning was much less likely to be present on case files. The lack of statutory obligations to provide services beyond 18 tended to mean that, even in the best-case scenarios, planning took the form of an exit strategy in preparation for case closure.

Where practitioners had established a rhythm of home visiting, however, the practical support provided was often greatly appreciated by young people. Social work activity tended to focus on young people's fundamental requirements for housing, finance, education and immigration. However, in some cases, wider issues were also being addressed, including efforts to finalise arrangements for counselling, where young people needed it, or helping young people to establish a broader base of social support before social services withdrew. In many cases, though not all, the timescales for planning were painfully short. In one dedicated housing and support agency, for example, planning took the form of a "to do" list that was implemented in the last two months before young people reached 18:

> *We've got a list of what we've got to do for young people, the basic requirements . . . It's a six-week plan to independence really . . . (although) I think six weeks is quite optimistic really . . . They've got to be independent by 18, that's our aim.*

Where links with social services had been weak over time, a common experience for young people living in unsupported housing, evidence of transition planning was often non-existent. In general terms, these young people were less likely to have been consistently participating in education, were likely to have weaker English language skills and to be more socially isolated. In many respects, therefore, they were the least well-equipped to make their way independently. Not surprisingly, they were also the most likely to experience an abrupt transition. Arrangements made at this stage were frequently formal and minimal. These included referral to or liaison with solicitors to seek extensions of leave to remain, referrals to NASS if young people met the eligibility criteria for support or referrals to Connexions or the Benefits Agency. Young people were notified (normally in person) that social services support would end, that they would be required to leave their property and referrals to other housing providers, including homeless persons units, were initiated. In better cases, practitioners offered advice and support to young people to negotiate these transitions while, in others, young people were just given referral letters and signposted to the relevant services. Left to their own devices, many young people had extreme difficulty negotiating the hurdles presented by these services. Although Meena's experience was not especially poor, it is illustrative of the limited planning that often occurred in these cases.

Meena was about to turn 18. She had lived in a shared house for two years and, although of poor quality, it had provided a stable base. She was studying A levels at college and was keen to continue. Although committed to her studies, she had limited direct social work support, had few friends, felt lonely most of the time and had insufficient money to socialise. The imminent end of her leave to remain was a major source of anxiety, although an application for an extension of leave had been made. She knew she would have to leave the house, but felt the offer of a hostel place, the only offer she had received, was far too distant from college. She felt powerless and frustrated at the uncertainty of her future. Although reluctant to criticise social services, she had felt confused about her entitlements throughout the time she had been supported:

In two weeks time I'm going to get kicked out of that house . . . I don't know where they are going to take me, I don't know what is going to happen, if I am going to be homeless again.

It's not a bad service, but no-one gives you advice, no-one tells you what is being done, what is going to happen, what they are going to provide you with, what rights you have . . . I never had a social worker sit with me and tell me.

Planning and immigration

Practitioners are necessarily engaged in a "multi-dimensional" planning process linked to the potential outcomes of the asylum process. Where young people had been granted ILR or ELR for a substantial period beyond 18, transition planning was generally made easier. Young people tended to feel a greater sense of security and were better positioned to envisage and plan for their future lives in the UK. Where positive planning was evident, young people's access to social housing, to benefits and the greater certainty attached to their plans for education meant the necessary steps along the pathway towards transition could be more easily achieved. Zola, for example, had been helped to settle into and furnish her council tenancy, which provided her with her first real sense of home, and, as a student in accountancy, she felt able to speak about her plans for a future career in banking.

A positive asylum decision often helped to lift a burden from young people's shoulders and reinforce the belief that they could control their own destinies. This was the view of Ana Paula's social worker, who felt this event had been the most influential factor on the lives of Ana Paula and her siblings:

I think they had indefinite leave very quickly . . . Once they had [this], they were just happy and moved on and focused on building up their lives here . . . I think that had a really positive impact, more than anything else. I think it really gave them confidence . . . Before that, she was quite reserved and then, around the same time, her character started coming out a little bit. It certainly had a positive impact on her mental health and well-being.

Although greater permanency assisted the planning process, it did not offer immunity to the effects of an abrupt transition. Where consistent support had been lacking over time, these young people were no less likely to experience difficulties at 18.

Kadjia's placement in shared housing (under s17) ended at 18 and her case was closed. Her *ad hoc* contact with social services over this time had been largely through office-based duty services. Although she had received ILR when approaching 18 and referrals were made to the homeless unit, Connexions and the Benefits Agency, these had not been properly planned and no-one had taken responsibility for supporting her through the process. Her difficulties with English combined with a lack of suitable interpreters at these agencies to create confusion and delay. In consequence, she spent several months being homeless, moving between acquaintances, before social services negotiated a more satisfactory solution.

Where young people were still waiting for an asylum decision, for the outcome of an appeal or an application to extend their leave, the sense of uncertainty was often overwhelming – 'my life is at a standstill waiting for their decision' (Abdulaziz). Some young people busied themselves in the present, trying not to look too far ahead. Others were more fatalistic, feeling that events were entirely outside of their control, while some continued to make plans in the hope of a positive outcome. Many young people identified the anxiety associated with a lengthy wait as *the* most difficult thing in their lives and as one that had adverse consequences for their mental health.

Practitioners were highly empathic to the tensions that were attached to the asylum process when, as appeared to be the case for the majority of young people, they desperately wanted to stay and make their lives here: *I think he is frightened of his life and I think he is always anxious about what is going to happen to him in the future . . . I have told him that his immigration status runs out at 18 and there's no guarantee that he will be staying here in the UK.* (Joseph's social worker)

Although many practitioners tried to address these fears directly, some young people (like Joseph) found it difficult to share their feelings or contemplate the different directions the future might take. In other instances, practitioners appeared to find discomfort in raising or, perhaps more appropriately, in continuing to raise the likely implications of a negative outcome for fear of creating further distress.

Uncertainty about the future inevitably had a negative impact on transition planning. There was evidence of practitioners endeavouring to create imaginative and flexible plans that tried to connect young people's needs in the present to the range of possible scenarios that might lie ahead in the future and to prepare young people, as best they could, to meet these challenges. Planning of this kind, however, was hard to achieve. Pathway planning is premised on encouraging young people to look into the distance. When that future is uncertain, any plans that are made can only be provisional:

It is very hard for a worker when you can't say, 'I can guarantee you this when you are 18', but you can't. You can't do anything. You don't want to lie to the child. All you can say is, 'you need to try and think what you want to do for your future', and try to address it in that way. It is very frustrating and very hard to develop a sufficient care plan when there are issues around immigration. (Amir's social worker)

Even where young people had been well supported, there were many cases where practitioners appeared to have difficulty preparing alternative plans that could be implemented if required:

We have got a plan for him if he stays . . . I don't have a plan for him if it goes the other way and the only thing is supporting him until that day, until we are [totally] sure what is going on. (Kamuran's social worker)

Planning stasis was most likely in relation to the prospect of return. Practitioners were aware that larger numbers of young people might fail to achieve permanency on reaching adulthood and be faced with this prospect. Some workers were trying to meet this challenge head on in their work with young people and prepare them as best they could for such an eventuality. They worried about what would happen to young people who went back. They worried about what risks young people might face, what support would be available from family, community or agencies, and, having invested heavily in reconstructing their lives here, how young people might make the cultural readjustments that would be necessary. In this context, time was spent exploring options with young people, trying to identify links in their home countries that might be helpful to them and encouraging young people to consider family tracing where these links were unknown or partially fragmented. Time was also spent trying to make young people aware of the harsh clandestine existence that might await them here if their application ultimately failed.

This work was not easy, especially where young people were firmly resistant to return and were focused on their present lives. For many practitioners, the enormity of these questions and the lack of an adequate social work vocabulary to describe them made it difficult to initiate (or revisit) these discussions with young people:

It's not something I broach really, unless it comes up. Unless somebody brings it up in a conversation first, I don't ask, 'How do you feel about going home?' Sometimes people say, 'I want to stay'. He hasn't said anything like that . . . I get the impression that most people in his situation will eventually be returned and it is only a matter of time. (Hassan's support worker)

Really [in the team] I think we're all at a complete loss. What can you do, except to make them aware that they might have to be returned? (Social worker, Area 1)

Although responses of this nature are understandable, they are likely to be less than helpful to young people and may lead to planning drift. With adequate preparation and time to reflect, some young people may choose to return; and there is work that has been done on the psycho-social processes involved in preparing young people to renew home country links, including preparation for voluntary return (Barnen, 2000). In any event, preparation for this eventuality should form one strand of "multi-dimensional planning" that takes into account, in parallel, all likely outcomes for young people on reaching adulthood. Transition planning needs to be realistic, undertaken over time (preferably from the point young people are first referred), have a multi-agency focus and provide young people with clear and accessible information to help them make informed decisions. In this context, Howarth's (in press) guide to planning for transition provides a range of helpful suggestions to inform planning of this kind, including support for those young people who have exhausted the appeals process and for whom the prospect of return is most stark.

Planning and legal representation

The possibility that more young people may be returned in the future makes it imperative that information is gathered to enable immigration officials to fully assess asylum applications and that claims are well presented (Ayotte and Williamson, 2001). Access to good lawyers with effective communication skills and to interpreting services has been problematic (Bann and Tennant, 2002; Rutter, 2003a). There is also evidence that this situation has been made more difficult by changes to the arrangements for legal aid funding in immigration and asylum cases (Bail for Immigration Detainees/Asylum Aid, 2005). Access to good-quality legal representation is of pressing concern to those seeking asylum, given the evidence that exists of inconsistencies in Home Office pro-cedures and decision-making for unaccompanied young people (Stanley, 2001).

Although social workers should not dispense legal advice, they have an important role to play in arranging solicitors, monitoring the progress of claims, supporting young people through these encounters and advoca-ting on their behalf. They also have responsibility for ensuring that applications are made "in time". Without accurate information about the state of claims, it is difficult to envisage how preparation and planning for young people's futures can be undertaken effectively.

These are tasks that overlay the normal range of duties associated with social work. Despite this, many practitioners worked diligently to monitor and keep young people informed about the progress of their asylum applications. The extent to which this occurred was, however, variable and where young people lacked support more generally, they often found it extremely difficult to access reliable advice:

> *Sometimes, even if I went to talk to them (social services) about my Home Office papers, no one has got any idea. They don't know, so they cannot give me any advice.* (Meena)

It is extremely difficult for young people to decipher the complexities of the asylum process. Some practitioners also felt that they themselves lacked sufficient knowledge of how the system worked to advise young people adequately or were left perplexed by the inconsistencies in Home Office decision-making for cases that were broadly similar:

> *We don't know enough about [the process]. I mean, I've been to one or two tribunals and I think, 'God, why has he got leave to remain?' I find it very unpredictable and I still can't work out why some do and some don't.* (Social worker, Area 3)

Young people also found it difficult to judge whether their legal represent- atives were working effectively on their behalf (see also Stanley, 2001). Representation was also subject to change, as practices closed or solicitors withdrew from individual cases. Liaison from social workers was therefore important. Practitioners found some solicitors to be insufficiently pro- active in pursuing claims and, in consequence, one team felt it necessary to make an organised push to chase up drifting cases:

> *We tried to rush the solicitors on. We'd lots of kids who weren't moving at all, so we had a blitz and tried to make them do a bit more.* (Social worker, Area 3)

However, responsibility for drift was not confined to legal representatives. More commonly it appeared to be associated with confusions arising from

Home Office inefficiency, and there were numerous examples where young people's papers had been lost or where forms had to be reissued, where asylum decisions were wrongly communicated to solicitors or social services or where essential communication had simply failed to take place. Drift also emanated from social services, usually in circumstances where practitioners failed to give sufficient attention to liaison and placed the onus on young people to negotiate their claims. This occurred with Abdoul, who had been waiting two years for an initial asylum decision and where it was suspected that his solicitor was of poor quality:

I've told him he needs to go into the solicitors and ask to look at all the letters that his solicitor has written to the Home Office. If there are loads, then fair enough, but if there's not, they're not doing their job properly . . . I don't know whether he's actually done that or not.

Quite how Abdoul, who lacked proficiency in English, was expected to do this was not clear. Where young people lacked sufficient support, delays and errors in the process were made more likely and transition planning was inevitably impeded. These young people were therefore more likely to experience an abrupt transition at 18 for which they had been inadequately prepared.

Transition at 18

What can be said from this study about the nature of the "after care" support provided to those aged 18 or over is necessarily limited. Although almost one-half of the sample (47 per cent; n = 99) were in this age group at the close of data collection, very few were in receipt of leaving care services. The majority of those who had been "looked after" were younger. Most were still living in placements and preparing for independence. However, three young people below the age of 18 were receiving some financial assistance under s24 of the Children Act 1989 after moving from care placements to live with relatives. Only three young people aged 18 or over were receiving some form of leaving care support. This support was helpful. It enabled them to continue living in supported settings, helped to ensure that financial arrangements were in place and that they could continue with their education. However, evidence of the day-to-day practical support that was being provided in these cases was scant.

The vast majority of young people in this age group (91 per cent) had been supported under s17 arrangements. As we have seen, for three-quarters of this group (77 per cent) social services responsibilities ended at the 18th birthday. Even where support continued beyond this point, it tended to be relatively short term and related to complications in young people's transition arrangements. It also depended on the commitment of individual workers to fight to keep cases open for a period of time or to offer young people informal advice and support:

> *It's closed on the database, but it's open to me. She's off the numbers, but the file is open to me for another six months.* (Aaliyah's social worker)

> *I'm sure it is much more about personal feelings and issues than it is professional. But I don't think I'm unique in that. I'm sure there are other workers here who still have contact with young people past 18.* (Abdi's social worker)

Many workers shared these concerns and did the best they could, despite the constraints imposed by their formal role and by the legal and funding environment. However, in overall terms, the evidence provided below relates primarily to the circumstances of young people no longer in receipt of formal social services support.

Transition to NASS

When young people who reached 18 were still seeking asylum or had an outstanding appeal, the majority (74 per cent) made a transition to NASS accommodation and/or financial support. In some instances, this difficult transition was managed well by social services. Attention was paid to NASS application procedures and time was spent reassuring young people, preparing them for what would happen and supporting them through the process. There were also examples of social workers, sometimes successfully, advocating on behalf of young people to prevent dispersal to protect their education, their access to health services, their place in settled accommodation or their social networks. In these cases, some support-only packages were negotiated. Where asylum teams had forged links with NASS housing teams this seemed easier to achieve, and there were examples of social workers working alongside NASS support officers to facilitate smooth transitions for young people. Efforts that are made to build links in this way, perhaps using multi-agency forums to link up services, may therefore prove helpful.

In some cases, however, little effort had been made to broker this transition. For these young people, transitions were often experienced as abrupt and traumatic. The formal duties of social services were usually met – NASS applications were made on time and young people were given notice of when accommodation and support by social services would end – but these cases conveyed a sense of young people being processed. Little attention had been paid to preparation and planning. In consequence, young people were often left confused about what to expect.

Chaotic transition arrangements were also linked to poor communication between the Home Office/NASS, solicitors and social services. In a minority of cases, young people were wrongly refused NASS support, inaccurate or lost documentation delayed the process of transfer or negative or positive asylum decisions that had been made some time previously were only discovered at the brink of transfer. For one sibling group, a decision to grant ELR that had been taken several months earlier was only revealed on the day they were packed and ready to leave their homes. Although asylum decision-making at the Home Office was often viewed by practitioners as mysterious, unpredictable and frequently inefficient, where practitioners were proactive in monitoring the progress of young people's claims the risks of a bewildering and distressing experience were (at least partially) reduced.

Irrespective of how the transfer was managed, young people tended to express dissatisfaction at the level of support provided by NASS, comparing it unfavourably to that provided by social services. Young people's income was reduced (to around £30 at this time) and social services subsidies for travel, clothing or other expenses ended. Although the quality of private sector shared housing provided by social services had been variable, those who had to move often felt that the standard of accommodation was worse. The role of NASS officers was also more restricted.

Both Walid and Diane felt that, whereas past social workers had visited them regularly and asked them about how they were faring in their placements, education, health and social life, this was no longer the case. Visits by NASS workers were more functional and restricted to their accommodation and finance. Entering the adult world of asylum seekers therefore involved a series of difficult adjustments for young people that had to sit alongside their anxiety about the future.

Patterns of housing, economic activity and social support

Table 8.2 shows, at the point of data collection, where those aged 18 or over were last known to be living, what they were doing and what sources of support were available from families, friends and their communities of origin. Inevitably, some caution is needed with respect to the accuracy of these figures, although they do provide a good indication of how young people were faring. With respect to housing and economic activity, the high proportion of cases marked "unclear" almost exclusively related to cases that had been closed some time previously and where case recording had ended at that point. Although the CLCA 2000 places an obligation on local authorities to monitor and report on the progress of care leavers, no such duty exists in relation to those supported under s17. In effect, these young people had been allowed to slip beyond the radar of social services after case closure.

Although Table 8.2 indicates that most young people had some form of home base, it also highlights the need for continuing "after care" support. At a minimum, around one in seven young people in this age group were not participating in post-16 education, training or work and a substantial minority of the sample had limited networks of social support. According to case file records, almost two-fifths of the young people (39 per cent) had no recorded support at all from family, other adults, friends or community. Making one's way in the world at the age of 18 is difficult enough. To expect young people to do so without reliable sources of informal support is unrealistic and reinforces the need to focus on strengthening young people's social networks while they are supported by social services and for a greater proportion of young people to have access to leaving care support.

Where young people's housing circumstances were known, fewer than

Table 8.2
Housing, economic activity and social support (age 18 or over)

Young people's circumstances*	*Per cent (n = 99)*
Housing	
• Supported housing	18
• Independent housing	41
• Kinship	5
• Unclear	35
Economic activity	
• Education	31
• Training	9
• Non-participation	14
• Unclear	45
Social support	
Has contact with:	
• Family	16
• Significant adults	7
• Friends	38
• Own community	43

*"Housing" and "economic activity" cover the whole sample (n = 99); "social support" records cases where case files showed evidence of contact with one or more sources.

one in five in this age group were continuing to live in supported accommodation. In just over one-half of these cases, this appeared to be a relatively short-term arrangement linked to complications in their transfer to independence or to NASS. Some young people, however, had a more settled base in hostels or supported housing. The majority of young people were living independently. Most were living in private sector shared housing of varying quality and, while some had been doing so since the point of referral, many had been required to leave their social services funded accommodation at 18 and move on without further support. Where young people had experienced an abrupt transition or where they had received a final negative asylum decision, a small number experienced periods of homelessness, staying with friends or acquaintances, or stays in homeless hostels. A few young people were discharged into homelessness. In these cases, abrupt case closure took place before a transfer to NASS or to independent accommodation had been completed and the barriers presented to young people in negotiating this transition had then proved insurmountable.

Some young people had moved into social housing. Access to council tenancies depended both on supply factors and on young people having leave to remain beyond the age of 18. Supply and housing policies varied across the three authorities. In Area 3, less pressure on council housing stock meant that young people with leave to remain were generally able to transfer to benefits and access council tenancies that provided greater security of tenure. In the other Areas, supply pressures were greater and more reliance had to be placed on the private sector. In Chapter 4, we highlighted the difficulties faced by local authorities in accessing good-quality private sector housing. Market rents were high and landlords were often reluctant to let to asylum seekers and those on Housing Benefit. In consequence, good housing providers were hard to find, contracts were difficult to monitor and enforce and young people were frequently subjected to relatively poor-quality accommodation and to sudden or inbuilt patterns of movement.

Developing leaving care services

In Area 2, recognition of these difficulties had led to a negotiated annual quota of council tenancies, shared with the mainstream leaving care service, and available to unaccompanied young people (whether s17 or s20) with leave to remain. However, this was insufficient for overall needs. In addition, supported hostels were used to cover periods when there were no vacancies and for young people waiting for the outcome of an application to extend leave. In Area 1, access to social housing was difficult, although a specialist housing officer had been appointed to negotiate bespoke arrangements for young people placed within and outside the authority. The only alternative route to council housing was the homelessness route. This was unsatisfactory, involving as it did quite lengthy stays in temporary housing with limited, if any, choice about the accommodation or its location at the end of it.

Initiatives to meet the transitional housing needs of young people require further development. The housing needs of unaccompanied young people, like other care leavers, are varied – even if options are inevitably more constrained for young people who are subject to immigration control. While many young people, including those arriving at 16 or 17 years of age, will benefit from the additional support available in family or, perhaps to a lesser extent, residential settings, some others will be less likely to do so and all will need to move on at some stage. Developments should therefore aim to address a continuum of needs, including supported lodgings, small supported hostels and floating support schemes. As was indicated in Chapter 4, supported housing with floating support tended to work more effectively when the support was provided by a dedicated social work team. Improvements to the range of available options will need sustained investment, cross-agency collaboration with statutory and voluntary housing providers to provide strategic planning and joint arrangements for needs assessment and tenancy allocations (see Stein and Wade, 2000). Towards the end of the study, signs were more encouraging. Strategies, such as those above, were being put in place to increase access to permanent tenancies and to develop directly managed supported housing in order to reduce the reliance of local authorities on private or community-based housing providers.

Initiatives are also needed in relation to education and training. Although many young people were highly committed to education, as we saw in Chapter 5, their experience of education was variable and a significant minority spent a large amount of time out of education or training altogether. Career planning that takes account of likely asylum outcomes is an integral part of pathway planning and should be given a higher priority for all unaccompanied young people. Effective career planning needs to build on the foundations of the past; it cannot be left to the transition stage. It also needs to equip young people with a range of transferable skills and qualifications against the possibility of return in the future. Like other care leavers, young people need a package of financial, practical and emotional support to enable them to sustain their participation in further or higher education (Jackson *et al*, 2005). Where young people were supported under s17 arrangements, in particular, this continuity was rarely provided and created additional anxiety for young people:

I am really worried about what is going to happen when I am 18. First of all, I don't know whether I can afford to go on to university. Secondly, I don't have any family and my friends aren't really there for my personal issues. I am worried that I will be left and that will be the end of everything. (Abdulkareem, age 17)

In practice, financial incentive schemes were limited and assistance to support young people's education was therefore largely discretionary and discriminatory. Strategies to create wider opportunities for young people through links with colleges, training providers and employers were also hesitant. This development work tended to be unsystematic and often dependent on the willingness of individual workers to seek out openings for young people in their care.

In relation to widening resources, there is much that could be learnt through closer collaboration with mainstream leaving care services. From uncertain beginnings, these schemes have developed an expertise and some success in developing resources to support leaving care work, especially in the areas of housing, finance and, albeit to a lesser extent, in education, training and health (Broad, 2003; Dixon *et al*, 2004; Hai and Williams, 2004). However, relationships between asylum and leaving care teams appeared uncertain, even in relation to those young people who had a longer-term or permanent right to remain. As a result, the potential for helpful joint working, shared initiatives or for exchanging ideas appeared limited.

The findings on transition as a whole reflect the limited engagement of local authorities at this time with the need to provide continuing "after care" support to unaccompanied young people. In effect, social services had delimited its responsibilities towards older teenagers, even allowing for the constraints that are imposed by immigration policies and procedures, and corporate leadership was generally lacking. Fortunately, in light of LAC(2003)13 and Hillingdon, this situation may be changing, as more older teenagers are formally accommodated and become "eligible" for leaving care support. Towards the close of the study, the combined effects of these changes were beginning to hold out some promise of positive improvement:

We didn't do pathway plans for children "in need" until the Hillingdon judgment last year. And now we've just been told that we've got to do pathway plans for all children "in need", which is actually a good idea. (Social worker, Area 2)

It will be good if we can get them into the looked after system, because then they will get support until they are 24. But at the minute, I personally think we are not doing them any favours because at 18 it just stops and they lose an awful lot. (Social worker, Area 3)

Most practitioners would welcome these changes. They were not happy with previous arrangements and, as we have seen, many were trying to do the best they could for their young people in testing circumstances. They were generally aware that young people needed more and continuing support, but were largely powerless to intervene. What these changes will mean in practice – how they will influence where young people live, what they can do and how they are supported – is, however, largely a question for future research and evaluation. Even though transition planning will always be complicated – and sometimes confounded – by asylum processes and outcomes, there is much more that could be done to smooth out young people's transition pathways to adulthood.

Summary

Given the age profile of unaccompanied young people, preparation and planning for adulthood should be at the heart of social work practice. Activities that help to meet young people's needs in the present (for placement, education, health and social support) are also important features of this preparation. Preparation should link into formal child-care planning and review systems.

The intersection of social services and immigration responsibilities makes pathway planning complex. A "multi-dimensional" approach to planning is needed, one that takes accounts of the specific overlapping needs of distinct groups of young people: a) those with long-term futures in the UK; b) those seeking longer-term futures; c) those who are refused permission to stay; and d) those who may choose to return to their countries of origin. Planning needs to be flexible, realistic and take account of this range of possible outcomes. Planning stasis was most likely in relation to the prospect of return. Careful monitoring of the progress of asylum claims by social workers and the actions of different players in the legal process is also critical to the well-being of young people.

Leaving care was an area of weakness for local authorities at this time. The use of written pathway plans was rare, even for those looked after. Timescales for planning were often too short. Furthermore, social services had largely delimited its leaving care responsibilities to most young people. For the vast majority of those supported under s17 (who formed the overwhelming majority of young people), case closure on reaching 18 was routine. In addition, where looked after young people move on to semi-independence before 18, their care status often changed to s17 and weakened (in practice) their eligibility for leaving care support. Continuing support beyond 18 for these groups often depended on the willingness of workers to offer informal help.

Most young people aged 18 or over were not receiving leaving care support (almost all had been supported under s17). Their circumstances, however, pointed to continuing needs. Although most had a home base, mostly in independent housing, a sizeable minority were not economically active and two-fifths had no documented support from family, friends or community. The lack of reporting requirements associated with s17 support meant that a high proportion of these young people had slipped from social services' view. Most practitioners recognised the need for continuing services and tried their best in difficult circumstances.

Further initiatives are needed to develop the range of supported accommodation options and to create wider opportunities in education and training. These will require sustained investment, partnerships with provider agencies and joint working arrangements. Financial incentives schemes should be improved and brought into line with those for other looked after young people. Towards the close of the study, some of these changes were occurring and strategies were being developed to increase the proportion of young people eligible for leaving care services. Most practitioners want this and recent policy developments that may increase the proportion looked after point in this direction.

9 Conclusion

The lives, concerns and circumstances of unaccompanied asylum seeking children and young people have started to be better understood and documented over the past few years. Those who arrive in the UK, often after long and arduous journeys, come to the attention of social services at ports of entry or at the duty desks of social services offices. Local authorities have clear duties under the Children Act 1989 and its associated guidance and regulations to provide assessments and appropriate services to children "in need". Unaccompanied young people, shorn of support from their parents or customary caregivers and making their way in an unfamiliar social landscape, are by definition in need of the particular care and protection that social services can provide.

This study took place at a time when the numbers of arrivals had risen, when new specialist children's asylum services were beginning to emerge and when, from a research perspective, very little was known about how social services were attempting to meet their responsibilities to these young people. The study has attempted to map out what was happening on the ground, to understand more about how young people negotiate the complex and difficult transitions that are associated with resettlement, how they are supported in this process by social services, how services have varied for different sub-groups within the overall population and with what effects for young people's lives. In doing so, the study carries a number of important messages about the kinds of services that appear helpful to young people, that assist them to re-centre their lives and move forward purposefully. These are reviewed in this final chapter.

The findings provide a benchmark for the state of social work services at the start of 2004, the point at which data collection largely ended. This is significant. At this time, our participating local authorities were still digesting the full implications of new Government guidance – LAC(2003)13 – and the findings from the Hillingdon Judicial Review. In light of these developments, services were in the process of review and realignment. The effect of these changes on the proportion of unaccompanied young people looked after and/or eligible for leaving care services lie outside the scope of this study, although they are important questions that require further assessment. Reorganisation and change are endemic features of social work practice in the asylum field. However, by focusing primarily on the more enduring aspects of social work relationships with unaccompanied young people, the study provides a range of messages to support good practice that should have lasting relevance, irrespective of twists and turns in the policy arena.

Service pathways

Most young people arrive in the mid-teen years and previous research has highlighted a tendency for those aged 16 or 17 to receive only a basic assessment of their needs and for them to be routinely placed in shared housing with limited social work support under s17 arrangements (Audit Commission, 2000; Stone 2000; Stanley, 2001). While this study broadly confirms these findings, patterns were more complex. In general terms, those aged under 16 at referral were more likely to have been assessed and supported by specialist children's teams and their subsequent careers were more likely to have followed a s20 pathway. Placement in care or with extended family members was positively associated with young people faring better in education and having stronger networks of social support. The statutory responsibilities associated with being looked after were also influential and these young people were more likely to have had allocated social work support, regular social work contact and a more comprehensive package of support linked to care plans and review arrangements.

Support arrangements for those whose careers followed an s17 pathway were highly variable and the vast majority of those aged 16 or 17 at referral (and some younger) were supported in this way. At one extreme, very basic assessments led to placements in unsupported shared housing that provided very limited (if any) social work contact and support. Placement and support arrangements were routine and resource led. At the other extreme, however, where support was provided by children's teams or, to a lesser extent, by dedicated support agencies, the overall package of support provided to young people was largely indistinguishable to that provided for looked after children. Although support and planning arrangements were often more informal, reflecting a lack of statutory duties, where assessments had been thorough and a rhythm of home visiting had been established over time, the responses to young people's emerging needs were frequently no less effective.

Nonetheless, it was generally the case that those supported under s17 tended to fare less well. They were more likely to spend time out of education or training, to experience social isolation and their lack of eligibility for leaving care services meant that the vast majority had to go it alone from the age of 18. **These findings reinforce the value of providing s20 accommodation and support to all unaccompanied young people, as presaged in recent guidance, even though the way this support is delivered to older teenagers may need to be both flexible and imaginative.**

Assessment

Assessment is pivotal to much that follows for young people. Getting this right and providing careful and well rounded assessments, provides a basis for service planning that is grounded in an understanding of the needs and aspirations of young people. Most young people did receive some initial assessment of their needs, although in some instances this appeared to have been based solely on a single interview. Core assessments in line with the Assessment Framework were rarely undertaken, amounting only to 8 per cent of the whole sample and 18 per cent of those who were subsequently looked after. These were more likely to have taken place for younger children supported by children's teams, for young people where signs of more complex health and welfare needs existed or for young people who were already placed informally at referral or were seeking reunification with relatives.

Different models of assessment were evident within and between the authorities.[1] A "procedural" model, following a standardised format to determine eligibility for services, was more likely for those aged 16 or 17 and often amounted to little more than a formal "screening process".

---

[1] See Smale and Tuson (1993) on models of assessment.

These assessments also resulted in standardised services for placement and financial support and allocated social work support was rare. These young people were the least likely to have awareness of their rights or of other options for placement and support that might have been available. An "exchange model" was more often adopted by specialist children's teams and was more likely to focus on children's needs rather than solely on their eligibility for services as an "unaccompanied asylum seeking child". **In the "exchange model" of assessment, practitioners tended to work alongside young people to inform them of their options, to help them articulate their own needs and aspirations and to release their own problem-solving potential through joint planning over time. Although these assessments were seldom perfect, and some young people found it difficult to raise issues of concern to them, this approach generally met young people's needs more effectively.**

Better and more rounded assessments were therefore generally under-taken in children's teams, by qualified social workers and most often involved younger children. This reflected the roles and responsibilities of the different asylum teams. Younger children were more likely to be referred to children's teams where qualified social workers undertook assessments and were more likely to adopt an "exchange model". However, based on ratings given by the research team, fewer than one-half of those referred below the age of 16 (48 per cent) received an "adequate or better" needs assessment and two-fifths (41 per cent) of assessments conducted by qualified social workers were "less than adequate". **Attention is therefore needed to raise the standard of assessments for all unaccompanied children and young people, but perhaps especially for those conducted with older teenagers. Consistent use of the current Assessment Framework and, in the future, of the proposed Common Assessment Framework envisaged by the Children Act 2004 may help to raise the overall quality of these assessments (Department for Education and Skills, 2003b).**

Age disputes concerning unaccompanied minors are not uncommon and young people may be refused access to a service until their age is clarified (Munoz, 1999; Dennis, 2002). Local authorities have lacked clear guidelines for conducting age assessments and, in any case, these assessments are subject to a considerable margin of error (Levinson and Sharma,

1999). Some informal or formal concern about age was evident in over one-quarter of cases (26 per cent), although this was not always acted upon. Age assessments were difficult to conduct and often appeared unsatisfactory. Decisions sometimes appeared to have resulted from a single meeting and case file records often failed to provide a clear (or any) rationale for age-related decision-making. A realistic appreciation of age is important if young people are to receive age-appropriate services. However, given the degree of difficulty attached to this process, further guidance and training to provide for greater consistency in the conduct of age assessments would therefore be welcome.

The assessment process itself was always challenging. Young people's initial encounters with social services were frequently marked by confusion and a degree of suspicion. While some young people needed to talk about the events that had led them to social services, others were more reticent and questions were met with silence, or with what workers perceived to be formal asylum stories that had been given to young people. Many workers were attuned to the complex reasons for silence and understood that it could be both protective and costly for young people (Papadopoulos, 2002; Kohli, forthcoming). Timing, proceeding at the young person's pace and sensitive questioning were features of good assessment practice. In these circumstances, young people generally felt reassured about the help that was at hand. While some workers harboured suspicions about the authenticity of young people's stories, most were sympathetic or agnostic, and initial assessments tended to focus on gathering basic information about young people's immediate needs for placement, finance, education and health screening. Although more complex questions about family and reasons for exile were often deferred for a more appropriate moment, many practitioners were alert to signs of acute anxiety and distress. In these circumstances (or where young people requested it) offers of counselling or family tracing were frequently made.

Deferring consideration of deeper emotional issues until young people are settled in placement may be a helpful strategy, allowing time for a more trusting relationship to develop. However, it was also the case that assessment was too often a one-off truncated event. Young people frequently needed to re-visit or re-tell their stories and new

needs emerged over time as their confidence grew in those around them. Initial assessments therefore need to be seen as provisional and should be subject to a continuing and careful process of formal and informal review.

Placement

For a majority of young people, their most pressing need was for a placement that could offer sanctuary and an opportunity to re-centre their lives and form new attachments. Although some young people had already found informal placements at the point of referral (with relatives, adults they had met or through community organisations), others were in immediate need and 47 per cent were placed on the same day as referral. How the placement process was managed depended on a number of variables: how and where young people were first identified (at port of entry or "in country"); their age; team policies and procedures; and the availability of placement resources.

While placement decision making was more likely to have flowed from an assessment of needs for those under 16, older males were the group least likely to have received any pre-placement assessment. **As other studies have found, many older teenagers, after only a basic assessment, were routinely placed in unsupported or low-level supported shared housing (Stanley, 2001; Dennis, 2002).** During the early phase of the study, in particular, reliance for initial placements on hotels or other forms of emergency accommodation was not uncommon. These were intended as temporary solutions (although some young people drifted for several months once they were placed) and stemmed from a confluence of limited placement options, high numbers of arrivals and weak team procedures. Practitioners recognised this practice as unacceptable and, over time, reliance on emergency accommodation was lessened as procedures for managing referrals, assessment and placements were tightened.

There was considerable variation in arrangements to assess and monitor the circumstances of young people placed with relatives, with informal community carers or in private foster settings. Where this was done well, sensitivity and skill was needed to establish the credentials of carers, the nature of their relationship with the young person and their capacity to provide good-quality care. Once assessments were completed, social work support often tended to reduce and undue reliance was sometimes placed on the sense of familial or community obligation that appears to exist within many refugee communities. Financial pressures and the effects of overcrowding sometimes created strain for families, support was not always forthcoming and some placements disrupted. **Kinship placements often provided young people with stable and familiar attachments and opportunities to re-build networks of support, strengths that were recognised by social workers, although arrangements for supporting placements in the community were inconsistent. Towards the close of the study, there was evidence of the use of s20 provisions for some placements with relatives or community carers. This has advantages for the additional support entitlements it provides and the greater protection it offers young people, especially for those placed informally with community carers.**

Consistent with previous studies, only limited use was made of residential provision (Williamson, 1998). These placements were mainly used for younger males for periods of assessment, to provide a bridge to assist their adjustment to life in the UK and to provide preparation for independence. Some young people found comfort and solidarity in their relationships with other unaccompanied young people. However, boredom and frustration often set in, especially when units were sited in rural areas or in areas far from young people's communities of origin. When planning residential provision, careful attention needs to be given to its location and purpose, the mix of residents and the culture of residential regimes (see Sinclair and Gibbs, 1998).

Foster care was the preferred option for younger looked after children needing placement. Foster placements could provide safety, security and an opportunity to build attachments to a substitute family. Practitioners were mindful of the benefits of providing culturally matched placements, although limitations in placement supply often made this difficult. As others have found, attempts were made to identify appropriate carers from within local refugee communities or to source them through independent fostering agencies (Williamson, 1998).

However, the desire to provide cultural continuities for young people sometimes overrode other important features of placement assessment. Although these cultural connections were desired and appreciated by many young people, placements should not be made without an adequate assessment of the carer's capacity to provide good-quality care (Department of Health, 1995; Ayotte and Williamson, 2001).

Most young people who were fostered moved into mainstream cross-cultural foster placements and some prioritised this to develop their English language skills. **Cross-cultural placements often involved a difficult period of adjustment for young people and carried some risk of cultural isolation.** Although these placements often lasted quite successfully and provided young people with a stable and supportive home base, cultural tensions sometimes resulted in breakdowns and, over time, some young people felt the need to move to more semi-independent settings in culturally mixed areas. **Little use was being made of provisions for independent visitors or befriending schemes, perhaps drawing on adults from within refugee communities who may have helped to mediate these tensions and offer guidance to young people.**

The majority of young people, especially those supported under s17 provisions, had a main placement in supported or unsupported housing. **Supported accommodation tended to work best when the floating support was provided by a dedicated social work team and was linked to comprehensive packages of care tailored to the needs of individuals.** Reliance on private landlords and housing agencies was considerably more problematic and often resulted in greater mobility for young people and highly variable accommodation and support arrangements. Inconsistencies in the support provided by agencies was a major worry for social workers and continuous monitoring and brokering of relationships between agents and young people was essential, but was not always undertaken. Contracts with housing providers were difficult to monitor and enforce and housing options were generally limited by financial constraints.

Decisions to place young people out of authority were primarily resource led and affected all categories of placement. However, it did force social services to place greater reliance on external agencies and had some effect on the consistency of support available to young people from support workers.

Previous studies have also pointed to discontinuities in the support provided by housing agencies, especially for young people placed at some distance from their local authority (Humphries and Mynott, 2001; Kidane, 2001a; Stanley, 2001). **It is difficult to escape the conclusion that these overall patterns were linked to the lack of statutory obligations for visiting, care planning and review when providing s17 accommodation and support.** Although, as we have seen, inconsistent support was by no means universal and some s17 packages of support were comprehensive and equivalent to those for looked after young people, it was nevertheless the case that these young people were more often left to fend for themselves.

Over the course of the study, the practice of teams evolved in response to new guidance and opportunities to take stock and review services. Strategies to improve the range of placement options and reduce reliance on private landlords and housing agencies were developing. **Unaccompanied young people are heterogeneous and their differing needs call for a flexible continuum of placement options. These include a need to expand the pool of local authority foster carers, especially those available from within refugee communities, and to increase the range of supported options available, including supported lodgings, small supported hostels and floating support schemes. Developments of this kind require specialist staff and the investment of time and resources to build partnerships with statutory and voluntary housing providers.** With respect to these developments, much could be learnt from the experience of leaving care schemes in developing supported housing options for care leavers (see Broad, 2003; Hai and Williams, 2004).

Education and training

Refugee and asylum seeking children come from diverse educational backgrounds (Candappa and Egharevba, 2000; Rutter, 2003a). This was true for our sample, although most had experienced some disruption to their education deriving from war, persecution, bereavement or from changes in family circumstances that had required them to work. A successful re-introduction to education is an important feature of the resettlement process. Not only is it essential for English language acquisition, it can also help young people to re-establish the everyday

225

rhythms of an ordinary life and provide a sense of purpose and direction as well as opportunities to reconstruct friendship networks. Supporting young people's education is therefore an important feature of the social work task.

Access to schools or colleges was frequently difficult, especially for those arriving in mid term or at age 15, and young people's adjustment to new educational environments also took time. Many young people experienced disorientation and anxiety, most needed intensive periods of English language support and some experienced bullying and racism. This is a time when young people need considerable support and reassurance from teachers, carers and social workers. Some young people lacked the confidence to seek help and practitioners need to be vigilant for signs of distress. **Clear links and communication with education services are necessary to ensure prompt access arrangements and that young people may benefit from the pastoral support, "buddy" or mentoring services that some schools and colleges provide.**

A majority of the young people were participating in full- or part-time education through schools, colleges or forms of alternative education provision. Limited use was made of accredited training schemes and opportunities for employment were extremely restricted, even for those with leave to remain. These patterns reflect, at least in part, the restructuring that has taken place in the school-to-work transition over recent decades and the expansion of educational opportunities associated with it (Coles, 1995; Furlong and Cartmel, 1997). They also reflect the emergence of specific funding streams to encourage courses and services targeted to the needs of asylum-seeking and refugee young people (Ofsted, 2003; Rutter, 2003b) and the lack of alternatives for those not wanting education.

Patterns of participation were not always continuous and a significant minority spent most of their time supported by social services out of education altogether. The likelihood of "non-participation" varied according to age at referral, region of origin, degree of placement stability and type of placement. Young people who mainly lived in care or kinship placements were much more likely to have experienced a continuous pattern of education than was the case for those who mainly lived in either supported or unsupported accommodation. Stable care and kinship placements tended to be protective and provide greater support for education and training. Young people placed in more independent settings, often under s17 arrangements, found it more difficult to sustain involvement in education. **These findings are consistent with those of other recent studies on unaccompanied young people (Stanley, 2001) and care leavers more generally (Biehal et al, 1995; Wade, 1997). They reinforce the value of providing unaccompanied young people with supportive and stable placements, of considering the educational impact of proposed placement changes and of giving educational support a high priority when planning for young people to live more independently.**

Many young people were resourceful, resilient and had a high commitment to education. Most young people also needed practical, financial and emotional support to maintain their motivation. **Sustained participation was more likely where professional support for education formed part of a comprehensive package of care that addressed most aspects of young people's lives in the round – linking education, placement, health and emotional well-being – and where young people had developed strong networks of support from family, significant adults or friends.** It may seem obvious to point out that, like everybody else, young people experience life as inter-connected rather than as segmented. What occurs in one sphere of a young person's life is likely to affect progress in others and, as such, support for education is likely to be more effective if it is situated in the context of support for their lives as a whole. **Furthermore, strategies that help to strengthen young people's social networks and that help to promote self-esteem, self-efficacy and resilience may also help the progress of their educational careers (see Daniel et al, 1999; Gilligan, 2001; Dixon et al, 2004).**

Although most young people, in addition to their weekly allowance, received some basic financial assistance associated with their expenses for education or training, others did not. For some aged 18, their transfer to NASS brought further financial hardship. Not all young people were aware of their entitlements and most financial support was highly discretionary. While it is the case that, for looked after children generally, there is variation in the level of financial assistance to support learning, the situation is improving with the introduction of clearer baseline procedures and guidance (Department of Health, 2001; Social Exclusion Unit, 2003). Leaving care services have also been developing financial incentive schemes to promote post-16 participation (Broad, 2003). **Unaccompanied young people have a right to clear information about their entitlements and there is a strong case for reviewing their financial entitlements, including those supported under s17, in line with those now available to young people in the care system, whose situation is very similar.**

Formal links with education services were more clearly defined for children of school age. Liaison arrangements for young people accessing further education or training were less certain. Connexions staff attached to asylum teams provided a helpful bridge and many workers had established informal links with teachers, college tutors and agencies providing specialist services. However, development work to expand resources and opportunities for young people tended to be *ad hoc*, often dependent on the individual commitment of already hard-pressed social workers. **There is a need for greater corporate leadership and for dedicated lead officers to identify and exploit opportunities with colleges, training providers and employers in order to broaden the range of options for young people.**

Health and well-being

Research into the health needs of refugee and asylum seeking children is limited (Mather and Kerac, 2002). Fragments of evidence from young people themselves suggest that they view their health in a broad way, linking separation from their families and worries about their welfare, poverty, social isolation, access to health care and school difficulties as factors affecting their health and well-being (Gosling, 2000). Although young people may carry with them a range of physical or emotional health problems arising from their past experiences, recent work has also emphasised their fortitude and resilience (Richman, 1998a; Ahearn, 2000; Kohli and Mather, 2003).

Initial assessments almost always included some screening of young people's physical health, although coverage of emotional well-being or of risks to which young people may have been exposed was less common.

Specialist children's teams were more likely than other asylum teams to conduct comprehensive health assessments and to have routine procedures in place for health checks. In these early encounters, practitioners often made attempts to gauge a young person's emotional state, including signs of anxiety or trauma, by listening to their stories and by assessing self-presentation and mood. In some cases, immediate concerns led to referrals for further assessment. In most, however, these signals were noted as issues to which practitioners could return once young people had settled in placement. Provided this follow-up does takes place over time, which was not always the case, this may be a helpful strategy for many young people, allowing them time to re-assemble their thoughts and feelings in a supportive environment, to decide what they can afford to share and with whom, and for fragments of their stories about themselves and their lives to emerge and "thicken" over time, as trust in those around them develops (see Kohli, forthcoming).

A majority of young people appeared to be physically healthy, but around one in eight were experiencing chronic health problems that affected their daily lives. **Health monitoring and support tended to be better for those who were formally looked after (s20) and for those supported in the community (s17) who were provided with an equivalent package of care. Health monitoring was facilitated where young people were living in stable placements, where carers and support workers gave priority to health concerns and where the rhythms of social work contact, planning and review were regular.**

Although a minority of young people may be sufficiently troubled to need psychiatric treatment, the majority may be helped through consistent care and strategies that help them to re-centre their lives and which promote their resilience and capacity to cope with the challenges of resettlement (Burnett and Fassil, 2002; Kohli and Mather, 2003). Many of the young people appeared to have settled well and were purposeful in their outlook, especially where they had a stable placement, were involved in education and had positive social support. However, almost one-third were continuing to experience some emotional turbulence. Anxieties about the past often articulated with resettlement difficulties in the present and concerns about an uncertain future to threaten young people's emotional resources.

Concerned practitioners were generally alert to signs of emotional distress and offers of counselling were commonly made. However, professional counselling raised quite complex questions for young people. Not all young people wanted, felt ready for or trusted therapeutic encounters. Where young people did feel able and ready to confide, counselling was often highly valued. Others, however, never got this opportunity, as their needs went unrecognised or their requests were ignored. **While counselling will be appropriate for some young people, it is unlikely to work for all, and more imaginative strategies for meeting young people's emotional needs may also be necessary. In this context, recent work on the concept of "therapeutic care" may be helpful (Papadopoulos, 2002; Kohli and Mather, 2003).** This envisages weaving therapeutic support into the daily lives of young people using the joint skills of carers and social workers, providing a safe environment in which young people may gradually feel able to speak about their experiences, and time, space and understanding for them to tell and re-fashion their stories at their own pace and in their own way. Through this process of bearing witness (Blackwell, 1997), it is hoped that young people may gradually use their own inner resources to promote self-recovery by re-weaving the threads of their lives that may have been fractured by experiences of trauma and displacement.

Information on health promotion work with young people in the areas of diet, substance use, leisure and sexual health was limited. However, most work in these areas tended to take place in the context of one-to-one casework or, in some instances, through the use of social groups. Essential help with diet, shopping and cooking was part of the core work undertaken by carers and support workers. Help of this kind was less often provided to young people living in more independent settings and, even where it was, it could be undermined by the low levels of weekly income they received. In some teams help was available to support young people's sport and leisure interests through leisure passes or small weekly grants. In other teams, however, financial support was discretionary and young people were not always made aware of entitlements they did have. **Given the Government's emphasis on promoting healthy lifestyles for young people, a coherent strategy to support and encourage young people to lead healthy, active lives is necessary. This may be strengthened** through partnerships with health promotion teams, peer education initiatives and through links with local projects working in the areas of sexual health, drugs and alcohol (Department of Health, 2000b; Robbins, 2001).

Social networks

Separation from parents, customary caregivers and the familiar is common to all unaccompanied young people. Their arrival in a new social landscape brings risks of social and cultural dislocation. Social workers have an important role in minimising this disconnection between young people's past and present lives by providing continuities with the past and opportunities for new social activities and relationships.

Many young people were socially isolated and were primarily dependent on support from social services and allied professionals. Those whose careers followed an s20 pathway, who were mainly placed in care or kinship placements, preferably within the local authority, and who were consistently involved in education tended to have stronger networks of social support. The additional sources of support in these settings had helped them to strengthen their social networks relative to those living more independently, usually under s17 arrangements. **Making an** *early* **investment in young people's social networks (through placement, education, family, friends and community) may help to improve overall well-being, reduce feelings of disconnection and, ultimately, help to reduce young people's longer-term reliance on support from social services.**

The arena of family and social relationships is sensitive ground. Uncertainty about young people's family histories, about their ordinary lives before exile and, in some cases, about their social relationships in the present, was quite commonplace amongst practitioners. However, just over one-third of the young people (36 per cent) were known to have relatives resident in the UK – with over half of these links being between siblings – and a small proportion (11 per cent) were known to have links with relatives overseas. In all, around three-fifths of young people (62 per cent) appeared to have no family contact of any kind.

Promoting links with relatives is important, wherever this is

consistent with a young person's welfare. Although contact may bring bad news as well as good, it may offer reassurance and help young people's adjustment in the present. Most of those who had links with relatives had received some support from social services to facilitate contact, although the level and quality of that support were variable. Offers of counselling or to attempt to trace missing relatives were frequently made, although some young people experienced continuing frustration that their requests for tracing had not been followed up by social workers. However, trust in the ethos of tracing agencies was also needed and some young people preferred to use informal community contacts to seek news from home.

Relationships between siblings were often *the* primary source of family identification and solidarity for young people and practitioners were successful in keeping sibling groups together. Where sibling groups were placed in more independent settings, some strains were evident for those in a primary care role and assessment of their ability to provide good enough care was not always undertaken carefully. Ongoing support also tended to be based on the needs of the whole group rather than on an appreciation of the needs of individual members and, in independent settings, the capacity of sibling groups to manage was severely tested.

A sizeable minority of young people (16 per cent) had also formed connections with other significant adults who, to varying degrees, had played an important role in their lives. Where young people lacked links with family or where social work support had proved unreliable, the presence of these figures tended to assume greater significance. Workers were not always aware of these connections or the importance of them for young people's overall well-being. Support to promote links of this kind was less common than for families. Initiatives to connect young people to mentors, befrienders or independent visitors were also not sufficiently exploited. Although these initiatives have resource implications, they may go some way to supplementing and reinforcing the formal support provided by social services.

Refugee children tend to have fewer friends than other groups of young people (Candappa and Egharevba, 2000) and their access to community or youth services is often constrained by lack of money, limited engagement in education, language barriers and racism (Cunningham and Lynch,

2000; Gosling, 2000; Stanley, 2001). These were common experiences for our young people, although many practitioners were mindful of the need for young people to connect with friends, with aspects of their own cultures and communities and with mainstream youth and leisure services. **Good friendships helped young people to re-orient their lives and provided an important source of company and emotional support.** Education and placement were the main arenas for broadening social networks, although friendships with citizen young people were often harder to make and sustain. **Placements in kinship settings, in same-culture foster placements and, to a more varying extent, in placements arranged through refugee agencies of community associations, tended to provide greater opportunities for young people to connect with their communities of origin.** Where social work support was limited, relationships made with peers in shared housing sometimes provided young people's only anchor in an uncertain world.

Comfort and companionship was also found through membership of churches and mosques and workers generally appreciated the benefits of this involvement and were willing to assist young people. **Young people's involvement in leisure activities and the extent of their social lives was heavily circumscribed by lack of money, especially for those living independently and managing on very low weekly allowances.**

Transition at 18

Most unaccompanied young people come to the UK in their mid-teen years. Preparation and planning for transition should therefore be at the centre of social work practice. Activities that help to meet needs in the present (for a settled placement, for education, health and social support) are also important features of preparation for adulthood. Transition planning, however, is often clouded by uncertainty about the future arising from the asylum process, creating a genuine tension for both young people and workers. A multi-dimensional approach to planning is required, one that prepares young people for multiple outcomes, including the possibility of return.

Pathways at 18 varied according to asylum status and the support arrangements provided by social services. Many young people were still seeking an asylum decision at 18 and most of these had transferred to the

National Asylum Support Service (NASS). Most of those granted exceptional leave to remain (ELR) had only been given leave to their 18th birthday and most were seeking an extension. Only a small minority had been granted leave to remain indefinitely. A small number of young people had received a negative decision, had exhausted their rights of appeal, but had not yet received removal directions. **Multi-dimensional planning has to embrace the differing needs of each of these groups and careful monitoring of the progress of asylum claims by social workers and of the actions of different players in the legal process is critical to the welfare of young people.**

Pathways at 18 were also profoundly affected by social services policies and procedures. Our information on post-18 transitions relates primarily to young people who had been supported under s17, who formed the majority of the sample (76 per cent).[2] For most of these young people social services responsibilities had ended at their 18th birthday, case closure was routine and reflected the lack of statutory duties to provide leaving care services. Where young people who had been looked after (s20) moved on before the age of 18 to live more independently or to join relatives, support arrangements were often changed to s17, thereby weakening *in practice* their entitlement to later leaving care support. In overall terms, therefore, social services had delimited its leaving care responsibilities to the vast majority of young people.

The intersection of social services and immigration responsibilities makes transition planning a complex, often confusing and challenging area of work. However, use of written pathway plans was rare, even for those looked after. Pathway planning is intended to bring greater clarity and transparency to the planning and review process, it provides an opportunity to think into the future with young people and to plan for different eventualities (Department of Health, 2001). Where it was used, workers often found it helpful in bringing focus to their work. **For young people, pathway planning provided access to realistic information, advice and guidance that helped to inform their decisions (see also Stanley, 2001; Howarth, 2005). Towards the end of the study,**

---

[2] Very few young people who had been looked after (s20) had reached 18 at the close of the study and most were still living in placements and preparing for transition.

implementation of pathway planning was being gradually extended and this is to be welcomed.

Research on leaving care has highlighted the relatively short timescales within which transition planning takes place, often compressed into the last few months of care (Biehal *et al*, 1995; Dixon *et al*, 2004). This was also evident in this study and, especially for those living more independently, too often took the form of an "exit plan" at 18. **Where young people's contact with social services had been weak over time, evidence of transition planning was often non-existent, transitions tended to be more abrupt and arrangements for case closure at 18 were brief and formal.**

Transition planning was made easier where young people had leave to remain that extended beyond 18. Arrangements could readily be made for young people to access benefits and social housing and to ensure continuity of education. Young people were able to envisage a future and make plans for their lives. Where leave to remain was uncertain, this sense of future was inevitably foreshortened and multi-dimensional planning became essential. Many practitioners tried to address young people's anxieties directly, provide information and explore options. Others, however, were more reluctant to raise the implications of a negative outcome for fear of creating further distress. Planning drift was most likely in relation to the prospect of return. However difficult it may be to find an adequate social work vocabulary through which young people can be helped to prepare for such an eventuality, it is an important dimension of planning. **Transition planning needs to be realistic, take place over time and take account of all possible outcomes so that young people may make the most informed decisions available to them.**

Amongst those aged 18 or over, there was considerable evidence of a need for continuing leaving care support. Although most young people had some form of home base, mostly in independent housing, at least one in seven was not participating in education or training and almost two-fifths had no documented support from family, friends or community. The extent of need, however, was difficult to determine. **Information about how young people were faring was often not available from case files. Local authorities are not required to monitor and report on the circumstances of those supported under s17 and, in consequence,**

many of these young people had disappeared from view after case closure. The vast majority were not receiving leaving care support. Even where (s17) cases remained open to workers after the 18th birthday, this usually depended on the willingness of individual workers to argue the case with managers or to offer continuing informal help for a period of time. Many workers were highly committed and were doing the best they could to support young people, despite the constraints imposed by their formal role and by the legal and funding environment.

Looking to the future

Leaving care was an area of weakness for these local authorities at the time the study was conducted. Given the age profile of unaccompanied young people at arrival, it may also represent an important test of how services are improving as a whole. In part, and in a context of constrained resources, this weakness has stemmed from factors specific to social services when faced with an increase in referrals from a relatively new client group. None of the local authorities were well positioned to meet these challenges. New policies, procedures and guidance were needed at a time when few signposts existed and, in response, new specialist children's teams emerged from these uncertain beginnings. Over the course of the study, as we have seen, these services have evolved and been realigned to tighten referral and assessment procedures, to improve the placement options for young people (including for those in transition), to reduce reliance on less adequate service providers and to increase the proportion of young people looked after (s20) and therefore eligible for leaving care services. These are welcome developments, reinforced by Government guidance and the Hillingdon Judgment, that give greater optimism for the future.

However, there is much more that could be done to support young people's pathways to adulthood in the future and it remains to be seen how the proposed wide-ranging reforms of the child welfare system arising from *Every Child Matters* will influence services for different segments of the population of unaccompanied young people. At present, the signs appear mixed. On the one hand, proposals for a common assessment framework, to provide a common core of skills and training and to promote multi-agency working through Children's Trusts are likely to be beneficial. On the other, the Government's maintenance of its reservation to the UN Convention on the Rights of the Child with respect to children subject to immigration control and its exclusion of immigration agencies from new duties to safeguard children's welfare and from involvement in local safeguarding boards, point to a continuation of a two-tier safeguarding framework that will adversely affect asylum seeking children. These inconsistencies are clearly unhelpful.

It is also the case that social services cannot do this work alone. The weaknesses in service provision, especially for those supported under s17, that have been identified in this (and other) studies also derive from the funding base for work with unaccompanied young people and, as indicated above, the tensions that are inherent in the interface between child care and immigration polices. Age-related distinctions in the Home Office Special Grant that primarily funds this work have influenced the shape of services and, in particular, the greater use of s17 arrangements for older teenagers. If, as guidance and evidence suggests, young people benefit from the greater protection afforded by the looked after system, this distinction appears untenable. In addition, the central thrust of childcare (and leaving care) legislation is on promoting social inclusion and forward planning with young people into the future. This sits in tension with the predominant drift of immigration policies and creates an uncomfortable and uncertain terrain for social work that makes effective planning and support more difficult to achieve.

Social services will inevitably have to work within the constraints imposed by immigration policies and procedures. However, the development of high-quality services will be enhanced through provision of a more consistent, equitable and facilitating policy environment, one that supports the efforts of young people to re-build and re-centre their lives and that enables them to take advantage of new opportunities. Most young people will stay and construct new lives for themselves in our communities. Even if return is ultimately necessary, however, the least we should do is provide effective services to help young people acquire the skills they will need to negotiate this journey successfully and to strengthen their fortitude and resilience to meet the challenges of the future, whether within the UK or elsewhere. It is what most young people would want and it is the least that they deserve.

References

Ahearn F. L. (ed) (2000) *Psychosocial Wellness of Refugees: Issues of qualitative and quantitative research*, New York: Berghahn Books.

Aldgate J., Heath A., Colton M. and Simm M. (1993) 'Social work and the education of children in foster care', *Adoption & Fostering*, 17:3, pp. 25–34.

Ali E. and Jones C. (2000) *Meeting the Educational Needs of Somali Pupils in Camden Schools*, London: London Borough of Camden.

Ames N. (1999) 'Social work recording: a new look at an old issue', *Journal of Social Work Education*, 35:2, pp. 227–237.

Audit Commission (2000) *Another Country: Implementing dispersal under the Immigration and Asylum Act*, London: Audit Commission.

Ayotte W. (1998) *Supporting Unaccompanied Children in the Asylum Process*, London: Save the Children.

Ayotte W. (2000) *Separated Children Coming to Western Europe: Why they travel and how they arrive*, London: Save the Children.

Ayotte W. and Williamson L. (2001) *Separated Children in the UK: An overview of the current situation*, London: Save the Children.

Bail for Immigration Detainees (BID)/Asylum Aid (2005) *Justice Denied: asylum and immigration legal aid – a system in crisis*, BID/Asylum Aid: Available: http://www.asylumaid.org.uk/Publications/Justicedenied.pdf

Bann C. and Tennant R. (2002) *Unaccompanied Asylum-Seeking Children*, Highlight Number 190, London: National Children's Bureau.

Barnen R. (2000) *Providing a Choice for Separated Refugee Children: A report on the value of renewing home country links*, Stockholm: Save the Children Sweden.

Berridge D. and Brodie I. (1998) *Children's Homes Revisited*, London: Jessica Kingsley.

Biehal N., Clayden J., Stein M. and Wade J. (1992) *Prepared for Living? A survey of young people leaving the care of three local authorities*, London: National Children's Bureau.

Biehal N., Clayden J., Stein M. and Wade J. (1995) *Moving On: Young people and leaving care schemes*, London: HMSO.

Biehal N. and Wade J. (1996) 'Looking back, looking forward: care leavers, families and change', *Children and Youth Services Review*, 18:4/5, pp. 425–446.

Blackwell D. (1997) 'Holding, containing and bearing witness: the problem of helpfulness in encounters with torture survivors', *Journal of Social Work Practice*, 11:2, pp. 81–89.

Blackwell D. and Melzak S. (2000) *Far from the Battle but Still at War: Troubled refugee children in school*, London: Child Psychotherapy Trust.

Bloch A. and Schuster L. (2002) 'Asylum and welfare: contemporary debates', *Critical Social Policy*, 22:3, pp. 393–414.

Bostock L. (2003) *Effectiveness of Child Minding Registration and its Implications for Private Fostering*, Position Paper 1, London: Social Care Institute for Excellence.

British Medical Association (2002) *Asylum Seekers: Meeting their health care needs*, London: British Medical Association.

Broad B. (1998) *Young People Leaving Care: Life after the Children Act*, London: Jessica Kingsley.

Broad B. (2003) *After the Act: Implementing the Children (Leaving Care) Act 2000*, Leicester: De Montfort University Children and Families Research Unit Monograph, No. 3.

Burnett A. and Fassil Y. (2002) *Meeting the Health Needs of Refugee and Asylum Seekers in the UK: An information and resource pack for health workers*, London: National Health Service/Department of Health.

Burnett A. and Peel M. (2001) 'The health of survivors of torture and organised violence', *British Medical Journal*, 322, 10 March, pp. 606–609.

Candappa M. (2000) 'The right to education and an adequate standard of living: refugee children in the UK', *The International Journal of Children's Rights*, 8, pp. 261–270.

Candappa M. and Egharevba I. (2000) *'Extraordinary Childhoods': The social lives of refugee children*, Chidren 5–16 Research Briefing No. 5, London: Economic and Social Research Council.

Carey-Wood J., Duke K., Karn V. and Marshall T. (1995) *The Settlement of Refugees in Britain*, Home Office Research Study 141, London: HMSO.

Cheung Y. and Heath A. (1994) 'After care: the education and occupation of adults who have been in care', *Oxford Review of Education*, 20:3, pp. 361–374.

Children's Legal Centre (2003) *Mapping the Provision of Education and Social Services for Refugee and Asylum Seeker Children: Lessons from the Eastern Region*, Cambridge: The Children's Legal Centre.

Children's Legal Centre (2004) *Care and Support for Unaccompanied Asylum Seeking Children*, Cambridge: The Children's Legal Centre.

Children's Legal Centre (2005) *Note on Home Office Position re Schedule 3 of the Nationality, Immigration and Asylum Act 2002 as it Applies to Unaccompanied Asylum Seeking Children (UASC)*; available at www.childrenslegal centre.com

Christie A. (2002) 'Responses of the social work profession to unaccompanied asylum seeking children in the Republic of Ireland', *European Journal of Social Work*, 5, pp. 187–198.

Clarke P. (2002) *By Private Arrangement: Inspection of arrangements for supervising children in private foster care*, Social Services Inspectorate, London: Department of Health.

Clayden S. and Stein M. (1996) 'Self care skills and becoming adult', in Jackson S. and Kilroe S. (eds) *Looking After Children: Good parenting, good outcomes*, London: HMSO.

Cleaver H. (2000) *Fostering Family Contact: A study of children, parents and foster carers*, London: The Stationery Office.

Coles B. (1995) *Youth and Social Policy*, London: UCL Press.

Corlyon J. and McGuire C. (1997) *Young Parents in Public Care*, London: National Children's Bureau.

Council of the European Union (2003) *Laying Down Minimum Standards for the Reception of Asylum Seekers*, Council Directive 2003/9/EC; available at: www. ecre.org/eu_developments/reception/recdirfinal.pdf

Cunningham C. and Lynch M. (2000) 'Understanding the needs of young asylum seekers', *Archives of Disease in Childhood*, 83, pp. 384–387.

Daniel D., Wasell S. and Gilligan R. (1999) ' "It's just common sense isn't it?" Exploring ways of putting the theory of resilience into action', *Adoption & Fostering*, 23:3, pp. 6–15.

Dawson A. and Holding S. (2001) *Young Separated Refugees in Yorkshire and Humberside*, London: Save the Children.

Dennis J. (2002) *A Case for Change: How refugee children in England are missing out*, London: The Children's Society/Save the Children/Refugee Council.

Denzin N. (1971) *The Research Act in Sociology*, Chicago: Aldine.

Department for Education and Skills (2003a) *National Statistics Bulletin, Statistics of Education: Care leavers, 2002–2003, England*, November, London: DfES.

Department for Education and Skills (2003b) *Every Child Matters: Green Paper on children's services, Cm5860*, Norwich: The Stationery Office.

Department for Education and Skills (2004a) *Aiming High: Guidance on supporting the education of asylum seeking and refugee children*, London: DfES.

Department for Education and Skills (2004b) *Draft Regulations and Guidance for Consultation: Care Planning and Special Guardianship: Adoption and Children Act 2002*, London: DfES.

Department for Education and Skills (2004c) *Unaccompanied Asylum Seeking Children – Leaving care costs: 2004/2005 Additional Guidance*, October 2004, London: DfES.

Department of Health (1995) *Unaccompanied Asylum Seeking Children: A practice guide*, London: Department of Health.

Department of Health (1997) *'When Leaving Home is also Leaving Care': An inspection of services for young people leaving care*, London: Social Services Inspectorate, Department of Health.

Department of Health (2000a) *Guidance on the Education of Young People in Public Care*, LAC(2000)13, London: Department of Health.

Department of Health (2000b) *Quality Protects Management Action Plans: A thematic review of leaving care services*, London: Department of Health.

Department of Health (2001) *Children (Leaving Care) Act 2000: Regulations and Guidance*, London: Department of Health.

Department of Health (2002) *Promoting the Health of Looked After Children*, London: Department of Health.

Department of Health (2003) *Guidance on Accommodating Children in Need and their Families*, LAC(2003)13, June, London: Department of Health.

Department of Health/Department for Education and Skills (2000) *Guidance on the Education of Young People in Public Care*, London: Department of Health/ DfES.

Department of Health/Department for Education and Employment/Home Office (2000) *Framework for the Assessment of Children in Need and their Families*, London: The Stationery Office.

Dixon J., Lee J., Wade J. with Byford S. and Wetherley H. (2004) *Young People Leaving Care: A study of costs and outcomes*, Final Report to the Department of Health, York: University of York.

Farmer E. and Pollock S. (1998) *Sexually Abused and Abusing Children in Substitute Care*, Chichester: Wiley.

Farmer E., Moyers S. and Lipscombe J. (2004) *Fostering Adolescents*, London: Jessica Kingsley.

Furlong A. and Cartmel F. (1997) *Young People and Social Change*, Buckingham: Open University Press.

Garnett L. (1992) *Leaving Care and After*, London: National Children's Bureau.

Gilligan R. (2001) *Promoting Resilience: A resource guide on working with children in the care system*, London: BAAF.

Goldsmith L. and Beaver R. (1999) *Recording with Care: Inspection of case recordings in social services departments*, Social Services Inspectorate, London: Department of Health.

Gosling R. (2000) *The Needs of Young Refugees in Lambeth, Southwark and Lewisham*, London: Community Health South London NHS Trust.

Hai N. and Williams A. (2004) *Implementing the Children Leaving Care Act 2000: The experience of eight London boroughs*, London: National Children's Bureau.

Hammersley M. and Atkinson P. (1983) *Ethnography: Principles in practice*, London: Tavistock.

Heath T. and Hill R. (2002) *Asylum Statistics United Kingdom 2001*, London: The Home Office.

Heath T., Jeffries R. and Lloyd A. (2003) *Asylum Statistics United Kingdom 2002*, London: The Home Office.

Heath T., Jeffries R. and Purcell J. (2004) *Asylum Statistics United Kingdom 2003*, London: The Home Office.

Hodes M. (2000) 'Psychologically distressed refugee children in the UK', *Child Psychology and Psychiatry Review*, 5:2, pp. 57–68.

Home Office (2000a) *Full and Equal Citizens: A strategy for the integration of refugees into the United Kingdom*, London: The Home Office.

Home Office (2000b) 'Age disputes', *Policy Bulletin 33*, October 2000, Immigration and Nationality Directorate, London: The Home Office.

Home Office (2002) *Unaccompanied Asylum Seeking Children: Information note*, London: Immigration and Nationality Directorate, Home Office.

Home Office (2004a) 'Transition at age 18', *Policy Bulletin 29*, Version 3.0, 25 February 2004, Immigration and Nationality Directorate, London: The Home Office.

Home Office (2004b) *Integration Matters: A national strategy for refugee integration: a draft for consultation*, London: The Home Office.

Howarth R. (2005) *Unaccompanied Refugees and Asylum Seekers Turning 18: A guide for social workers and other professionals*, London: Save the Children.

Humphries B. and Mynott E. (2001) *Living Your Life Across Boundaries: Young separated refugees in Greater Manchester*, London: Save the Children.

Jackson S. (1994) 'Educating children in residential and foster care', *Oxford Review of Education*, 20:3, pp. 267–279.

Jackson S. (2002) 'Promoting stability and continuity in care away from home', in McNeish D., Newman T. and Roberts H. (eds) *What Works for Children?* Buckingham: Open University Press.

Jackson S., Ajayi S. and Quigley M. (2005) *Going to University from Care*, London: Institute of Education.

Jones G. (1995) *Leaving Home*, Buckingham: Open University Press.

Kagle J. (1984) 'The contemporary social work record', *Social Work*, 28, pp. 149–153.

Khan P. (2000) 'Asylum-seekers in the UK: implications for social service involvement', *Social Work and Social Sciences Review*, 8, pp. 116–129.

Kidane S. (2001a) *I Did Not Choose to Come Here: Listening to refugee children*, London: BAAF.

Kidane S. (2001b) *Food, Shelter and Half a Chance: Assessing the needs of unaccompanied asylum seeking and refugee children*, London: BAAF.

Kidane S. and Amarena P. (2004) *Fostering Unaccompanied and Asylum Seeking Children: A training course for foster carers*, London: BAAF.

Kohli R. (2001) 'Social work with unaccompanied asylum seeking young people', *Forced Migration Review*, 12, pp. 31–33.

Kohli R. (forthcoming) *Social Work Practice with Unaccompanied Refugee Children*, Basingstoke: Palgrave Macmillan.

Kohli R. and Mather R. (2003) 'Promoting psychosocial well-being in unaccompanied asylum seeking young people in the United Kingdom', *Child & Family Social Work*, 8:3, pp. 201–212.

Levenson R. and Sharma A. (1999) *The Health of Refugee Children: Guidelines for paediatricians*, London: The Kings Fund/Royal College of Paediatrics and Child Health.

Marsh P and Peel M. (1999) *Leaving Care in Partnership: Family involvement with care leavers*, London: The Stationery Office.

Mason J. (1994) *Qualitative Researching*, London: Sage.

Mather M. and Kerac M. (2002) 'Caring for the health of children brought into the UK from abroad', *Adoption & Fostering*, 26:4, pp. 44–54.

McCann J., James A., Wilson S. and Dunn G. (1996) 'Prevalence of psychiatric disorders in young people in the care system', *British Medical Journal*, 313, 14 December, pp. 1529–1530.

Meltzer H., Corbin T., Gatward R., Goodman R. and Ford T. (2003) *The Mental Health of Young People Looked After by Local Authorities in England, Summary Report*, Norwich: HMSO.

Melzak S. and Kasabova S. (1999) *Working with Children and Adolescents from Kosova*, London: Medical Foundation for the Care of Victims of Torture.

Miles M. and Huberman A. (1994) *Qualitative Data Analysis: An expanded sourcebook* (second edition), California: Sage Publications.

Milner J. and O'Bryne P. (2002) *Assessment in Social Work*, Basingstoke: Palgrave Macmillan.

Mitchell F. (2003) 'The social services response to unaccompanied children in England', *Child & Family Social Work*, 8:3, pp. 179–189.

Monck E., Reynolds J. and Wigfall V. (2004) 'Using concurrent planning to establish permanency for looked after children', *Child & Family Social Work*, 9:4, pp. 321–331.

Munoz N. (1999) *Other People's Children: An exploration of the needs of and the provision for 16- and 17-year-old unaccompanied asylum seekers*, London: Children of the Storm and London Guildhall University.

Norton R. and Cohen B. (2000) *Developing Youth Work with Young Refugees*, Leicester: National Youth Agency.

Ofsted (2003) *The Education of Asylum Seeker Pupils*, Norwich: Ofsted Publications Centre.

Okitikpi T. and Aymer C. (2003) 'Social work with African refugee children and their families', *Child & Family Social Work*, 8:3, pp. 213–222.

Packman J. (1993) 'From prevention to partnership: child welfare services across three decades', *Children & Society*, 7:2, pp. 183–195.

Papadopoulos R. (2002) *Therapeutic Care for Refugees: No place like home*, London: Karnac.

Parker J. (2001) 'Social work with refugees and asylum seekers: a rationale for developing practice', *Practice*, 12:3, pp. 61–76.

Philip K., Shucksmith J. and King C. (2004) *Sharing a Laugh? A qualitative study of mentoring interventions with young people*, York: Joseph Rowntree Foundation.

Philpot T. (2001) *A Very Private Practice*, London: BAAF.

Pinkerton J. and McCrea R. (1999) *Meeting the Challenge? Young people leaving care in Northern Ireland*, Aldershot: Ashgate.

Raychuba B. (1987) *Report on the Special Needs of Youth in the Care of the Child Welfare System*, Toronto: National Youth in Care Network.

Refugee Council (2000) *Helping Refugee Children in Schools*, London: Refugee Council.

Refugee Council (2005) *Ringing the Changes: The impact of guidance on the use of sections 17 and 20 of the Children Act 1989 to support unaccompanied asylum seeking children*, London: Refugee Council.

Remsbery N. (2003) *The Education of Refugee Children*, London: National Children's Bureau.

Richman N. (1998a) *In the Midst of the Whirlwind: A manual for helping refugee children*, London: Save the Children.

Richman N. (1998b) 'Looking before and after: refugees and asylum seekers in the West', in Bracken P. and Petty C. (eds) *Rethinking the Trauma of War*, London: Save the Children.

Robbins D. (2001) *Transforming Children's Services: An evaluation of local authority responses to the Quality Protects Programme, Year 3*, London: Department of Health.

Roberts K. and Harris J. (2002) *Disabled People in Refugee and Asylum Seeking Communities in Britain*, Bristol: Policy Press.

Rushton A., Dance Q., Quinton D. and Mayes D. (2001) *Siblings in Late Permanent Placements*, London: BAAF

Russell S. (1999) *Most Vulnerable of All: The treatment of unaccompanied refugee children in the UK*, London: Amnesty International.

Rutter J. (2003a) *Supporting Refugee Children in 21st Century Britain: A compendium of essential information*, Stoke on Trent: Trentham Books.

Rutter J. (2003b) *Working with Refugee Children*, York: Joseph Rowntree Foundation.

Rutter J. (2003c) *The Experiences and Achievements of Congolese Children in Camden Schools*, London: London Borough of Camden.

Rutter J. and Jones C. (1998) *Refugee Education: Mapping the field*, Stoke on Trent: Trentham Books.

Ruxton S. (2000) *Separated Children Seeking Asylum in Europe: A programme for Action*, London: Save the Children/United Nations High Commissioner for Refugees,.

Saunders L. and Broad B. (1997) *The Health Needs of Young People Leaving Care*, Leicester: de Montfort University.

Save the Children (2003) *Young Refugees: A guide to the rights and entitlements of separated refugee children*, London: Save the Children.

Selwyn J., Sturgess W., Quinton D. and Baxter C. (2003) *Costs and Outcomes of Non-infant Adoptions*, Report to the Department for Education and Skills, London: DfES.

Separated Children in Europe Programme (2004) *Statement of Good Practice* (third edition), International Save the Children Alliance in Europe/UNHCR; available at www.savethechildren.net/separated_children/good_practice/index.html

Silove D. and Ekblad S. (2002) 'How well do refugees adapt after resettlement in Western countries?', *Acta Psychiatrica Scandinavica*, 106:6, pp. 401–402.

Sinclair I., Gibbs I. and Wilson K. (2004) *Foster Placements: Why they succeed and why they fail*, London: Jessica Kingsley.

Sinclair I. and Gibbs I. (1998) *Children's Homes: A study in diversity*, Chichester: Wiley.

Sinclair R., Garnett L. and Berridge D. (1995) *Social Work and Assessment with Adolescents*, London: National Children's Bureau.

Smale G. and Tuson G., with Biehal N. and Marsh P. (1993) *Empowerment, Assessment, Care Management and the Skilled Worker*, London: HMSO.

Smith C. (1994) *Partnership in Action: Developing effective aftercare projects*, Westerham: Royal Philanthropic Society.

Social Exclusion Unit (2003) *A Better Education for Children in Care*, London: Social Exclusion Unit.

Spencer Y. (2002) 'A right to education: schooling for refugee and asylum-seeking children', *Childright*, 192, December, pp. 8–9.

Stanley K. (2001) *Cold Comfort: Young separated refugees in England*, London: Save the Children.

Stein M. (2004) *What Works for Young People Leaving Care?* Barkingside: Barnardo's.

Stein M. and Carey K. (1986) *Leaving Care*, Oxford: Blackwell.

Stein M. and Wade J. (2000) *Helping Care Leavers: Problems and strategic responses*, London: Department of Health.

Stone R. (2000) *Children First and Foremost: Meeting the needs of unaccompanied asylum seeking children*, Barkingside: Barnardo's.

Triseliotis J., Borland M., Hill M. and Lambert L. (1995) *Teenagers and Social Work Services*, London: HMSO.

United Nations High Commissioner for Refugees (1994) *Refugee Children: Guidelines on protection and care*, Geneva: UNHCR.

Wade J. (1997) 'Developing leaving care services: tapping the potential of foster carers', *Adoption & Fostering*, 21:3, pp. 40–49.

Wade J. (2003) *Leaving Care*, Quality Protects Research Briefing, 7, Dartington, Department of Health/Research in Practice/Making Research Count.

Wade J. and Biehal N. with Clayden J. and Stein M. (1998) *Going Missing: Young people absent from care*, Chichester: Wiley.

Who Cares? Trust (1993) *Not Just a Name: The views of young people in foster and residential care*, London: National Consumer Council.

Williamson L. (1998) 'Unaccompanied – but not unsupported', in Rutter J. and Jones C. (eds) *Refugee Education: Mapping the field*, Stoke on Trent: Trentham Books.

Williamson L. (2000) 'Unaccompanied refugee children: legal framework and local application, in Britain', in Bloch A. and Levy C. (eds) *Refugees, Citizenship and Social Policy in Europe*, London: Macmillan.

Index*

---

* Note: page numbers in bold indicate material in tables. Page numbers followed by n indicates a footnote.

Index compiled by Elisabeth Pickard